A SOCIETY TO MATCH THE SCENERY

A SOCIETY
TO MATCH THE SCENERY

Personal Visions of the Future of the American West

Gary Holthaus, Patricia Nelson Limerick,
Charles F. Wilkinson, and Eve Stryker Munson,
editors

A project of the Center of the American West,
University of Colorado at Boulder

UNIVERSITY PRESS OF COLORADO

Copyright © 1991 by the University Press of Colorado
P.O. Box 849
Niwot, Colorado 80544

10 9 8 7 6 5 4 3 2 1

The University Press of Colorado is a cooperative publishing enterprise supported, in part, by Adams State College, Colorado State University, Fort Lewis College, Mesa State College, Metropolitan State College of Denver, University of Colorado, University of Northern Colorado, University of Southern Colorado, and Western State College.

Library of Congress Cataloging-in-Publication Data

A Society to match the scenery: personal visions of the future of the American West / Gary Holthaus
. . . [et al.].
   p. cm.
   "A project of the Center of the American West, University of Colorado at Boulder."
   Includes bibliographical references and index.
   ISBN 0-87081-241-6
   1. West (U.S.) — Description and travel — 1981- 2. West (U.S.) — Civilization — 20th century. I. Holthaus, Gary H., 1932- II. University of Colorado, Boulder. Center of the American West.
F595.3.S63 1991
978'.033 — dc20   91-24957
                                                        CIP

For further information contact:
Gary H. Holthaus, Director
University of Colorado
Campus Box 401
Boulder, CO 80309 (303) 492-1876

CONTENTS

— CONTENTS —

— CONTENTS —

— CONTENTS —

LIST OF ILLUSTRATIONS

PREFACE

This book is the first publication of the Center of the American West, established in January 1990 by the University of Colorado as a project of the College of Arts and Sciences. The study of the American West is a fascinating field blessed with a rich history, a vigorous body of literature, and extraordinarily diverse human and natural resources. The working premises of the center include the ideas that events in the region are best understood as being a continuum of past, present, and future, and that understanding is best achieved by meshing objective data, the perspectives offered by the arts and sciences, and robust policy analysis and debate. The essays presented in this volume grew out of presentations made at two major symposia in which we attempted to apply the ideas just summarized. The symposia — "A Society to Match the Scenery: Shaping the Future of the American West" (October 1988) and "Inhabiting the Last Best Place: Limits, Opportunities, and the Future of the American West" (March 1990) — were both well received, with a total of nearly fifteen hundred people in attendance. As the table of contents to this volume amply demonstrates, the participants included many of the most knowledgeable and creative minds in the region.

We have many thanks to offer to those people who helped bring this project to fruition. First and foremost, we wish to extend our appreciation to Eve Munson. Eve served as the editor for this volume and carried the primary responsibility both for the general organization and for editing the manuscripts. We also extend our gratitude to our authors, who undertook the task of rewriting their symposia speeches into these printed essays and who responded to our various requests with speed and good spirits. Ann FitzSimmons, Dodie Udall, and Marie Wilwerding all performed valuable staff work on this book and on the symposia.

The University of Colorado at Boulder has been exceedingly supportive, both with the Center of the American West in general and with this book in particular. James N. Corbridge, chancellor, Charles R. Middleton, dean of the College of Arts and Sciences, and Bruce Ekstrand, vice chancellor for academic affairs, have been most generous with their time, suggestions, and financial contributions. The symposia, and this volume, would not have been possible without two substantial grants from the Colorado Endowment for the Humanities. We also appreciate the fine working relationship that we have had with the University Press of Colorado and its director, Luther Wilson. Last, we would like to extend our heartfelt thanks to Richard Hart and Alvin Josephy. They were the heart and soul of the wonderful conferences sponsored every summer from the mid-1970s through the mid-1980s in Sun Valley, Idaho, by the Institute of the American West. Those dynamic interdisciplinary gatherings were the inspiration for the Center of the American West and for the collection of personal visions presented here.

Gary Holthaus, Director
Center of the American West

Patricia Nelson Limerick, Board Co-Chair
Center of the American West
Associate Professor of History

Charles F. Wilkinson, Board Co-Chair
Center of the American West
Moses Lasky Professor of Law

PART ONE

Introduction

SPEAKING OF THE WEST

In 1929 at age thirty-six, Joseph Wood Krutch published his despairing book, *The Modern Temper*. Although he would later move to Arizona, where the desert would lead him to a new kind of hope, Krutch in 1929 felt sure that humanity had landed itself in a big mess. Science and rationality had eroded faith in the modern world; thoughtful people had to learn to live with a kind of emotional malnutrition, getting by on skepticism and alienation.

On a lecture tour to publicize his gloomy book, Krutch went to Detroit, where he was met by the president of a women's club. "She approached me," Krutch remembered, "only after every other descending passenger had left the platform. 'Are you Mr. Krutch?' 'I am.' Her face fell. 'But you do not look as, as — *depressed* as I expected.' "[1]

Had she been able to attend the Center of the American West's symposia at the University of Colorado in the 1980s, the president of the Detroit women's club would have had a similar response. In October of 1988, at the symposium "A Society to Match the Scenery: Shaping the Future of the American West," and in March of 1990, at the symposium "Inhabiting the Last Best Place: Limits, Opportunities, and the Future of the American West," speakers squarely confronted the problems of the American West. And yet the spirit of the exchange was by no means one of despair and depression. For the Westerners assembled in Boulder on those two occasions, the exploration of common ground and common concerns provided considerable pleasure. While the ideas and convictions expressed at the microphone, and now printed here, were frequently stimulating, the energy of the conversations taking place all around the hall was equally impressive. In breaks between sessions, as participants clustered for animated discussions, those exchanges demonstrated the remarkable process under way in the late twentieth-century West: quite literally, the reexploration of the region and the reconsideration of the habits and customs of Westerners. This is, in the best sense, a matter of second thoughts, a reconsideration of what humans, in the last four centuries, have done to this place and to each other, and a weighing of choices for the centuries ahead.

The West, many of the speakers agreed, has a troubling record in resource use. Too often, Westerners have approached their remarkable region with, as Philip Burgess put it, an attitude of "rape, scrape, and run." Acting in haste, Westerners have used resources recklessly and apportioned them unfairly, and that, despite the shift in attitude embodied in the conservation movement, is a pattern of folly that persists into our times.

We cannot, moreover, reverse that pattern with a sudden and simple change of our intentions and goals. Choosing to preserve a resource by no means leads to a clear path of action. Jim Carrier makes this point in his discussion of the fires at Yellowstone. Efforts to preserve scenery and wildlife often collide with the needs of people trying to make a living.

Human relations with nature are, after all, only half of the riddle of Western American life; the other, necessary half of the riddle concerns relations *among* humans. As the participants of these symposia pointed out repeatedly, one of the West's most valuable resources is its people, with their wonderful diversity. By one habit of thought with a deep historical root system, that diversity is seen as a problem — which indeed it sometimes has been. But a key part of the reexploration of the American West is the repicturing of that diversity — as an opportunity, a chance to make everyday life an intellectual adventure, an occasion for the most down-to-earth and direct education.

While falling short of unanimity, the speakers converged on a shared definition of the West: It is a place distinctive for its aridity, its open spaces, its rich natural resources, and its instructive mix of cultures, human skills, and perspectives. This region does not go out of its way to make the definer's job easy. The northern parts of the Pacific Coast have, at times, abundant rainfall; cities are as significant a part of the Western landscape as wide, open rural spaces; natural resources are, to say the least, random in their distribution; and, despite the historical fact of human diversity and complexity, it is perfectly possible to find pockets and enclaves of Westerners living solely with "their own kind," indifferent to the fate of the "others" with whom they share this region. Still, many places and parts of the West share enough in the way of common characteristics to make regional thinking possible and productive, even necessary.

In this collection, Sally Fairfax is alone in discounting the distinctiveness of the region, arguing that all parts of the country have beautiful scenery of which the inhabitants are proud. But in the West, a combination of aridity and remoteness has forced humans to leave greater chunks of the scenery alone; suburbs and cities can indeed seem dwarfed by a landscape where the human imprint, while substantial and significant, still remains subtle. The scenery may not be "better" in the West (depending upon one's penchant for green vistas, manicured land-scapes, or ocean views), but it is more insistent.

Despite abundant opportunities for visual pleasure, the West, as most of the symposia participants agree, is a region of stern limits. Vast expanses of it remain without human habitation. This landscape, harsh and arid as it is, is what many love most dearly about the West. As Jim Carrier put it, "I still feel an exhilaration when I get into the jeep and drive out of Denver into the landscape that, for me, continues to hold the magic and meaning of the West."

Magic notwithstanding, this landscape has given certain American ambitions and habits a rough ride. Reaching the hundredth meridian, the line where rainfall drops below twenty inches per year, the home-stead ideal collided with reality. As Bruce Babbitt points out, the results were of broad national significance as Western homesteaders "expected to plow the soil into a checkerboard extension of the Middle West. But for the most part it would not happen." From this failure came "two opposing concepts of land tenure." The first held that public land was to be given away or sold to promote development. The second, Babbitt argues, was "a new concept, that public lands should be retained in permanent ownership and managed for public purposes."

The participants in these symposia are, however, far from agree-ment on the proposition that public ownership of land has served a public good. Babbitt is not the first to point out that inept and even corrupt management has sometimes reduced "the public good" to a veil concealing flawed practices. Still, he argues, if we take "the next step in the evolution of public land-use policy," replacing the concept of multi-ple-use management with one of "dominant public use," we can have careful management of limited resources. Daniel Kemmis, however, makes a counterargument: because so much of Western land is con-trolled by Washington, D.C., we in the West have shrugged off responsi-bility for it. "The West will not be ready for its own politics," he asserts, "until it is ready to claim its own land." But Kemmis's proposition does not quiet the fears of those who see a long-term association of "local decision making" with the practice of short-term extraction.

The issue of resource limits and public policy dominates the sympo-sia discussions, as it does public exchange throughout the West. Adrian Bustamante uses the controversy over the federal government's Waste

Isolation Pilot Project (WIPP) in New Mexico as an example of the hard choices the West faces and the bitter social divisions forced on us by limits. In New Mexico, he notes, people in Santa Fe and Albuquerque have voiced strong opposition to the plan to store low-level nuclear waste in the southern part of the state. Trucks loaded with deadly cargoes will travel through densely populated urban areas, and this prospect understandably alarms city dwellers. On the other hand, "people in Carlsbad want it because the potash mines gave out and now they need jobs." With its appearance of having unused "waste" spaces, the American West will always be the leading candidate for waste disposal; the conflict swirling around WIPP and other nuclear-waste sites will remain a part of the political and social landscape for decades to come.

Ed Marston, in his discussion of life in a small town on Colorado's Western Slope, makes a comparable point on the difficulty of reconciling the need for jobs with the need for a safe environment. Residents of his hometown, Paonia, and towns like it, do not dare to look too hard at the environmental effects of mining, because a mine offers the most lucrative jobs in the region. Without mining, a lot of workers would confront hard times — indeed, times hard enough to provoke a move elsewhere. Similarly, Western Slope residents are ambivalent about efforts to improve education in the region; given the educational opportunities, a better education for their children too often leads to the children moving away in order to put that education to use.

Jo Clark gives several poignant examples of hard political choices forced by the limits in the West. For example, she speaks about the anguish of George Sinner, who as governor of North Dakota was asked to sign a certificate of need for a home for the elderly for the Turtle Mountain Chippewa, a group that does not pay state taxes. The request arrived on the governor's desk right after state residents, beleaguered by an economic depression caused by a national bust in energy and agriculture (the two biggest sources of revenue in the state), had voted to roll back state taxes. As Clark tells it, Sinner remarked, "I can't approve a new obligation when I'm having to cut so many programs, but how can I deny a population which I know is probably the neediest in the state?" In economically depressed areas, Clark argues, doing the right thing approaches impossibility.

Thomas Noel places this idea of limits into the context of a national consumer culture based on wastefulness — what he calls the disposable society. He suggests that this is particularly inappropriate in the West and makes a specific plea for historic preservation as "part of a larger ethic, an idea of preserving, of saving, of fixing things up rather than having disposable cities, disposable office buildings, disposable shopping centers, and a disposable past." Regrettable in environmental terms, waste is one component of social injustice. Calling American Indians "the poorest of the poor, living in the richest country on the planet," Walter Echo-Hawk puts the spotlight on the ways in which social injustice and environmental injustice run on parallel tracks.

A confrontation with limits is not, however, necessarily a confrontation with gloom. Daniel Kemmis, quoting Wendell Berry, suggests that the West's "hardship is its possibility." "Hard country," Kemmis argues, "breeds capable people — capable, among other things, of genuine democracy." It is here, Kemmis says, that "the West has the capacity to contribute something deep and important and lasting to the history of politics and civilization. Simply because we have for so many generations worked on the project of living together in hard country, we have, although we don't recognize it, developed among ourselves certain patterns of behavior, which amount to shared values."

Hardy folk living in hard country — the image certainly does characterize some parts of the West, but its application to Denver or Albuquerque is more questionable. As Bill Hornby, the son of a U.S. Forest Service superintendent, points out, in spite of our enchantment with the beauty of the outdoors, most of us in the West live in cities. He points to himself as an example. He grew up in Montana, went to Stanford, and spent time in Wyoming and New Mexico before settling in Denver. Even though he spent "some time in the woods," learned to fish, and has "been out in a wheat field," he has spent most of his life in towns and cities. And yet, he says, the city "is the place most Western historians don't want to think about." Preoccupied with the mountains, the resources, the water, "we really can't work in the cities when we're talking about the West." If most of the people in the West live in cities, then to keep the West liveable, we have to see that cities are liveable. The urban West and the rural West may seem to be separate places, but their destinies are tightly interwoven.

"We have been unwilling to imagine the possibility of a good city," Kemmis argues, and therefore "we believed — we still believe — that we can somehow escape ourselves by slipping into the mountains, avoiding the hard task of facing up to ourselves in cities." Using the Classic Maya culture as an example, Davíd Carrasco echoes this point, arguing that if a society fails to recognize and deal with the problems of cities, the entire landscape and culture can collapse. As he says, "cities are the greatest forces of ecological transformation . . . the style centers of the world, controlling life in the countryside. . . . Even though people in the West think they live in rural America, on the edge of the wilderness . . . they actually live in a world determined more and more by cities."

Reckon with the significance of Western cities and you reckon as well with what may be the most important resource in the West — its many people and its mingling of many cultures. This is no easy reckoning, to be sure. Many of the symposia participants write about the historical injuries and injustices that come in a package with the West's cultural diversity. Walter Echo-Hawk sums up a long, painful legacy when he notes: "Historically, as we all know, the white man has taken things that belonged to the Indian in a one-way pattern that must now be reversed, if for no other reason than that the Indian no longer has much left to give."

With an unflinching look at injustice in the Western past, Camille Guerin-Gonzalez writes of a West "where large groups of people have been and continue to be disenfranchised on the basis of their race, their gender, and their language." An overemphasis on the appeal and mystique of nature, she feels, can provide indirect support to that injustice, leaving humans dwarfed by the power of the landscape. She agrees with Kemmis that

> the world spirit is alive in Western valleys, but it is alive in people, and not a place; in the white settlers, women, men, children, who created a life for themselves with hard work; in Mexicano migrant farm-workers in the beet fields of Colorado; in Hispano and Eastern European miners; in Central Americans in the Los Angeles garment district; in Indian peoples throughout their land, struggling to survive European concepts of democracy and freedom; in Southeast Asian immigrants and in African-Spanish and African-American settlers. If hardship is possibility, then it is in these people and their continuing hardship, as Herbert Marcuse argued thirty years ago, where those powerful concepts of freedom and democracy might finally be realized.

Even today, as Judge Raymond Jones points out, many who have settled in the West "speak of it as frontier, as though it were empty, as though it were no one's home." If we are to be serious about the West, he argues, "One of the factors that must be considered is the extent to which we will include all of the people." With deep affection for both place and people, Jones recounts the history of his family in the region. "Blacks," he insists, "have a place in this place." The very fact that he needs to make this assertion is a poignant reminder that African-

American people have been much overlooked in popular thinking about the West.

The people of the West are an enormous resource, a point many symposia speakers make. In spite of ongoing legal tensions between whites and Indians over land, water, and fishing rights, observes David Getches, "Most Westerners would consider it a tragedy if Indians were swirled into the melting pot of American society"; their disappearance into the American mainstream would rob us all of "the lessons drawn from their successful survival in this rugged, but fragile, mostly dry place." After listing dozens of groups that call the West home, Terry Tempest Williams writes, "If there is a miracle in the West, it is in the fabric these subcultures create."

The human diversity of the West remains, however, a conversation waiting to happen. We have, heaven knows, enough to talk about; whatever our ethnic backgrounds, we share a set of environmental dilemmas, economic frustrations, and social tensions. Just as important, we have a treasure trove of compelling stories to tell each other, pooling the pieces and parts of a powerful regional history. We have, as well, a shared future to envision — a future in which both collaboration and conflict are likely prospects, depending on the choices we make together.

The participants in the symposia offer a lot of questions that Westerners need to discuss frankly, directly, and openly. How do we live with the physical limits of the land? What kind of stewards of the land will we be? How do we deal with the nuclear waste that heads West as if drawn by a magnet? How can we live in harmony with the land in a way that will allow rural Westerners to survive economically? How do we preserve the character of communities as they vie for badly needed "development bucks"? How, in the face of movements like the call for English as the official language, do we make a persuasive case for the positive value of the region's ethnic diversity? What mistakes, in the very useful question Barbara Sudler raises, are we making that our grandchildren will judge us for, in the same way that we are judging our grandparents? Can we, in the late twentieth century, become genuine *settlers*, and not unsettlers, of this region?

Mark Trahant says we need to learn to ask even harder questions. He speaks as a journalist concerned that too many of his professional colleagues have been co-opted into celebrating, rather than carefully examining, what we call progress. He suggests that we distance ourselves from the process so that we can cast an appropriately critical eye upon it. Babbitt and Hornby suggest that we need new laws in order to make public servants more accountable and to move ourselves away from the unworkable notion of "first come, first served."

Ed Marston calls upon universities in the region to develop expertise in regional issues, giving Westerners a place to turn for help in gathering and interpreting data on the region's problems. University of Colorado Chancellor James Corbridge joins Marston in this hope: "Our Western society calls out for a celebration of its distinctive contribution to American culture. By responding, the Western university will not, as some fear, diminish itself. Rather, the university community will seize the most promising chance of reaching its full potential."

In a variety of projects, the Center of the American West aims to play its part in the reexploration of the American West, under way at the end of the second millennium and the beginning of the third. The tone and spirit of that reexploration are probably best captured in the essays here by William Kittredge and Wallace Stegner: a clear-eyed assessment of the achievements, losses, gains, errors, benefits, and injuries of the Western past, and an equally clear-eyed assessment of the prospects for the future. Composed by master writers, those two essays make it clear that the West is still a place of poetry and drama, a kind of poetry and drama a great deal richer than the tinny stories of the stereotyped "Old West." The old style of Western adventure — the pursuit of short-term profits in extractive industries — has run its course. In the most crucial passage in this entire collection, Wallace Stegner invites Westerners to take the opportunity presented by this moment in history: the opportunity to "dream other dreams, and better."

As Stegner's invitation reminds us, Westerners have not run out of opportunities for courage and heroism. If, like Joseph Wood Krutch, the participants at the symposia in Boulder did not seem as "depressed" as one might have expected, then this surely is the reason. Closing the door on one variety of Western enterprise, a reckoning with the region's limits opens the door to a new, and better, Western adventure.

Gary Holthaus, Patricia Nelson Limerick, Charles F. Wilkinson
Boulder, Colorado
February 1991

THOUGHTS OF MY DESERT HOME

for you

I would walk beside you
on warm New Mexico dirt
sometimes redpacked clay
sometimes silkwaves of sand

where no moss or willows
brazen about in moist excess.
　　　Just we two
in sun where desert's dry
and clear but fertile.

Over windshaped monuments of stone
a cloud might explode and surprise us
to hang free in infinities of blue.

No shock in sagebrush
insistent, deeprooted and lingering
like the lovely walk remembered.

Cordelia Candelaria

SUMMER RAIN IN ASPEN

———

Unexpected this dry summer
it sounds like the dismal roar
of an idling engine

just another version of the rush
of the Roaring Fork cutting
through the urgent Rockies.

And just as that shower of melted snow
drowns itself in whitewater
the rain attacks its own puddles
in dinning torrents this dusty August.

And just as you start to listen in surprise

the rain slows

to a stunning silence

Welcome wetness greening the drought.

Cordelia Candelaria

ROUGH PASSAGE ON I-80

We are travelling through the country
where "Thank you Oh Lord
for the deal I'm about to receive"
is chiselled into the blacktop
like a crow's incantation.

It's minus 3 degrees
on the Count Fahrenheit scale.
It would be Boraxo country
except there ain't no Boraxo.
And no mule teams. Here the mules drive.

Those rolling hills out there
are full of coal and oel and moly
a lota moly, that's lybdenum
the kind of denum the cowboys
around here wear. Around here everybody's
a cowboy with no cows
and every cow is without boys.
The boys have all gone to Rock Springs
to drill and to get shot.

   Low trailers hunkered in the Winde,
the big snau-blower. Scrap rock, like deinosaur fins
strung along the saurian freeway. Ah,
to endeavor to gain what another endeavors
to gain at the same time — competition!
eight barrelled, sharp clawed!

The graft is longbed style, Shot the Sheriff
fur shure, plus some shot the D. A. types,
they're all here. Tractor hat Stranglers,
Drive-up Drinkers, Mobile Snorters,
Pass on the Right Siders — mega rednek,
and for good reason — they've lynched all the Lavender
Neks.
More dangerous than Beirut.
They don't take hostages,
they don't take anything alive.

White rock laces, Four-Wheelers,
Big Dealers, Slim Jim Peelers,
Teased Hair Squealers! YaaHoo!
beller the Yahoos, it's where
they make the springs rock —
they don't call it Rock Springs for nothin'.

RADIO: White Christmas scrap,
Der Bingle baritone in motheaten night-cap.
We see through the landscape:
black rubbermaid crows
sail past a turquoise trailer, cold aluminum
hunched under the guns of the winde.
Inside the sleeping resident turns
on a couch of Budweiser cans
lips frozen turquoise, wrenched,
limbs on the pike to gangrene.

RADIO MUSAK: Gordon Lightleg!
dulcimerland, vests on pennywhistles,
Folkak, Blusak, Rucksak Rock.

On to Rollins and Riggins.
Steel mosquitoes probe an oel poule.
Deinosaur blood, black and crude,
the awful, devious oleo-olfactory
death odour, atomic weight 32, low and volatile,
driven by the pistons of hell,
the transfusion of the red roadmap,
where those stumping bags of the autoperiod
were once given to roam. Out the window

the Prontosauris Oil Company
sits next to the Horny-toed Boot Factory,
Overthrust Belt getting looser and looser now
after the gas these "Big Boys with popcorn teeth"
sucked out of the mantle.

On the asphalt cinch, rolling along,
kidneybelts tightened, the Kenworth Tractorsaurus
stampede into Wamsutter, Lusk, Dittlebone
and other such turquoise-eye-shadow towns.

The Wamsutter Hotel is totally electric.
Gas, permanent vacancy,
Conoco, Amoco, nowhere to go.
That Big Trailer over there
is where the Mayor lives,
pole light on all night,
prowling dogs, cringe and slobber
for an ankle to crush — not the friend of Everyman.
All this would be on a hill but there ain't none.

Gay Johnson installations
on both sides of the Strip.
The Howard Johnson of the High West.
A woman built like a stack of tires
fills up her coupé — SIGN
"Gay Johnsons, Buses Invited, Tobacco."
On second thought, Howard Johnson
doesn't deserve
to be the Gay Johnson of Wyoming.

Roadkill scattered like throwrugs
on blacktop. All the groundrunners
are either smart (located elsewhere)
or dead at the wheels of the heavy hitters.

Speedy schools of pickup trucks
scatter ahead of hunter packs of tractorsaurus,
Terribledactyl birds,
ghosts of old clavichord players
swoop with heavy grecian wings
to snatch up flat rabbit fleeces

from the altar of the tar, Wyoming crêpes
dredged in pea gravel crude.

RADIO: Governor of Wyoming Safety Bulletin:
Recommends strapping skis bottomup
on roof-rack in case of flip-over.
Woman held in tract house by unidentified
Gillette Krak Dealer — across town six onlookers
killed when police check out false report
and man rains lead on the unpaved avenue.

    State Trooper ahead between the strips,
coffee thermos in officer's fist.
His police shield doubles as Red Badge of Courage.
Snow fences, like arthritic twigs of protozoa
vanish into the vale of snow — the world is getting colder
as the transmitted propaganda says it is getting warmer.

TRANSMISSION FROM GILLETTE: The Razor City.
Serious roadkill this time — they're digging with backhoes
and throwing the victims in.
Gillette: people have been known
to go there just to have their throats cut
AD: "Trucker's Mistress,"
a truckstop item hooked to cigarette lighter
with concertina wire stretching to vitals
for over-the-road Mechanical Head —
available in truckstop gilt shops
with Chain Wallets and Turquoise Buckles —
"A real herpie saver."

    Laramie exits flash by like marked cards.
University of Wyo. What do they teachem there?
Nothin' works with ranchin' anyhay these days.
There they go, canterin' to the subcafeteria
in search of teflon heffers. Say!
What do you do when a Wyoming Cowboy
throws you a pin? Run like Hell!
because the grenade in his mouth
is about to go off!

Willie's on again . . .
all the truckertops and lesser heavy hitters
singing along under parts-shop, feedstore web hats,
the houseflies washed out in the strenuous amphetewake.
"On the Rode Again . . ."
Three Hundred pound Choir Boys
with eyes like strawberry-coconut donuts.

Crawling to Little America in Cheyenne.
Twenty-six degrees below Count Fahrenheit.
The transmission from Gillette fallen silent.
Cut off by the authorities no doubt. Somebody asks
how interesting can a town afford to be?
The soft, reasonable talk of Denver
supplants the airwaves, the jittery compromise of the city
crowds out the spontaneous stix.

A yellow ivory ball of pollution
hangs above Cheyenne's fibreglass air.
The Santa Claus-bright Gettysaurus Reks Refinery
is strewn along our approach, blowing
not so symbolic mushrooms, MX Missile Burgers,
the biggest meat in Strip Town.

Martyrs are a dime a dozen around here.
The best ones have been dead a long time.

Edward Dorn

— PART TWO —

Mr. Jefferson in 1803

THE AMERICAN WEST:
A PERSONAL DREAM FROM THE VANTAGE
POINT OF MONTICELLO IN 1803

Citizens of the Territory of Louisiana: It is with pleasure and some trepidation that I appear before you this morning. Trepidation, because in my own lifetime I never came West, although I was the foremost architect of our westward vision and the purchaser in 1803 of the Territory of Louisiana. I was never able sufficiently to disengage myself from the disagreeable burdens of politics to explore this vast territory myself. Although I dreamed of coming here to conduct an inventory of a continent on behalf of the Enlightenment, I spent my whole life huddled on the Eastern seaboard and was limited to a vicarious enjoyment of the achievements of my young friend Mr. Lewis. His great achievement is, I think, incapable of hyperbole. His suicide in 1809 was a loss to science, to his family and friends, and in particular to me.

I also come with trepidation because I am unused to public speaking. I am not an orator like that evil genie of American political life, Mr. Hamilton, or Patrick Henry, who I said spoke as Homer must have written. In my own lifetime I gave virtually no public addresses. When I reluctantly permitted my friends to forward my candidacy for the presidency in the year 1800, I made no speeches, I submitted to no interviews with the press, I published nothing, and of course there was no physical likeness of me available to the American voters. In the year 1880 the American citizens voted for their president on the basis of

---

Thomas Jefferson was portrayed during the symposium "Inhabiting the Last Best Place" by Clay Jenkinson. Jenkinson has given his scholarly interpretations of Jefferson to members of Congress and fourteen state legislatures, to judicial conferences, to academic audiences, including law schools, and at hundreds of community auditoriums in about forty states. Jenkinson speaks spontaneously, without script or notes. The quotations from Jefferson are sometimes, therefore, approximate.

political principle. Accordingly, I was able narrowly to defeat my good friend and predecessor, John Adams. I was therefore called upon to make an inaugural address. I prepared it carefully. On the morning of March 4, 1801, virtually alone, and unembarrassed by a military escort, I walked from the boarding house in which I was staying to the unfinished capitol building in our unfinished national capital on the Potomac. There I took out from my pocket a paper on which I had articulated my vision of America and read — to a hushed gathering of well-wishers and legislators — my inaugural address. Unfortunately I mumbled, and was so little audible that no one in that chamber heard my vision of America except my Virginia cousin, John Marshall, the Supreme Court chief justice, and he did not like what he heard. Earlier in the day he had written one of his arch-federalist friends about the change in political order that I liked to call the Second American Revolution. He said, "Mr. Jefferson's Republicans can be divided into two groups: theoretical visionaries and absolute terrorists. Among the latter," he said, "I am not disposed to classify Mr. Jefferson."[1] The rest of those who had gathered in the Senate chamber, having heard nothing of my vision, were forced to rush out afterwards and consult printed copies in the street. Moreover, as the third President to the United States, I broke with the emerging tradition of my predecessors and sent my annual messages by courier to Congress. It seemed to be monarchical and also an inefficient use of time to go over in a splendid horse-drawn carriage to deliver an annual address in person like some potentate from the Old World. In view of some of your more recent annual addresses, perhaps you would like to reinstate this admirable and restrained institution in your time.

I further feel trepidation because I am warned on good authority that many of you are lawyers. Late in life, a young man, a member of Congress from the commonwealth of Virginia, wrote to me at Monticello and said, "Why is it, Mr. Jefferson, that nothing gets done in Congress?" I said, "Sir, whenever you gather one hundred fifty lawyers into one room at one time, nothing good can come of it. These are, after all, men who are paid to talk by the hour, to yield nothing, and to argue about everything. No sir, to expect good sense and good government from a body of lawyers is to expect something that never has been and never can be in the history of the world."

I consider myself primarily a scientist, a natural philosopher, secondly a farmer, and a politician only reluctantly. I said once, "Whenever a man casts his eye longingly on public office, a certain rottenness of character is sure to creep in."[2] I wrote, "My whole life has been a war against my natural inclinations. The creator fitted me to be a scientist by rendering that my supreme delight."[3] So it is with pleasure that I turn from political issues to the West.

I saw the West as the guarantor of American liberties, a buffer of security for a fledgling republic, a growing space for our national expansion to the thousandth generation, and a zone for the maintenance of a healthy political economy in the United States. What I want to talk about briefly today are three issues: Indians, revolution, and agriculture. When I purchased Louisiana somewhat reluctantly in 1803, I saw it as a means of keeping at arm's length all potential enemies — the Spanish, the British, and the French. The West would be a buffer for this frail little experiment in self-government. I also saw it as a virtually infinite land into which we could expand in simple agriculture. I said to Mr. Madison in a letter from Paris that as long as there was free land in the West, this experiment in approximate democracy would prevail, for then every man who wished land on which to subsist could have it. But once we filled the West — I thought it would take many hundreds of years — then we would need to begin reluctantly to redistribute the wealth of the country from time to time. As long as there was free land in the West, I said, we would not crowd into cities, which are so many open sores on the face of the landscape. The acquisition of Louisiana meant we would not need to submit to Hamiltonian empire and industry. Empire is easy, republic a moral struggle. In my America, most able-bodied men and women would live quietly on land, close to their creator, in tune with nature, and this experiment in liberty would triumph.

That, in essence, was my vision of the West.

Before I go on, however, I must say that the British were right in one respect about the difficulties of moving westward. They were well aware that there were already sovereign inhabitants of this continent: the Indians, the so-called savages of the West. It seemed to me all of my life that if we created our own utopia in the West by systematically violating the rights of the aboriginal inhabitants of the continent, then we would have failed to live according to the principles of justice and respect and fair play without which America is a meaningless concept. In my second inaugural address, I devoted a long paragraph to our aboriginal neighbors. I said, these people deserved our commiseration; they only wanted to be left undisturbed. My own policy with respect to Indians was simple. It seemed to me that, in the short term, they ought voluntarily to yield their lands in the Ohio Valley and move out into this infinitude of Louisiana. This would give them breathing space, for it was my observation that every time white pioneers encountered a sovereign Indian village, they destroyed it, sometimes purposefully, more often not, with disease and alcohol and other systematic exploitations. Most tribes who had the misfortune to stand in the way of white pioneers were extinguished or diminished. Stone-age cultures did not apparently mix well with the land-hungry scions of Europe. So my hope was that, rather than removing these people entirely from the rolls of existence, we could encourage them instead to remove themselves voluntarily to the West, where there would be time for them to develop at their own pace, unembarrassed by white frontiersmen. They would, of course, benefit from certain European technologies — the wheel, the alphabet, phosphorescent matches, the plow — but they would be able to incorporate these blessings of culture into their admirably anarchic tribes at a pace more nearly their own. If sovereign peoples did not choose to yield their eastern territories, we would not force them to remove.

Second, I hoped that they would put down the war hatchet and the hunt and take up the plow like white farmers. Agriculture is the most sacred approach to economic life. Those for whom the hunt and warfare are the core of existence will always remain primitive. Nor are they truly civilized. My hope was that Indians would in the short term withdraw and begin to learn the superiority of sedentary agriculture, and when at last our white citizens reached the Mississippi River, our native brothers would be waiting with their own enlightened communities, as it were, with their own Parthenons and their own distinguished literature. Then we would intermingle and intermarry to produce an amalgamated American race, full of a lusty desire for natural rights, and yet with those trappings of European civilization that were in keeping with the simplicities of our republican vision. I could not conceive of expanding across the continent at the expense of our native brethren. I admit that this proved to be more difficult to avoid in practice than in the rational vision of Monticello.

Agriculture, it seems to me, is the only truly natural approach to life. I wrote only one book in my lifetime, *Notes on Virginia*, a set of responses to a series of queries put to me by the secretary of the French legation at Philadelphia. In it I said, "Those who labor in the earth are the chosen people of God, if God ever had a chosen people, whose breasts he has made his peculiar deposit for genuine and substantial virtue."[4] Farmers are the chosen people of God for two reasons. First of all, as the physiocrats teach us, farmers produce the basic wealth of the nation. They cooperate with creation and bring forth bounty and give it freely to the larger good of their community. They alone produce real wealth. Mr. Hamilton's minions, his capitalists, his bankers, his creditors, his manufacturers, and his tradesmen do not produce real wealth. They only spin their own fortunes from the wealth of the farmer. Second, farmers are the chosen people of God because they are closer to nature than the rest of us. They have their hands in the soil, they cooperate with creation. They look up to the sky, to the realm of meteorology, with deep respect, they nurture frail animals and frail plants, their hands are dirty from the humility of agriculture. The class of farmers generally, I said to Mr. Madison, have never been corrupt in any society whatsoever. A farmer is more free, more independent, and more truly happy than any other citizen. And every step you take away from your garden or your farm into abstraction or professionalism is a step away from good sense into dependency, loss of virtue, and certainly a loss of happiness.

I envisioned the American West as primarily a paradise for simple farmers. My idea of a farmer is of one who subsists, who feeds and clothes himself and his family, who is truly independent of Mr. Hamilton's mercantilist grid. If, at the end of the year, this Virginian pastoralist enjoys a tiny surplus, it is removed to the nearest village and bartered if possible for something that the farmer cannot produce for himself — a violin, books and paper, a pair of shoes. And then, having been engaged as little as possible in the money economy, the American Adam returns to his farm and lives free for another year. During his leisure hours at night, he reads Homer in the original Greek.

I saw the West also as a possible solution to the ugly problem of slavery. It was clear that slavery was the plague of the American experiment, a taint in our national crusade of innocence. Unfortunately we were unable in my lifetime to emancipate our Negro brethren. But if we could at least keep slavery out of the West, I believed, the nation would eventually become a slaveless society, if only because the Western states were destined to grow more powerful in the political arena than the original federation. Tobacco culture was corrupt, economically inefficient. It exploited land and it exploited people. It seemed to me only a matter of time before its usefulness was entirely lost. So if we could keep slavery huddled on the Atlantic side of the Appalachian mountains, the outrage of Negro servitude would not plague us into the future. This was the point of my Plan for the Government of the Western Territories (1784), which, had it passed, would have prohibited slavery from crossing the Appalachian mountains anywhere in the United States. When, at the end of my life, I saw slavery cross the Appalachians in a purely sectional fashion, I wrote in despair that this surely was the death knell of the nation.

I saw the West as a solution to the class conflicts that had riddled the Old World for centuries. Samuel Johnson, the great British lexographer, said that subordination and hierarchy in society are not only inevitable but essential to order and happiness. I disagreed. I felt we must move as quickly as possible to a classless society. And as long as there was free land in the West, there would be no basis for those subordinations that cities represent and promote. To me, the West offered almost infinite possibilities for individuals to pursue their own happiness, unencumbered by government or taxation or the sort of irreason that is inherent in city life. The West promised an egalitarian opportunity for the United States. I also thought that our administration of the West would show to a skeptical world that colonization is not the inevitable pattern of human expansion. I considered the West not an empire for Hamiltonian economics, not a Napoleonic empire for personal power and the glories of war, but rather an "empire for liberty such as the world has never previously seen." And it seemed to me that the West would show the world that it was possible to expand without subjugating our frontier neighbors. I was the principle author of the Plan for the Government of the Western Territories of 1784. That bill envisioned the incorporation of new territories on an equal basis with existing states. As soon as a new territory contained a minimum number of citizens, it began to govern itself and take part in our national councils. My whole life was devoted to the notion that our Western brethren must not be dependent on New York, or Boston, or Washington, but must pursue their own destinies in range after range of decentralized republics. Local control, states' rights, and decentralization were the themes of my political life. It seemed to me that we must even cheerfully anticipate the time when Western states would secede and form rival republics dedicated to their own conceptions of happiness and their own needs. Finally, I thought of the West as a "tabula rasa," in John Locke's terms, a blank slate, on which we could inscribe utopia. And it is on this theme that I wish to close.

In the Old World, in France in particular, the philosophers began their lives as reformers but almost immediately were frustrated by the root-bound cultures in which they grew. They therefore descended into literature and satire, and their reformist movements were stillborn. But in the New World, men of letters could be utopians and have some reason to believe that their utopian visions would be inscribed on an actual landscape. I was the principal author of the notion that our national capital should not be in Boston or Philadelphia or New York, but in the wilderness. If we maintained the capital in Philadelphia, our national center of power would forever bear the fragrance of its colonial past and of European tyranny. But if we carved out a capital in the wilderness, it would symbolize a new nation dedicated to a repudiation of the failures of the Old World. The Eastern seaboard, interesting and unique as it was, still maintained the ambience of political and cultural dependency on Europe, particularly Britain. But the West was unencumbered by the past. I saw the West as a blank slate, on which for the first time in human history a republic of reason and good sense and justice could be etched without the bloody revolutions that attend reform movements in the Old World. Thomas Paine said in his book *Common Sense*, "We have it in our power to begin the world over again."[5] I gave my life (reluctantly) to political statesmanship, not because I sought power but because it seemed to me that I lived in a unique time in history when a thoughtful statesman truly could help to shape a nation in a wilderness. That nation, in my view, should be peaceful, isolationist, and pastoral, should supplement its agriculture with the smallest possible manufacturing apparatus, should permit little or no permanent military establishment, should eschew the political struggles of the Old World, and should export nothing but agricultural produce and the idea of America. Our citizens should support themselves as much as possible on agriculture, live quietly according to the dictates of reason and nature, seek harmony with their Indian brethren, and prefer Enlightenment to wealth and power. Each citizen should participate in self-government and hasten the time when no government will be required whatsoever. My agrarian state would revolutionize itself every twenty years, either through peaceful constitutional revision or armed rebellion. "I like a little rebellion now and then," I wrote. "It is as important in the political world as thunderstorms in the natural world."[6]

Let me say, finally, that my most important doctrine was written in a letter to Mr. Madison from Paris in during my five years as the American minister there. To my closest friend and political lieutenant, I wrote, "The earth belongs in usufruct to living, not the dead."[7] The dead have no right to impose their vision on the future. The United States will be a great revolutionary nation, insofar as it breaks from time to time with the misguided habits of the past, including its own habits. We must make it possible for our children to begin the world over again according to their dreams and needs. We fought our revolution for the right of consent. We insisted that we consent to any form of government that coordinated our activities and taxed our labor. Each generation, like each nation, has a natural right to govern itself according to its will. Anything else is tyranny. I suggested to Jimmy Madison, therefore, that we tear up the constitution every nineteen years. I settled on a term of nineteen years as the effective life of a generation after consulting the Comte de Buffon's mortality tables. If in 1990 you impose upon the future your constitution, your positive law, and especially your national debt, you will be as guilty as George III of tyranny, and much more clever. The world belongs in *usufruct* to the living. Usufruct is a feudal legal term meaning that the occupant of an estate has a right to the fruits of that estate, but he must not degrade the carrying capacity of the land that has been entrusted to him. He must pass his sliver of the earth with all of its fruitfulness to his children.

I leave you with a question: Do you in 1990 enjoy Louisiana in usufruct, or are you in fact degrading its long-term carrying capacity and therefore tyrannizing your children without their consent? If you are doing the latter, I suggest revolution.

Clay Straus Jenkinson

— PART THREE —

The People

THE BOWL

There was a woman who left the city, left her husband, and her children, left everything behind to retrieve her soul. She came to the desert after seeing her gaunt face in the mirror, the pallor that comes when everything is going out and nothing is coming in. She had noticed for the first time the furrows under her eyes that had been eroded by tears. She did not know the woman in the mirror. She took off her apron, folded it neatly in the drawer, left a note for her family, and closed the door behind her. She knew that her life and the lives of those she loved depended on it.

The woman returned to the place of her childhood, where she last remembered her true nature. She returned to the intimacy of a small canyon that for years had loomed large in her imagination, and there she set up camp. The walls were as she had recalled them, tall and streaked from rim to floor. The rock appeared as draped fabric as she placed her hand flat against its face. The wall was cold; the sun had not yet reached the wash. She began wading the shallow stream that ran down the center of the canyon, and chose not to be encumbered by anything. She shed her clothing, took out her hairpins, and squeezed the last lemon she had over her body. Running her hands over her breasts and throat and behind her neck, the woman shivered at her own bravery. This is how it should be, she thought. She was free and frightened and beautiful.

For days, the woman wandered in and out of the slickrock maze. She drank from springs and ate the purple fruit of prickly pears. Her needs were met simply. Because she could not see herself, she was unaware of the changes — how her skin became taut and tan, the way in which her hair relaxed and curled itself. She even seemed to walk differently as her toes spread and gripped the sand.

All along the wash, clay balls had been thrown by a raging river. The woman picked one up, pulled off the pebbles until she had a mound of supple clay. She kneaded it as she walked, rubbed the clay between the palms of her hands, and watched it lengthen. She finally sat down on the moist sand and, with her fingers, continued moving up the string of clay. And then she began to coil it, around and around, pinching shut each rotation. She created a bowl.

The woman found other clay balls and put them inside the bowl. She had an idea of making dolls for her children, small clay figurines that she would let dry in the sun. Once again, she stopped walking and sat in the sand to work. She split each clay ball in two, which meant she had six small pieces to mold out of three balls she had found. One by one, tiny shapes took form. A girl with open arms above her head; three boys — one standing, one sitting, and one lying down (he was growing, she mused); and then a man and a woman facing each other. She had re-created her family. With the few scraps left over she made desert animals: a lizard, a small bird, and a miniature coyote sitting on his haunches. The woman smiled as she looked over her menagerie. She clapped her hands to remove the dried clay and half expected to see them dance. Instead, it began to rain.

Within minutes, the wash began to swell. The woman put the clay creatures into the bowl and sought higher ground up a side canyon, where she found shelter under a large overhang. She was prepared to watch if a flash flood came. And it did. The clear water turned muddy as it began to rise, carrying with it the force of wild horses running with a thunderstorm behind them. The small stream, now a river, rose higher still, gouging into the sandy banks, hurling rocks, roots, and trees downstream. The woman wondered about the animals as she heard stirrings in the grasses and surmised they must be seeking refuge in the side canyons as she was — watching as she was. She pulled her legs in and wrapped her arms around her shins, resting her cheekbones against her knees. She closed her eyes and concentrated on the sound of water bursting through the silence of the canyon.

The roar of the flood gradually softened until it was replaced by birdsong. Swifts and swallows plucked the water for insects as frogs announced their return. The woman raised her head. With the bowl in both hands, she tried to get up, but slipped down the hillside, scraping the backs of her thighs on rabbitbrush and sage. She finally reached the wash with the bowl and its contents intact. And then she found herself with another problem: She sank up to her knees in the wet, red clay, only to find that the more she tried to pull her foot free, the deeper she sank with the other. Finally, letting go of her struggle, she put the bowl and her family aside, and wallowed in it. She fell sideways and rolled onto her stomach, then over onto her back. She was covered in slimy, wet clay, and it was delicious. She stretched her hands above her head, flexed her calves, and pointed her toes. The woman laughed hysterically until she became aware of her own echo.

Her body contracted.

She must get control of herself, she thought; what would her husband think? What kind of example was she setting for her children? And then she remembered — she was alone. She sat up and stared at the coiled bowl full of clay people. The woman took out the figurines and planted them in the wash. She placed the animals around them.

"They're on their own," she said out loud. And she walked back to the spring where she had drunk, filled up her bowl with water, and bathed.

The next morning, when the woman awoke, she noticed that the cottonwood branches swaying above her head had sprouted leaves.

She could go home now.

Terry Tempest Williams

THE POET LETS HIS TONGUE HANG DOWN

A one-question interview from Bean News

I would enquire of you
The Slinger leaning forward askt
One of the 4 Great Questions
Least troubling my mind since my arrival:

WHO ARE THE BARBARIANS?

As if in a space elapsed
between our sighting then hearing a jet
The Poet grew pale
and his blaring transistor fell
from his Ivory Fingers
    four of whom
    jumped off at the knuckles
    and ran off with all his rings
    and straightway sent notes
    to the six who stayed
    expressing contempt and dismay
And the temperature fell in his veins
and his mouth weakened
and grew slack
and his left eye left the track
and wandered about the landscape
unlocused and his tongue
fell out over his chin
and his nose migrated
even as Gondwana too gorged

on the immensities of time to be observed
so that its movement is proven
by the striations of its slippage
as they are the scars of the Earth
And his ears floated upward
as if Helium was all they heard
and his feet came off and sped over the horizon
leaving even the wings of his ankles
    and his shoes filled with dust
    an instant ghost town complete
    with banging shutters and peeling posters
    of those of us wanted, dead or alive
Then his hair flew away
in a dust bowl condition
    like in the *Grapes of Wrath*
    and things what they were
    all the people of his barren scalp
    packed up and found their way to California
    around the craters of this once rich terrain,
And his brain snapped shut like a greasy spoon
when the last customer has et his chops
    then gone out the door wiping his chin
    with one hand while the other buys "The Times"
    which he reads standing on the corner
    toothpick in his mouth "Rams clobber Lions" in his eye
    and turns the pages to the comics where Rex Morgan
    is performing and can't be reached
    as his hand comes up from scratching his ass
    to catch the pages in the Michigan Winde
But the poet's Head was during this lapse
busy with alterations
and when the job was done
the bang of hammers
the whine of bandsaws gone
And all the baffling pulled off
his Head was a pyramid
the minimum solid

    And one of his eyes came home
trying to look like the trip had been a bore

when signs to the contrary were all over the floor
and he smiled
But the Eye on top of his pyramid
would say no more

Edward Dorn

PLAINSONG AT CROWHEART BUTTE

1

Near this place they fought, Shoshoni
and Bannock against the Crow . . . this river
basin harbored buffalo . . . today
blond boys gallop in the spring ride
here on herefords beneath this morning's sun pale
men in Stetsons peddle hardware in
Dubois Conoco and Exxon promise antlers
for a tankful of supreme . . . near this place
they fought . . . Shoshoni and Bannock
against the Crow . . . this
river basin harbored buffalo.

And near this place the strut macabre . . . thus
suppose a moon . . . suppose it full exquisite
absolute . . . its light . . . the corpses . . . Shoshoni Bannock
Crow . . . Washakie conquering Shoshoni chief cuts
the heart from one dead Crow and
jabs it on his lance . . . suppose his rush the thrill
the killer's thrill of life the taste the salty
taste of sweat like blood damp upon his lip his
eyes *his eyes* his own heart pumping
breath into the night his veins
so flushed that they distend . . . suppose
beneath the moon he raises to its light
the skewered heart and chants, his lucid
song suffusing night like moonlight . . . far off
perhaps the Crow as well beneath indifferent

phases of the full indifferent moon, benign and
absolute, perhaps the Crow, far off, hearing
know . . . *among some tribes the custom*
is to eat the heart or liver of
a worthy foe . . . the Crow, far off, hear perhaps and
know . . . Washakie his eyes and blood aflame, chants
holding high his bloody lance and
leads the ancient dance beneath the moon
full and absolute . . . there are those perhaps
who, far off, hearing know . . . this place the
strut macabre . . . they call it Crowheart Butte . . .
here Shoshoni and Bannock fought the Crow
this river basin harbored buffalo

2

And near this place while Washakie
"displayed" a dead Crow heart and danced Jake
Astor's boys passed through unperturbed . . . John
Jacob Astor never saw Astoria still
we must suppose he was amused . . . at Washakie
his bleeding heart and strut beneath the moon . . .
Tell my man he's number one Astor
winking told his crew keep a sharp eye out for beaver
and the swivel oiled your
gatling gun will get you through . . . Oh
yes Astor said crossing silken legs and
savoring an elegant cigar We
are much amused . . . spread the word . . . today
this roadside point of interest self-interestedly
proclaims "Washakie a mighty warrior . . . a wise chief
friendly to the whites . . ." inviting tourists to
return with us to Yesteryear and his faithful
Indian companion making highways to the sea
for *in this chief's teepee* we are told
hung no white man's scalp . . . Jake Astor never
saw Astoria but the ledger
shows he was astute . . . this monument
was easy . . . the sign says Crowheart Butte.

And Washakie we must suppose was much obliged
at something so grandiose as "history"
treating him so fine . . . how
could he know he grinned a Stepnfetchit grin and
danced a soft shoe shuffle sporting
that awesome heart upon his eagle feathered lance and
singing bravely as he danced, *I*
feed your heart to dogs Crow they
shit upon your grave. Astor placed his fine cigar
between his teeth and smiled as he applauded. That boy's
good I think he can be used . . . and
"in consideration of the local chief" wise
and mighty chief supreme arbiter of this basin's
buffalo almighty shaker of a dead Crow
heart upon a stick in consideration as they say of
the local chief they call this fort
Fort Washakie . . . today with Astor's blessing
I pass blandly through this land that that
Crow's heart like Washakie's beat to have . . . and
under Astor's moon a moon so big
it bathes a continent in exquisite silver
light last night I took a leak and dumped
where willows mark both their graves . . . down the road
there is this place where Washakie was silly
while Astor was astute . . . this monument
was easy . . . they call it Crowheart Butte.

3

Moonset flight of the owl sunrise cicadas sing
Wind River in the spring
I bathe ablution in the high spring run
horses grazing ablution in the cold fast waters
thank you Bannock and Shoshoni thank you for this place
in the morning's golden sun Fort
Washakie spelled out in stones
whitewashed on the hill Fort
Washakie sanctuary to white men fugitive
from Sioux white men Sacacawea Fort
Washakie her grave Sacajewea her grave this grove

defiled my clean white body defiles
this blest indifferent grove because Sacajewea
Sacacawea Sacajewea Sacacawea because
Sealth Seattle Sealth because Joseph
Hinmaton Yahlatlat Joseph because Crazy Horse Crazy
Horse said yes the interpreter said no because
the bayonet the corporal's bayonet in his
side because Napoleon was
a corporal because Hitler was a corporal because Old
Hickory was a corporal because this
grove is real estate because Sacacawea Joseph Seattle
Captain Jack Crazy Horse Wounded Knee Sand Creek Saigon Fort
Washakie because we couldn't get the lingo or
wouldn't even E.P. thick skinned and bold let
not the daughter no nor any of us
burnish what is tarnish the sins too
will teach us because E.P. the dazzle of
sweat and coin fixed rightly in his third eye who
learned nine languages ancient and
modern east and west and knew King James
precisely for what it was collaboration
hegemony of the rich and righteous because E.P. lamenting
this half savage country couldn't get the lingo
nor the fathers of our country not
Jefferson his dictionary awash in Chesapeake Bay
not Jackson who put the Creeks in their graves and
sold the plots in Philadelphia because
not any of us could get the lingo or would because Shakespeare
maker of beauties even on the edges of civilization
bedazzled us and John Wilkes Booth with blank verse and
Cicero in his mouth bedazzled us because
spelled sixteen different ways Shakspeer Shakespere Shakespeare
Shakespear he Washakie in whose tipi hung
no white man's scalp he Washakie
shook his spear jabbed on it the fresh heart of a dead
Crow his enemy the Crow and danced because in celebration
he Washakie enemy of Sioux and Crow and Nez Perce
succor (sic) of white men because killer of none he Washakie
namesake and hero of this grove defiled wise
and mighty chief he Washakie learned our lingo carved

the heart of one good Crow because because
thank you Bannock and Shoshoni thank you
ablutions in this morning's golden sun thank you
high spring waters thank you cicadas thank you sunrise thank you
flight of the owl thank you moonset moonset moonset because

Peter F. Michelson

MOTEL SUPERBO

A sleepwalker from Continent I
prints out the contract
and hands me a key attached
to a leg iron.
The drapes, heavy with fire retarder,
won't quite shut. The air condish
is clogged with breath of dead carpet.
Kim Basinger is crazy for sex
on HBO, gimme mo say Steamboat Springs.
Dodge Rams charge and butt
along the main drag.
The blasé traffic lights control
with cold indifference the snarling,
big pipe packs, sends them along
and then pins them to the tar
where they whine and gnash
at the electronic tether,
sending tics through the ignorant sleepers.

Edward Dorn

PROGRESS OR DECLINE?
JUDGING THE HISTORY OF WESTERN
EXPANSION

On a flight from Cody, Wyoming, I met the person for whom Western history worked out perfectly. Sitting next to me on the plane was a very tanned fellow with a very nice fringed leather jacket and a handsome black cowboy hat. White ones pick up dirt too fast, he told me, which seems to me heavily symbolic of something.

This fellow, the owner of a prosperous real estate company in Florida, had recently decided *not* to go all out in the Miami real estate game, but to pull back on his way to the top and instead buy a dude ranch on the way to Yellowstone. So now he spends half the year outside Cody and half the year in Miami. He was also very taken — understandably — with the area around Carmel, and he was very close to buying property there and bringing dude ranching to Monterey Bay (which, under the power of a considerable urge for a Freudian slip, I initially typed into this text as "Monetary Bay").

I have a couple of reasons for bringing this fellow to your attention. The first reason hit me as he was talking of his pleasure in riding horses through the hills outside Carmel and in the mountains outside Cody. This carried echoes of Richard Henry Dana on horseback during shore leave in California, and echoes of Teddy Roosevelt recovering on horseback in the Dakotas from the loss of his mother and his wife. And it suddenly seemed to me that sitting next to me on the plane was the primary beneficiary of the whole process of Anglo-American Western expansion. Partly to test the theory, and partly to test his ego, I said, "You are it, aren't you? The culmination of the whole business? Jedediah Smith, Narcissa Whitman, John C. Fremont, George Armstrong Custer — they made you possible. You're the one it all worked out for." And, with black hat firmly in place (the etiquette of whether cowboys should remove their hats while riding the open ranges of the air has apparently not been settled), my traveling companion fully and heartily agreed that he was the culmination, the consummation of the Western enterprise. It seems a curious outcome for a cause in which so many have died.

And that is the first reason I wanted to describe this fellow today: because there are moments when all of the struggles and sorrows of Western expansion seem to have borne their principal fruit in the creation of an economic structure that gives more packages of pleasure and privilege to people who are already over their heads in pleasure and privilege.

While no one chose the date of this conference, October 19, for strategic, symbolic purposes, it *is* the anniversary of the 1987 stock market crash. I think that is all for the best; there is simply no reason to meet all day in order to be Pollyannas, in order to devote ourselves to "feeling good" about the American West and its past and present and future. This is a pretty fine group of people assembled today — the audience as much as the speakers — and the risk of having such a pleasant group assembled is that it could make us giddy, swept away by our own collective good nature into unreasonable optimism. So the fact that the newspapers are filled today with one-year-after-the-crash stories seems to me all for the best. Anyone who begins to get giddy and hopeful can simply leave the room, get a newspaper, and come back to reality. Or, to stay within the airplane frame of reference, those who begin to get giddy with hope can think back to their departures from the airports of most major Western cities — think back to the improbably grand physical setting for those cities, think back to the painful, brownish aerial scum that blankets them, think back to the spread of suburbs that can, if you are in the wrong mood, make the earth look exactly as if it has come down with a bad skin disease with an undiscovered cure. A year ago I flew out of Los Angeles, south, down the coast, and looked at that stunning set of beaches, that grand meeting of continent with Pacific, coated with warehouses and oil tanks and motels and overall dense smog, until I was utterly convinced that Western history was tragic, a terrible twist on the myth of Eden. Instead of getting thrown out of Eden, Adam and Eve in this version stayed, and ruined paradise. And when God came back to check on them, He could barely recognize the place, with abandoned cars and piles of tires on fire and coal-fired electrical generating plants on the site where the tree of the knowledge of good and evil once stood, and with Adam and Eve sitting around looking quite proud of themselves.

That brings me to the second reason I have begun with my Cody, Wyoming, airplane companion. I do think that in many ways Western

American history is the story of a group of people going to hell in a handbasket, but over and over again. The conversation from Cody to Denver was simply another reminder of this: One has frequent occasions to think that the company, in this ill-destined handbasket, is great. There are moments, living and traveling in the West today, when one simply thinks, "We are, from all impressions, in a mess, but one could not ask for better companions."

Regrettably, embarrassingly, I *liked* my Cody airplane companion — he was, no doubt, an invader and intruder from Florida, but his brief tour of duty in the West had changed him and given him some characteristics — and certainly some *clothes* — that are not everyday sights in Miami. More important, he was a good sport in an argument, and his sense of humor, put to the test by our argument, was in fine shape. One can only hope, on behalf of the Adam and Eve of the original story, that during their transportation out of paradise they were able to enjoy such a pleasant and stimulating conversation; one can only hope, on behalf of the ancients, that during the decline and fall of the Roman Empire, the art of conversation was as well developed and as much enjoyed as it was on the trip from Cody. This may seem to some of you a superficial point — that in the midst of a troubled time, opponents can still sit next to each other for two hours and enjoy each other's company and conversation, but to me this is the only basis for hope we have.

Peter Hassrick, the expert on Western art, shows and describes a painting by Frederick Remington called "In Search of Geronimo." It shows troopers and their horses on a narrow, desert mountain path. "Artist in Search of Geronimo," Hassrick muses, and goes on to note that Remington himself, in the writing that accompanied the painting, remarked of the search for Geronimo, "Thank heavens, we haven't found each other yet." The elite white Eastern painter, and the resistant and determined Apache warrior — it is probably just as well that they did not find each other in the nineteenth century, because the conditions for conversation were not good in those times. But now, whether or not we want it that way, we *have* all found each other; Remington's kin have met Geronimo's kin, and even if the conditions for cross-cultural conversation are still not ideal, they are immeasurably better than they were in the nineteenth century.

Each incident, then, in which Westerners of these various backgrounds and convictions defy the odds and choose not to attack each other, nor to evade each other, but to *converse* — each of these incidents seems to me powerfully freighted with hope. But those moments of hope still must be set against those moments of despair, when parts of Western America, from the air, seem to say, clearly and directly, that humanity is an infection of the earth, and this region has come down with a bad case of it.

As to this gloomy picture I am presenting, let me make a long story short, a story probably familiar to many of you here, and say, that interpretations of Western American history have gone through a recent revolution. Western American history used to be what I will call, not altogether kindly, Happy Face History, Have a Nice Day History, because it was so firmly centered on Anglo-Americans, and because it seemed to end so well, with white people in charge of the continent and with a lot of natural resources converted into cash in white people's pockets. That is not the version of Western American history we teach now. The recognition of the importance of Indian people, of Hispanic people, of Asian people, of black people, and of white people who did not necessarily succeed in their enterprises has ended that "triumph of civilization" school of history for all time. And just as important, environmental history has knocked over the "triumphant mastery of the wilderness" school of Western history by showing the complex and complicated ways that white pioneers, sometimes out of innocent motives, launched a landslide of unfortunate physical events: soil erosion, the depletion of minerals, the pollution of streams and rivers, the scarring of landscapes, the destruction of wildlife, the devastation of forests. I can convey this reorienting of Western American history, away from happy endings and toward tragedy, most vividly by quoting from a friend, the Western historian Donald Worster, author of *Dust Bowl* and *Rivers of Empire* (who is, in this quotation — just to demonstrate the happy and productive level of scholarly exchange in Western history — actually describing my own book, *Legacy of Conquest*, but putting the idea more vividly than I believe I did myself): "[T]he dream of conquest itself has begun to go sour among the white conquerors. They are losing the very property they won to the forces of environmental deterioration, and they are losing their cultural dominance to a resurgence of minority self-confidence and influence. The West thus becomes the region where the white man destroys his own world — at the very moment of victory."[1]

Now that is rather forcefully put, more forcefully than I put it myself in *Legacy*, but it does indicate how far Western history has traveled from the old celebration of the Anglo-American triumph over the continent. What is beyond dispute now is this: that westward-moving Anglo-Americans, while they thought they were making progress, were also making a mess: a mess in their relations with nature; a mess in their relations with native Indian people, with both native and, later, immigrant Hispanic people, with immigrant Asian people; and, from time to time, in conflicts over the allocation of resources and the allocation of profits from those resources, a mess in their relations with each other, between groups and individuals we too often lump into that monolithic category, "white people."

We can choose, so far, between two clear responses to the fact that progress and decline came in a mixed package. One response rests on this premise: Despite a few unfortunate side effects, the pioneers thought they were making progress, and indeed they were, because the bedrock definition of progress means the greatest good for the greatest number. This may at first seem like a resurgence of Happy Face History, but I think it is more than that. There is simply no denying the fact that the West has meant and means opportunity for an enormous number of people — not only for emigrants from the eastern United States and European immigrants, but also for Asian and Mexican immigrants down to this day. Mexican immigrants, after all, have a *reason* for taking on the risk and sacrifice of crossing into the American West. Even though the conditions they find are far from ideal, American wages are indeed far better than Mexican wages. The "progress as the greatest good for the greatest number" argument is not, then, necessarily ethnocentric, but it is necessarily reductive — dismissing the hardships and inequities that came in the same package with the opportunities, and dismissing the environmental prices paid to provide them.

If one rejects this first response, then, to the reinterpretation of Western history, the pattern has been that one is then catapulted to an opposite response, a response where the operating premise is this: The pioneers were ruthless exploiters and extractors whose Judeo-Christian heritage supported them in their belief in the rightness of their own power and privilege, and who set about tearing up nature and ruining the natives with something close to purpose and intention.

There is no question that Western history provides some candidates for this ticket. In some ruthless episodes of war, in mining camps where nature had only the role of the package in which treasure came (a package to be discarded like Christmas wrappings when the treasure was removed), in the exploitation of timber where loggers ripped through forests as if forests were indeed the home of Satan, response number two seems like the accurate one. There were indeed participants in Western expansion who look as if they took their training courses in pioneering from urban street gangs, from thieves, from arsonists, from criminals who specialized in the malicious destruction of property.

But that is not the whole story. Neither the forgiving "greatest good for the greatest number" response nor the condemning "greedheads out on a round of destruction" response comes anywhere near to giving a full portrait of the complexity of the nineteenth-century participants in Western expansion. Both responses, in fact, share one premise in common: that in America, money talks. Response number one: money talks, but in human hands, that more or less works out for the best, and the majority of people in the West end up okay. Response number two: money talks, and this vicious force drives an engine of environmental and cultural destruction.

Well, certainly money matters, and no interpretation of the West can go anywhere without that recognition. But other things matter too, and mattered in the nineteenth century as well. White Americans who entered the West then and set themselves to work developing the resources had a clear idea that they were agents of progress. Of course, the hope for financial gain played its role in this, but there was also a strong component of the mind, a considerable faith in the word they used frequently, the word "improvement." Putting resources to use was certainly a route to financial profit, but it was also, in their minds, "improvement" — and living under the power of that idea was one way of wearing blinders. There are unfortunate consequences, outcomes, results of their actions that are glaring and visible to us, but the power of the idea of "improvement" — taking waste places and putting them to human use — was so strong that those side effects could hardly be seen. I think, then, that many of the white settlers (or invaders or conquerors, according to your point of view) would have been astonished by response number two, the damning of the pioneers for their clear, conscious violence and destruction. "Us, destroyers?" they would think. "This isn't destruction, this is improvement."

Recognizing this blindness to consequence does not mean that we have to adopt blindness ourselves. Recognizing their viewpoint is, of course, only fair, only justice to the dignity of humans in our past. But I should say that this is the part where some of the Western historians I respect most say that I am pulling my punches, turning soft and mushy-minded, letting the settlers (or invaders or conquerors) off the hook.

But there is another point on which I would not budge — the "improvement" school of Western expansion was by no means universal in the nineteenth century. Clearly this faith was not winning a lot of fans among Indians or Hispanics, but it was far from universal even among Anglo-Americans. In a book called *Witnesses to a Vanishing America*, Lee Mitchell has traced a history of regret of some white Americans who noted and lamented the "price of progress" as early as the 1830s. In fact, one can go back before that, back to the era before Anglo-Americans reached the Trans-Mississippi West, and see some of the same thing

— in Puritan leaders lamenting the injury to community that came from the geographical spread of colonists looking for more land, in British colonial governors wringing their hands over the damage done to Indian relations by irresponsible colonial land-hunters. Contrary to simple-minded images of American history, there was never universal national glee over Western expansion — the era of the Mexican-American War, for instance, had a full share of anxious, worried Americans concerned about the morality of the conquest of the present-day Southwest and concerned about its effect on the troubling question of slavery and its expansion. There was, in other words, always a group or several groups inclined to see Western expansion more as a matter of decline than of progress, and we are not imposing late twentieth-century hindsight in raising the question today.

For anyone who is today a "regretter," who has moments of thinking, "What a continent it once was," moments of wondering whether the addition of toxic waste, pesticides, engines dependent on fossil fuel, and nuclear waste has been altogether an improvement, then the good news is that you have a distinguished pioneer heritage as well. You too have a lineage reaching back through the decades and even centuries, a lineage of "regretters."

There was, moreover, something about Western expansion that made it the most fertile possible ground for regret. The rapid, irreversible change of territorial expansion and resource development carried a predictable side effect in nostalgia; such a headlong pace of change made it inevitable that before-and-after contrasts would haunt people's memories, and a large number of people would thus find themselves yearning for what was, yearning for what had been, and out of that yearning would come an almost irresistible urge to romanticize the past, to imagine lost and impossible golden ages of harmony or bravery or nobility or opportunity. Westerners developed the habit of plunging forward into the future with their eyes cast backward, over their shoulders, into a vanished Eden, lost before it ever fully existed.

There is, in addition, a pattern of thought that has been growing in power over the twentieth century, the pattern of thought by which one looks at the Flatirons bordering Boulder and then looks at the roads and the cars and the shopping malls, and thinks, "Oh dear, this hasn't worked out well at all."

That is the perspective implied in the title of this book — *A Society to Match the Scenery*, with the apparent assumption being that, up to this point, the scenery has considerably outscored the society. The scenery, by and large, looks better than the society. But we are only able to make that observation — we are only able to find the society wanting

— because the whole economic and political structure that Western expansion built allows us to be here to judge it so harshly. We can raise the question of what sort of society *would*, actually, suit the scenery, because we live in a society that asks those questions. It is almost as if the participants in Western expansion struggled and worked and fought and extracted and exploited, all so that we could come along in 1988 and pick on them and point out their flaws and their sins and the multiple ways in which they thought they were making progress, but were in fact making a mess.

Bill Hornby from *The Denver Post* wrote a column about this conference, and in the column he expressed the hope that we would not end it in despair, that we would instead find grounds for continuing to think of the West as, in Wallace Stegner's phrase, the geography of hope. I'm not sure if this is exactly what he had in mind, or if he will settle for this, but I will return to my earlier notion, that we may be going to hell in a handbasket, but the company and the opportunity for conversation are both excellent in that journey. And (here is where the hope comes in) it still seems to me that if we make that conversation frank and direct and open, and if we face up fully to the decline as well as the progress recorded in Western history, we may be able to change the direction of our collective vehicle, or at least to slow it down and give ourselves more time to talk.

Patricia Nelson Limerick

A SOFT WIND BLOWING THROUGH THE AMERICAN WEST

Pima. Papago. Apache. Navajo. Hopi. Zuni. Cochiti. Zia. Santa Domingo. San Carlos. Jicarilla. Mescalero. Jemez. Acoma. Comanche. Crow. Blackfoot. Bannock. Sioux. Dakota. Oglala. Teton. Osage. Assinowan. Shoshoni. Ute. Goshute. Paiute. Arapaho. Cheyenne. Shawnee. Pawnee. Kiowa. Gros Ventre. Nez Perce. Pomo. Klamath. Miwok. Mono. Yakima. Tewa. Tegwa. Mojave. Shivwits. Walapi. Havasupi. Hispanic. Asian. Black. Slavic. Scandinavian. Irish. Italian. Greek. Basque. Mennonite. And Mormon.

A chant of regional diversity that calls these people into being. A mantra of just some of the subcultures of the American West.

And what is the value of such disparate voices? I maintain it is in the stories we tell; the stories that bind us to the land.

I recall hiking in the Jedediah Smith Wilderness, on the western slope of the Tetons. A man joined me on the trail. We struck up a conversation and I asked him where he was from. He looked at me with a twinkle in his eye and began whistling like the wind. I didn't know what to say. Puzzled, I shrugged my shoulders. He smiled.

"Laramie," he said.

This man knows his place and the wind that blows through his country. And he has a story.

A story keeps things known. It is the umbilical cord that connects us to the past, present, and future. A story allows us to envision the possibility of things. It draws on the powers of memory and imagination. It awakens us to our surroundings. It reminds us who we are and where the source of our power lies.

Native peoples have always known this — that the earth is a storied landscape.

Luther Standing Bear, a Lakota, recalls:

Lakota children, like all others, asked questions and were answered to the best ability of our elders. We wondered as do all young, inquisitive minds, about the stars, moon, sky, rainbows, darkness, and all other phenomena of nature. I can recall lying on the earth and wondering what it was all about. The stars were a beautiful mystery and so was the place where the eagle went when he soared out of sight. Many of these questions were answered in story form by the older people. How we got our pipestone, where corn came from, and why lightning flashed in the sky were all answered in stories.[2]

Maria Chona, a Papago woman, explains how a child learned among her people: "My father went on talking to me in a very low voice. This is how our people always talk to their children, so low and quiet, the child thinks he is dreaming. But he never forgets."[3]

And then I remember asking Renny Shortbull, a Sioux boy of twelve, where he would take me in his country.

"I would take you to the St. Francis Mission because that is where the storytellers are. They know the ways of our people. I would take you there first."

Renny Shortbull knows that stories grow out of community, that they define, elucidate, and inform our world. They teach us what is possible, what we can count on, what we can hold on to in the midst of change.

Story maintains a stability within that community, providing common knowledge as to how things are; how things should be. Knowledge based in experience. A story has a composite personality that becomes the conscience of the group. It belongs to everyone.

Breathe deeply. It is the smell of sage we share in the West, the mutuality of stories that tell us who we are.

The Kalahari Bushmen have said, "A story is like the wind. It comes from a far-off place and we feel it."

It was going to be a long ride home for fifteen Navajo children. Dropping kids off five, ten, and twenty miles apart is no small task. We were committed for the night. The sun had just vanished behind Giant's Knuckles, causing those in the back of the pickup to huddle close.

"It gets cold in the desert," I said.

"It's winter," one of the children replied. They covered their mouths with their hands, giggling, as we continued to bump along the dirt roads surrounding Montezuma Creek. What did the driver and I know? We were Anglos.

We had been down by the river for the afternoon. A thin veneer of ice had coalesced along its edge. The children, bending down, would break off pieces and hold them between their thumbs and forefingers. Before the ice would melt, some brought the thin sheets to their eyes as a lens, while others placed them in their mouths and sucked on the river. Still others winged the ice sheets across the cobbles, watching, listening to them shatter like glass.

Life on the river's edge was seen in whirligig beetles, water skaters, and caddis fly larvae under stones. Canada geese flew above the channel, landing for brief intervals, then continuing on their way. The children followed tracks, expecting to meet a pack of stray dogs hiding in the tamarisks. Our shadows grew longer with the last light of day reflecting on river rapids and willows.

The hours by the river were well spent. Now, in the back of the pickup, the children told tales of days when a horse could enter a hogan and leave as a man; of skinwalkers disguised as coyotes who stalk the reservation with bones in their hands, scratching white crosses on the doors of ill-fated households. They spoke of white owls, ghostly flashes of light that can turn the blood of mice into milk.

Just then, my friend hit the brakes. Those in the back fell forward.

"Did you see that?"

"What?" we all asked.

"A mountain lion! It streaked across the road. I'll swear it was all tail!"

The children whispered among themselves, "Mountain Lion . . ."

We filed out of the truck. My friend and I walked a few feet ahead. We found the tracks. A rosette. Five-toed pads, clawless, imprinted on the sand, in spite of the cold.

"No question," I said. "Lion. I wonder where she is now?"

Looking into the darkness, I could only imagine the desert cat staring back at us. I looked over at the children. Most of them were leaning against the truck as headlights approached.

"What's going on?" a local Navajo man asked as he rolled down the window of his pickup with his motor idling.

My friend recognized him as the uncle of one of the children. "We think we saw a mountain lion," he said.

"Where? How long ago?"

The other man in the cab of the truck asked if we were sure.

"Pretty sure," I said. "Look at these tracks."

The men got out of their vehicle and shined their flashlights on the ground until they picked up the prints. One of the men knelt down and touched them.

"This is not good," the Navajo uncle said. "They kill our sheep."

He looked into the night and then back at us. "What color of eyes did it have?"

My friend and I looked at each other. The Navajo elder began reciting the color of animals' eyes at night.

"Deer's eyes are blue. Coyote's eyes are red." His nephew interrupted him. "Green — the lion's eyes were green."

The two men said they would be back with their guns and sons tomorrow.

We returned to the truck, my friend driving with a handful of kids up front and the rest in the back around me as we nestled together under blankets. The children became unusually quiet, speaking in low, serious voices about why mountain lions are considered dangerous.

"It's more than just killing sheep," one child explained. "Mountain Lion is a god, one of the supernaturals that has power over us."

Each child gave away little bits of knowledge concerning the lion: that it chirps like a bird to fool you; that parts of its body are used for medicine; that in the old days, hunters used the sinew of lion for their bows. The children grew more and more anxious as fear seized their throats. They were hushed.

We traveled through the starlit desert in silence, except for the hum of the motor and four wheels flying over the washboard.

In time, from the rear of the pickup, came a slow, deliberate chant. Navajo words — gentle, deep meanderings of music born out of healing. I could not tell who had initiated the song, but one by one each child entered the melody. Over and over they sang the same monotonous notes, dreamlike at first, until gradually the cadence quickened. The children's mood began to lighten, and they swayed back and forth. What had begun as a cautious, fearful tone emerged as a joyous one. Their elders had taught them well. They had sung themselves back to *hozho*, the place within where the world is balanced and whole.

After the last child had been taken home, my friend and I were left with each other, but the echo of the children's chant remained. With many miles to go, we rolled down the windows in the cab of the truck, letting the chilled air blow through.

Mountain Lion, whose eyes I did not see, lay on the mesa, her whiskers retrieving each note carried by the wind.

We have much to learn. And there are other stories.

In 1910 Tsuru and Kinji Kurumada left Japan and immigrated to Richfield, Utah. Kinji Kurumada was a farmer. He loved the Utah soil, which yielded robust harvests of potatoes, tomatoes, melons, and corn. Day after day he worked the land. But perhaps Mr. Kurumada was best known for his canyon lettuce and for how he supplied neighboring counties each year with his greens. There were family priorities. Each spring the lettuce was planted way into the night, as it had to be harvested before the Fourth of July. The moon would shine. The seeds would be folded into the earth. And as ritual would have it for more than thirty years, the canyon lettuce grew and was harvested early, just as the community had come to expect year after year.

Mr. Kurumada also had an uncanny gift for recognizing soils. It grew out of his intimacy with the land. It was a game with residents, bringing the old man samples. They would hold out their hands, dirt in both palms, and ask, "Where are these from?"

He would look at them, mull them over in his own fingers, and then reply, "This is from Monroe Mountain — and this soil belongs to Capitol Reef."

And then other locals would come forth with two more handfuls. The old man would make a clod from the loose dirt. "Glacial till. Draper, Utah. And this — looks like Big Cottonwood Canyon."

He was usually right. Kinji Kurumada knew his ground, establishing a firm sense of place for himself and his family.

In the spring — March 15, 1942, to be exact — June Kurumada, son of Kinji Kurumada, was on a bus for California. He was traveling with members of the Japanese-American Citizen's League. The bus was stopped. June was pulled off, arrested, and jailed. It was the beginning of the internment camps for Japanese-Americans. Had Kinji Kurumada been around to check the soils, he would have found two handfuls; one from Topaz, Utah; the other from Heart Mountain, Wyoming.

There are problems in the American West. It has never been easy.

I recall traveling to northern New Mexico, taking the high roads from Santa Fe to Taos. I stopped in the Spanish village of Chimayo and entered the *santuario*. Back home, my grandmother was very ill. I sat on the wooden pews carved by a villager and prayed. An elderly woman sitting next to me took my hand and said, "Vente; come."

I followed her down the center aisle past the altar of candles into a small room. There was a hole in the floor where the earth was exposed. She knelt beside the red, sandy soil and took some in hand. I watched her gently rub her palms together with the blessed earth and then cross herself. She looked up at me, placed her hand on my shoulder, rose, and left.

Alone, I knelt down as she had, took some of the red earth as she had, and rubbed it between my hands with my grandmother in mind. I marked my forehead and prayed in the manner I was accustomed to.

Out in the courtyard, the Hispanic woman waited.

"*La tierra cura*," she whispered. "The Mother Earth heals."

"Gracias," I replied, and we parted ways.

La tierra cura. The earth heals.

A woman from Chimayo knows. Navajo children who sing themselves back to health know. So does the son of a Japanese farmer who has in his *tokunoma* (the gallery where beauty is displayed) river stones and soil samples from the canyon where his father harvested lettuce.

Stories. More stories. We remember where the source of our power lies.

Could it be, as Frederick Turner suggests in *Beyond Geography*, that the true story of the Western settlement is a spiritual one?

Five generations back, when Mormon colonizer Brigham Young stood on the threshold of the Salt Lake valley and said, "This is the place," my ancestors understood that their lives depended on the grace of the Great Basin to feed their souls as well as their bodies.

I share their sentiments, and after 141 years of continual settlement; a residency of Dixons, Blacketts, Romneys, and Tempests, this is my home. I choose to dig in, knowing eventually my bones will lie next to theirs.

I am talking about a spirit of place, and the human necessity to realize itself through community, which is in direct correspondence to the land. The subcultures of the West have either adapted to a homeland or are in the process of adopting one, and it is this relationship between landscape and community that is best articulated through story.

It is a matter of becoming native — not Navajo, Hopi, or Sioux, but rather recognizing within whatever subculture we belong to that there is a sense of place. We can articulate our relationship to the land, honoring our own natural autobiographies, realizing wild rivers run through our veins.

D. H. Lawrence speaks of the "future primitive," the man and woman courageous enough to see in the land their destiny and brave enough to engage in it. He says:

> They went like birds down the great electric direction of the west, lifted like migrating birds on a magnetic current. They went in subtle vibration of response to the new earth, as animals travel far distances vibrating to the salt-licks.
>
> They walked a new earth, were seized by a new electricity, and laid in line differently. Their bones, their nerves, their sinews took on a new molecular disposition in the new vibration.

They breathed a savage air and their blood was suffused and burnt. A new fierce salt of the earth, in their mouths penetrated and altered the substance of their bones. Meat of wild creatures, corn of the aboriginal earth, filled and impregnated them with the unknown America.[4]

In many ways, the unknown America, this unknown America, still exists. As Herman Melville tells us, "It is not down in any map; true places never are."[5] And so, as Lawrence goes on to say, "now we wait for the fulfillment for the law in the west, the inception of a new era of living. . . . We wait for the miracle, for the new soft wind."[6]

Disparate voices, speaking on behalf of the land — we hold this sprig of sage and remember.

If there is a miracle in the West, it is in the fabric these subcultures create; the tension and strength woven together through regional diversity; the warp dressed by individual communities and the weft created by the landscape that binds us.

It is here we must identify our clout, our regionality, as a philosophical and political entity. Not out of provincialism, but out of the Jeffersonian model that "united we stand, divided we fall." Monoculture in the West is a by-product of laziness and grief, a lack of passion with no homeland to love.

La tierra cura. The earth heals.

We speak of these things, to the mutuality of our stories and stand our ground.

Peter Schragg, in an editorial for the *Oregonian*, June 7, 1988, writes, "It is time for the West to stop playing to the East, just as the East, stop playing to Europe. The American orientation from the fifteenth century, well before there was an America, always has been that of East facing West. In a sense, the East imagined the West into being as much as Western reality shaped the East's imagination. The East still looks to the West, primarily for curiosities and aberrations, rather than for comprehension and perspective. Unfortunately, the West has been too ready to oblige."[7]

Standing ground. The West has its issues: environmental, economic, social, and cultural. They are compounded by the subcultures more often than they are reformed. We need to find common ground, ways of expressing ourselves and of articulating national interests in our own terms. We need a geopolitics of this region, and its seeds may be found in story.

In 1950 government agents proposed to get rid of prairie dogs on some parts of the Navajo reservation in order to protect the roots of the sparse desert grass and thereby maintain some marginal grazing for sheep. The Navajo objected, insisting, "If you kill off all the prairie dogs, there will be no one to cry for the rain." The amused government officials assured the Navajo that there was no correlation between rain and prairie dogs, and they carried out their experiment.

The outcome was surprising only to the government officials. Today, the area near Chilchinbito, Arizona, has become virtually a wasteland with very little grass. Without the ground-turning process of the burrowing animals, the soil has become solidly packed, unable to accept rain. The result: fierce runoff whenever it rains. What sparse vegetation was once there has been carried away by flooding waters.

"If you take away the prairie dogs, there will be no one to cry for the rain." Earth wisdom inherent in stories.

Ralph Waldo Emerson 115 years ago said, "We have listened to the courtly muses of Europe. We declared an intention to walk on our own feet, work with our own hands and speak with our own mind."[8]

If there is a mind of the West, perhaps it is the mind of the land, as diverse and rich as the communities that inhabit it. If we lose our spiritual tie to the West or, in some cases, never find it, we become the tumbleweed that blows across the interstate. No sense of place. No stories to evoke who we are and all we are connected to. No communities to keep us whole. Cultural diversity is lost and the land is given away. Stories give us residency. We are just now in the process of digging in, and I believe we have it in us to become native.

A few days ago, I was at the Pack Creek Ranch in Moab, Utah. A friend of mine had come west to see the canyon country. We had spent the day hiking Courthouse Wash in Arches National Park and were having a relaxed dinner. Utah is a small place, especially in the desert. Everyone knows everyone else. And so, one by one, friends started popping in. I introduced them to my friend, and we began talking, telling stories of where we had been and where we wanted to go. Finally my companion said, "Stop, wait a minute. Do you hear yourselves? You people out here talk about the land as though it was a person. You talk about the land as though it had character."

May I suggest that we are involved in a renaissance of thought and action, that we are in the process of creating a new subculture in a landscape of many. And in the landscape that I am a part of, where canyon walls rise upward like praying hands, a country of red rocks and ravens, we have a model: Coyoté.

When the Navajos speak of Coyoté they do so hesitantly, looking over their shoulders, checking the time of year, so they won't be heard. They know his stories are told only after the first frost and never after the last thaw. Their culture has been formed by Coyoté. He is profane and he is sacred. A bumbler and a hero. He straddles the canyon walls with wild oats in his belly. And they know him by name, "Ma'ii," the one never to be taken for granted. They understand his fickle nature, how he seduces fools into believing their own myths that they matter to the life of the desert.

Coyoté knows we do not matter. He knows rocks care nothing for those who wander through them; and yet he also knows that those same individuals who care for the rocks will find openings, large openings, that become passageways into the unseen world, where music is seen through dove's wings and wisdom is gleaned from the tails of lizards. Coyoté is always nearby but remains hidden. He is an ally because he cares enough to stay wary. He teaches us how to survive.

It is Coyoté who wanders naked in the desert and leaves his skin on the highway, allowing us to believe he is dead. He knows sunburned flesh is better than a tanned hide, that days spent in the desert are days soaking up strength. He can retrieve his coat and fluff up his fur after a day in the wilderness and meet any man, woman, or child on the streets of Moab and seduce them for dinner. Coyoté knows it is the proportion of days spent in wildness that counts in urbane savvy.

Coyoté's howl above the canyon says the desert may not depend on his life, but his life depends on the desert.

We would do well to listen.

The canyons of southern Utah and elsewhere are giving birth to a Coyoté Clan — hundreds, maybe even thousands of individuals who are quietly subversive on behalf of the land. And they are infiltrating our neighborhoods in the most respectable ways, with their long, bushy tails tucked discreetly inside their pants or beneath their skirts.

Members of the clan are not easily identified, but there are clues. You can see it in their eyes. They are joyful and they are fierce. They can cry louder and laugh harder than anyone on the planet. And they have enormous range. The Coyoté Clan is a raucous bunch: They have drunk from desert potholes and belched forth toads. They tell stories with such virtuosity that you'll swear you have been in the presence of preachers. The Coyoté Clan is also serene. Its members can float on their backs down the length of any river or lose entire afternoons in the contemplation of stone. Members of the clan court risk and will dance on slickrock as flash floods erode the ground beneath their feet. It doesn't matter. They understand the earth recreates itself day after day.

Same tribe. The Coyoté Clan harbors myriads of stories that evoke a sense of place, a sense of belonging to something much larger than ourselves.

La tierra cura. The earth heals.

The value of regional diversity lies in the mutuality of our tales. Disparate voices articulating the land, remembering, discovering where the source of our power lies.

A new soft wind blowing through the American West is paving the way for the "future primitive." It is as potent and irresistible as the ritual of burning sage.

Terry Tempest Williams

HEALTHY ENVIRONMENT, HEALTHY ECONOMY: AMERICAN INDIAN LESSONS

I have a basic premise that there can be no healthy economy in the American West without a healthy environment. It is a premise based on the experience of the West's oldest residents — the American Indians. When one contemplates the American West, whether it be of the past, the present, or the future, it is impossible to round out the picture without taking into account the Indian tribes. When we look into the more remote backyards of each of the Western states, we find a large number of self-governing Indian tribes that are alive and well, that enjoy unique cultures found nowhere else in the world, and that are in possession of large tracts of land called Indian reservations. And though the tribes are stricken with chronic poverty, these Indian reservations hold vast natural resources, and therefore American Indians have a role to play in the American economy.

Under the stewardship of the Indian tribes, much of these lands remains in a pristine, undeveloped condition. As such, these Indian lands are among the last vestiges of the true American West in its natural state. We therefore believe that the tribes truly inhabit the last best place in America.

But what does the future hold for American Indians — their culture, their lands — as we advance into the next century? Will we continue to exist in the American West one hundred years from now, as we do today? This is a question that is on our minds.

In 1492 Christopher Columbus first came to these shores.

It has been almost five hundred years since the first Euro-Americans arrived. Maybe it is time to take stock of where we are at this point in history. In that relatively short time span, Manifest Destiny has run its course. That is to say, you guys now own everything here from coast to coast. The white man has subdued the tribes, has tamed the wilderness, has altered the environment to suit his preferences, and now exercises complete and absolute dominion over the beasts and birds that inhabit the American West. What now is left to be done, and what kind of stewardship over the land will now occur? These are issues that vitally concern all of us, including the American Indian. As we begin to enter the next century together, after five hundred years of occupation of, and presumably adaptation to, this land, can we now hope for a maturing society and a maturing economy? Can we now hope, for example, for a kinder, gentler economic system that is less harsh on the environment? One part of that maturing process is the need for society to come to terms with the American Indian.

Contrary to popular belief, the "vanishing red man" theory of the last century was erroneous. We never did vanish. The tribes are still here and have no intention of leaving the American West. In fact, most traditional Indian beliefs are that we will be here long after the white man has gone. Nevertheless, the red man continues to remain a virtual mystery to his non-Indian neighbors. Our religion, our culture, our hopes and expectations all remain a mystery. And what will be the place and the role of the American Indian in our ever-maturing society as we go side by side into the next century? Certainly our roles and our relationships must change in fundamental ways. Historically, as we all know, the white man has taken things that belonged to the Indian in a one-way pattern that must now be reversed, if for no other reason than that the Indian no longer has much left to give. The American Indian contribution to this relationship, as we know, has included the giving of Indian lands and natural resources. Even our religions and cultures have been deemed expendable. Even our dead have been taken from us and treated as America's archaeological resources. This pattern of exploitation must cease as we approach our five-hundred-year anniversary, and a new racial relationship, a pattern of coexistence, must be founded.

Why is this so? For one thing, it is simply not good for one race to socially or economically exploit another. The American Indian is a miner's canary when it comes to American liberties, just like the American eagle is the miner's canary when it comes to the environmental health of the land. As Felix S. Cohen, the father of federal Indian law, once wrote, "The Indian plays much the same role in our American society that the Jews played in Germany. Like the miner's canary, the Indian marks the shifts from fresh air to poison gas in our political atmosphere; and our treatment of Indians, even more than our treatment of other minorities, reflects the rise and fall in our democratic faith."[9] Bearing that in mind, it is my hope that the freedom of American Indians to be themselves and to enjoy their own religion and culture will be protected and respected throughout the American West, at least to the same extent that the federal laws protect the endangered snail darter or the American eagle, so that our tribal peoples and our irreplaceable ways of life will not perish. It is only through a genuine understanding and mutual respect that our different peoples can coexist.

But what do these things have to do with economic development in the American West? Perhaps nothing at all, for, as I mentioned earlier, we are the poorest of the poor, living in the richest country on the planet. We are strangers to economic development. But perhaps there is some relationship, at least insofar as a healthy environment and a healthy economy are connected with one another. It is here that American Indians, if they are allowed to exist, can offer at least some small spiritual guidance. Whether we like it or not, Westerners must acknowledge the long-standing spiritual relationship of the American Indian to the land. And maybe in that regard we have something to offer to the dominant element of American society, which, maybe, has not quite yet adapted to the land as well as it must if we are to survive and flourish.

Sioux Chief Luther Standing Bear, noting the recent arrival of the white man and the need for adaptation, once said:

> The white man . . . does not understand America. He is too far removed from its formative processes. . . . The man from Europe is still a foreigner and an alien. And he still hates the man who questioned his path across the continent.
>
> But in the Indian the spirit of the land is still vested; it will be until other men are able to divine and meet its rhythm. Men must be born and reborn to belong. Their bodies must be formed of the dust of their forefathers' bones.[10]

Let me close by citing an excerpt of a speech of Chief Seattle. These comments were made more than one hundred years ago, in 1854, to American government negotiators who were asking to buy Chief Seattle's land near the present-day city of Seattle.

> Every part of this soil is sacred in the estimation of my people. Every hillside, every valley, every plain and grove, has been hallowed by some sad or happy event in days long vanished. Even the rocks, which seem to be dumb and dead as they swelter in the sun along the silent shore, thrill with memories of stirring events connected with the lives of my people, and the very dust upon which you now stand responds more lovingly to their footsteps than to yours, because it is rich with the blood of our ancestors and our bare feet are conscious of the sympathetic touch. Our departed braves, fond mothers, glad,

happy-hearted maidens, and even our little children who lived here and rejoiced here for a brief season, will love these somber solitudes and at eventide they greet shadowy returning spirits. And when the last Red Man shall have perished, and the memory of my tribe shall have become a myth among the White Men, these shores will swarm with the invisible dead of my tribe, and when your children's children think themselves alone in the field, the store, the shop, upon the highway, or in the silence of the pathless woods, they will not be alone. In all the earth there is no place dedicated to solitude. At night when the streets of your cities and villages are silent and you think them deserted, they will throng with the returning hosts that once filled them and still love this beautiful land. The White Man will never be alone.[11]

Walter Echo-Hawk

LAND, COMMUNITY, AND SURVIVAL: LESSONS FOR THE WEST FROM AMERICAN INDIANS

We should be glad that the law recognizes special rights for American Indians. Indian law — that body of treaties and statutes defining the legal status of Native Americans — is a tool that has helped Indians hold fast to at least some of their land. Because land and resources are the foundation of Indian culture, saving some vestiges of their former homeland also kept alive cultures and traditions that define Indianness. We all should rejoice in that. The most basic Indian tradition — a philosophy of permanence — can inspire the success of our own society. Let me explain.

Westerners suffer a kind of schizophrenia about Indians. There is considerable hostility toward the preservation of special Indian legal rights. Non-Indians whose immediate self-interest is pinched resent the Indians' legal entitlements to water, or to fish, or to land — coveted resources in the West. These extraordinary rights are often condemned as "un-American." One court in Washington likened them to "titles of nobility" that are contrary to the United States Constitution.

The other side of the Western personality, however, is glad that there are still Indians here, a romantic reminder of people living close to the earth, a colorful culture with enviable traditions. Most Westerners would consider it a tragedy if Indians were swirled into the melting pot of American society.

Only because Indians have been able to cling to their lands and resources have they had the equipment needed to survive. Without the shield of sometimes-resented legal rights, that would have been impossible.

Understanding the role of land and resources in cementing together Indian cultures and communities, and in ensuring the material, cultural, and spiritual survival of Indians, is important to our own survival as a society in the new West. These lessons are the greatest gifts that Indians have to offer us, the lessons drawn from their successful survival in this rugged, but fragile, mostly dry place. We can borrow from the experience of Indian societies to find ways to give permanence and quality to our own existence in the West.

Culture and its accoutrements give societies their identity and their continuity. Culture embodies the wisdom of ancestors telling us how they learned to survive and how to enjoy life. Many of us have roots set shallow in the West, and perhaps the continent, a heritage of less than two generations for a majority of Westerners. Many of our parents left behind a deeper heritage in Europe. Our ancestors' experience there and in the industrialized East used cultural equipment that was not fully adequate for life in the West.

American Indian societies can help us find and define our culture in the West. Their experience teaches us how to understand our adopted home and how to find permanence here, if we will listen to their story. We should think of them as surrogate ancestors, here to impart cultural understanding to us immigrants, we who lack a complete culture of our own, searching for identity, community, and survival.

The cultural contributions of Indians are often mentioned but their real value is rarely understood. A schoolchild can tell you that the Indians gave us corn and tobacco (gifts that may cancel out in their respective values to society). Indian cultural contributions are not limited to these commodities. They extend to names — Arapahoe Road, a town called Niwot (after the great chief who frequented this area). Indian-style architecture abounds in the Southwest, like the University of New Mexico School of Law's kiva design. And the art and jewelry and dress of the region are traceable to Native Americans. Jack Weatherford's new book, *Indian Givers*, goes farther, documenting American Indian breakthroughs in agriculture, medicine, food and fiber, and government that have been vitally important to the New World and Europe.

More valuable than any of the other cultural gifts Indians offer, though, is their basic philosophy. That philosophy enabled them to survive in an arid environment, a place where islands of rich resources were separated by long distances. We need to understand the Indians' philosophy of permanence and how it guided their relations with one another and with the environment. The West's future may depend on how well we learn these lessons.

Indians forged their groups tightly around ties of family and community. Individually and in their communities they adapted their existence, their economies, and their lifestyles to the ways of the land rather than trying to tame the land. Westerners need to ask whether we value our independence and self-sufficiency too much. Every one of us who has lived through a tough winter storm in the Rockies or had a car break down on some back road in the middle of the plains has learned the frailty of the individuality that open spaces make possible, has learned the importance of being able to depend on others for help and support.

Indian tribes and some Hispanic communities in the Southwest successfully irrigated a hostile land using collective systems. The early settlers ignored their example and tried to irrigate their lands by going it alone. They failed at first, with the exception of the Mormon pioneers, who were dedicated to working together. Irrigation finally succeeded when settlers joined their efforts.

The West's Indians knew, too, that they must learn to live with nature's whims. This is a place always in flux, always subject to natural disasters, to droughts, to floods, to earthquakes. Survival requires knowing the place and adapting to it. Instead, we newcomers compounded natural risks with our own disasters and boom-and-bust economies. Ambitious schemes exploited natural resources: Mining, damming, draining, and clear-cutting changed the face of the West in one way or another. Much of the old West is lost. Old-growth timber stands are museum pieces; heaps of mine tailings mar the landscape; canyons have become lake bottoms; whole species have disappeared.

We did not have to indulge these excesses; we could have listened to the Indians. They had their own excesses, too, generations ago. The Anasazi found the limits of artificial irrigation and their society died. They learned the hard way. Many experiences like these were long ago embedded in the Native American cultural message, their ideal of a permanent relationship with the land. Why should we repeat mistakes that imperiled ancient peoples? Need we reprove the truths they teach about the land?

The two most vexing issues in the West today, survival of communities and stewardship of resources, are tied together. Failure on one issue is failure on both. Indian cultures offer wisdom on addressing both.

First, people in the West need to find their community, their ties of tradition and ceremony and values. They can use their communities to support one another and, at times, to allow one another precious individuality.

Second, Westerners need to keep an eye on the landscape, the surroundings that bind them together as communities and can give them spiritual and material sustenance. Survival depends on understanding the land. We need a collective understanding and an implicit agreement not to overexploit and destroy the resources that sustain us — land and water. Those resources are at risk. If they are exhausted, or damaged, or spread among too many people, the West loses sustenance and the cultural nexus for its communities.

Today people throughout the West are coming together and defining their communities around the resources that are important to them and that can give them permanence here. Folks on Colorado's Western Slope — farmers, ski instructors, ranchers, and storekeepers — rally together to resist a big city's scheme to de-water their homeland. A similar story is unfolding in the San Luis Valley.

People are beginning to sense the natural limits of the region's ecology. We have made some progress as a region and as a nation in securing a permanent place where we can live harmoniously with our surroundings and our neighbors.

The interrelatedness of everything in our environment is a truth strange to European culture. But we are groping toward an understanding of it and reflecting it in laws like the National Environmental Policy Act that insist on looking at the big picture before unleashing development. We have had the will to set aside some lands forever as wilderness, some rivers as wild, places that only half a century ago were symbols of hostility and enmity. We are getting serious about stemming the loss of any more species, bringing back otter and buffalo — and maybe even wolves. We have a sense that doing these things is essential to our permanent survival in this region. The essence of this place is at risk if we do not do them. Indians knew this all along.

Fortunately — fortunately for us — the law gave tribes some security for some of their homelands, enough to keep alive a culture shaped to the land. If we hope to live out our days here and consider it a place for our grandchildren, too, we should listen to and learn and teach the wisdom on which Indian societies were long ago built.

The survival of Western culture may depend upon adapting ourselves and adopting some of the lessons of our surrogate ancestors. Their adaptability and success in surviving with dignity is a model for the West. Just as we accept and internalize and act on the lessons of our German, English, Irish, Scandinavian and other ancestors, we ought to gain strength and knowledge from the lessons of our surrogate Indian ancestors. Listen to their drum, too. Our strength to embrace the future and to seek permanence for a society in these parts depends on integrating all these lessons.

David H. Getches

THE AMERICAN WEST
FROM THE EAST AND THE SOUTH

By the title of these remarks, I don't mean the East and the South the way some of you may think of it. As a Chinese person growing up in China, I had vivid images of the American West. Much of that came from the movies we were allowed to see. My parents allowed us to see one movie a year. That was our New Year's treat, and we inevitably looked for movies that featured cowboys and Indians. So, unfortunately, we were part of that legacy of the West, the West of cowboys and Indians, and I don't think I have to explain to you who were always the good guys and the bad guys in those movies.

But there was also another American West that was so much a part of us. We'd all heard of or had family and friends who went to the United States to work, and particularly to a place called The Golden Mountain, which was, of course, San Francisco. That was the other American West that all of us had in the back of our minds. So when my parents took us to California as immigrants — and, mind you, my parents were extremely well-educated Chinese — the image that they gave us and the rationale that they offered us for why we should go to California was that the streets of California were paved with gold. They selected a town called Palo Alto because of the good public schools and because, they told us, we all were going to go to Stanford University. Stanford, of course, was built with money made by Leland Stanford — money made from the railroads and from the exploitation of Chinese labor. So that was my view of the American West as a child.

Then there is the view of the American West from Mexico. There is a saying that captures the relationship between Mexico (particularly northern Mexico) and the United States (particularly the western and southwestern parts of the United States): "Poor Mexico, so far from God and so close to the United States." What they're thinking of is this ambiguous, ambivalent, bittersweet relationship that Mexico has always had with the United States, especially the western and southwestern United States. For instance, it was only very reluctantly in the late nineteenth century that the United States allowed the railroad tycoons to extend the railroad from the American West into Mexico.

In my studies of the Indians of the northern part of Mexico, the Yaqui, I discovered that part of what we call the American West, the Mexicans thought of as their north and their northwest. So this idea called the American West is not something that they share in Mexico. They view the American West as part of their national territory. They have extended, or tried to extend, Mexico into the American West. They have lost a lot of that territory. If you go to the American West, there are peoples from both sides of the border who shared a common heritage, but with very different perspectives.

Evelyn Hu-Dehart

DRAWING STRENGTH
FROM THE DIVERSITY OF THE WEST

I am a son of the West. My grandfather, the Reverend Matthew Shadrack Jones, who, with his bride, America Jones, came to western Kansas in a covered wagon in the nineteenth century, homesteaded 140 acres outside of Friend, Kansas — a farm that we still have — and began to preach in the Baptist churches up the Arkansas River valley, up as far as Colorado Springs. Even now, forty years after his death, in places such as Manzaneras, and La Junta, and Trinidad, and Walsenburg, people who are now old still speak in reverent terms of the Reverend Shadrack Jones and of the black Baptist churches he founded that still thrive to this day. My father, born in 1903, himself became a man of this place, working on the railroad between Chicago and Albuquerque until, on a stop in Pueblo, Colorado, he encountered this tall, foxy woman from Kentucky who had come to Pueblo. She had come to take care of her great-aunt, my great-great-aunt, Aunt Susie, who had come to Pueblo after the days of slavery to make her way. Finding this woman, so the story is told, my father got off the railroad and settled in Pueblo and found his place.

A lot of different things can help you find your place. Blacks, too, have a place in this place. It would be well for all of us, as we consider the American West, to reflect on the way in which it has been shaped, and the way it has been exclusive in the past. One of the factors that must be considered is the extent to which we will include all of the people in this place. We have not been good at that. We are 100 or 150 years too late in discussing this. Not that we are too late in the absolute sense — not that we ought not to be discussing this — but there were duly constituted societies present in this place, societies that had worked through the rigors of this place and were living in balance with it, people who knew how to live off the land and knew how to make the land prosper while they themselves prospered. Yet when our forbearers saw this place, they saw frontier. Even today we speak of it as frontier, as though it were empty, as though it were no one's home. They saw something, and still today we see something that we call the frontier, which is there for the taking. Certainly it was treated that way — as something there for the taking and something to be given in reward. We didn't see other peoples' homes, we didn't see other peoples' sacred places, we didn't see animal habitats in ecological balance with the whole. We didn't see animals at all — animals that lived and thrived and enabled human inhabitants themselves to thrive.

We must take a regional view of this place. We are long, long too late in approaching the West as a region that must be seen as a whole socially and economically. Certainly we have been beaten and bludgeoned into looking at our water in those terms. But we devastated the land in many other ways before we had the foresight to look upon it as an interrelated region. As we look at the democratization of the world, at *perestroika* and what is happening in Eastern Europe and China and soon to be happening in South Africa, it is important for us to bring that imperative home to the West, to undertake a kind of democratization of this region and develop a sense that it is populated by people who are of this place, who know this place, who are comfortable and in balance with this place, and who have been shaped by this place. It is important that we recognize the mistakes that we made in not including those whose home it was before. It is important that when we talk of shared values, we are very careful to include all of those who have made a contribution in this place.

We have made mistakes. We are now talking about concepts that we might have profited from talking about 150 years ago. Let us now, at this late date, act on these concepts and act on these ideas. Let us use the strength that this place has put in us and truly make this place, this region, this American West, a great thing of beauty.

Raymond Dean Jones

DEVELOPMENT AND CULTURAL SURVIVAL

Recently the movie *The Milagro Beanfield War* made its debut. If you haven't seen it, I suggest that you do. Even if you don't see it, please read the book. It's richer, it's deeper than the movie. The idea conveyed in the book is that "development" means at least two different things. It means, to certain groups of people, power, social enhancement, profit, success. To other groups of people, however, it means something totally different. It means a challenge to their economic and cultural survival. And that is where we are today. We're caught in this conflict between development and, in many cases, economic, political, and cultural survival of different groups.

The question to us is, how do we respond to this changing complexion of the West and Southwest? Do we respond as California and Texas did in the mid-1970s, when, because of the fear of the new immigrants, they enacted laws that would bar undocumented — they called them illegal — schoolchildren from entering public schools? Do we respond through what has been a movement of the 1980s that is directly linked to that anti-immigrant hysteria, with an English-language amendment, as has been done in various states across the Southwest and West?

Linda Chavez, one-time president of the group U.S. English, resigned from that group's governing board. When you read the memo that prompted her resignation, you understand why. In that memo, the author, John Tanton, raised the question of whether Hispanics are as educable as Asians. And he worried that the high birthrate among Hispanics would make this "the first instance in which those with their pants up are going to get caught by those with their pants down!"[12] There's a bias there, clearly. But these are not biases that are shared solely by groups such as U.S. English with its drive for an English-language amendment.

How do we respond to such movements? This is the "fourth wave" of immigrants to arrive at our shores, the Asians and Latinos. But how do we respond? I had the opportunity to be on a committee in Dallas, the Greater Dallas Community Relations Commission, a multiracial, multiethnic group of about twenty individuals. Our primary objective was the resolution of conflict between racial and ethnic groups in Dallas. This is one effort that was positive, an effort that looked the problem squarely in the face.

Racism is a topic we don't like to address because it makes many people feel uncomfortable. I know this because I teach a course called "Race and Ethnic Relations in the United States" at the University of Colorado. On the first day of class I ask my students, "Do you feel that you are completely nonracist, somewhat nonracist, color-blind, somewhat racist, or totally racist?" Only 20 percent said that they consider themselves to be somewhat racist. I don't know whether that is good or bad. About half consider themselves to be color-blind. During the course they begin to look within themselves, to examine their own biases, to examine how they relate to other people, to examine how they relate to issues of public policy. Can they make those connections?

In California, because of the overwhelming change in demographics that is taking place now, there is a new organization called California Tomorrow, just instituted, that will examine racial and ethnic questions, the changing characters of the schools, and solutions to problems throughout the state. These are steps that are serious and that point us in a direction of positive change. These are only first steps. Again, we cannot change unless we examine our own biases, our own misgivings, our own preconceptions. It's a difficult thing to do, but necessary.

Estevan T. Flores

THE HUMAN ELEMENT IN THE WEST: CONTRADICTIONS, CONTRADICTIONS, CONTRADICTIONS

Sometimes we forget people in trying to protect the environment. I come from a culture that was there when "there" wasn't even "the West" — it was northwestern Mexico. And I admit that the culture was mishandling the environment. It was a very poor society and the only way they could accrue wealth, the only way they could make a living in most of that arid land, was to bring in sheep. Of course, the range became overloaded with sheep. I'll be the first one to admit this. But there was a need there. There was a need.

I'm glad now that demands on the environment have been balanced off, to a degree. But when I go sometimes to look at some of my cousin's cattle up in the mountain meadows, I go on horseback because I'm a poor hiker. I've got a bad knee. I get these dirty looks from people who are hiking along the trail. I'm intruding. My horse is intruding by defecating on the trail. I feel sorry for them because, if I were a hiker, I'd hate to get out of the way for a horse, so I give them a meek little smile. We're always going to have these problems. We all have our agendas. Every group has its agenda. We can hope that we will continue dialogues and try to make something out of the mess we're in, because we *are* in a mess.

Santa Fe has been pointed out as a place that has maintained its values in spite of its being a recreation town. I really have to differ. Santa Fe is one of the towns in the West whose centers have died. The plaza, for example. (And I wave the flag for the chamber of commerce. Folks, we're poor in New Mexico. We need your money. Come and vacation in New Mexico.) The problem is that the plaza is dead because, as our ex–state historian put it recently, "It's been artsy-crafted to death." It is now full of galleries, one gallery after another. My favorite drinking place is gone. The old Plaza Bar where I used to go and shoot pool with some of the old-timers is not there anymore. The old guy in the red baseball cap who taught me how to play nine-ball with aplomb is gone. I don't know where he drinks now. I haven't found him, and Santa Fe's a small town.

The people have been fleeing the center of town because of tourism. The local people are excluded from what used to be the center of life in Santa Fe, which is the plaza. I find the same thing in many, many other towns. You go to Durango, Colorado, and other places, and you get the impression that they're trying to create an artificial environment so that other people can enjoy it. The attempt is to bring back that nostalgic era, that era of the way it probably was. That lies heavily on many, many local people.

This was brought home to me by a friend of mine, Ivan Illich, who wrote *Deschooling Society*. I was showing him around Santa Fe. I was showing him our famous Canyon Road and he asked me, "Adrian, is it real?"

"What do you mean, is it real?"

"Is your town real?"

It hit me like a ton of bricks. We had created an artificial Santa Fe to maintain what some people thought Santa Fe should be.

We're doing this all over the West. Why? Commercialism. We need the tourist dollars. But how do we solve this problem? I don't have any answers. I'm trying not even to look into the future, because I'm a historian. So I'm copping out. But how do we solve these problems? They're very basic problems.

One saving grace is that the little towns, the villages that were supposedly dead in the 1950s in northern New Mexico, are still alive. They are still alive and functioning well. I remember in driving between Las Vegas, New Mexico, and Santa Fe, I'd see one or two or three lights in a town — Bernal, for example. Today, when I drive through there, there are maybe fifty lights in that town. That town has grown since the time when they had already given the eulogy for it. It bounced back.

The problem is that most of those people are depending on the nuclear research going on in Los Alamos for jobs. So you see the contradiction there. We have people making a living. How are they making a living? They are carpenters and welders and everything else, helping scientists who are doing nuclear research. Nuclear research needs to be looked at. WIPP — the Waste Isolation Pilot Project — is a big problem in New Mexico. A lot of people don't want the garbage from Los Alamos and other areas put in the Carlsbad area, which has some salt beds that supposedly would contain the radioactivity of the waste.

The people in Carlsbad want it because it will provide jobs. The people in Santa Fe and Albuquerque don't want it because trucks carrying that waste have to pass through their towns, and suppose an accident occurred? People in Carlsbad want it because the potash mines gave out and now they need jobs. Contradiction, contradiction, contradiction.

So does anything really change in the West? I don't know. We have got to see what we can reclaim and how we can reclaim it, and reclaim it rationally. Not with so much passion that we tear things up — we must plan rationally. How do we plan, how do we do it? I don't know. I'll try to record it as past if I'm still around in the future. Meanwhile, I'm very concerned.

Adrian Herminio Bustamante

NEW SETTLERS IN THE RURAL WEST

I bring to you an on-the-ground report from the rural West — one grass root.

A radio talk-show host from Denver called early one morning to wish *High Country News* a happy twentieth birthday. I was told to stand by, only to hear: "Now we leave the glamour and glitz of Aspen for humble Paonia . . ."

Well, it isn't hard to be humble in my town.

It's a small town, just 1,400 souls, with twenty churches. It's a hopeful place these days. Even the local Rotary Club is growing. It has a woman member. It's the kind of laid-back Rotary where members ask the group to sing to celebrate some event. One member named Wally, who is close to eighty, recently asked the Rotarians to sing "Happy Birthday" to his mother. Looking at Wally, who totters about on cowboy boots, a fellow Rotarian asked how old his mother was. She'd be 104, came the answer, if she were alive.

I don't think *High Country News* could be better situated than in this working town close to the West Elk Wilderness. You can see the economic and cultural flip-flops up close. Paonia has lost some 850 mining jobs in the last decade, freezes have shut out the peach crop more often than not, and ranchers have sold out. Yet, after two or three years of holding on, the town renews itself and turns over its businesses. Greater fools, perhaps, march in with large fortunes and proceed to spend most of them fixing up a ranch or home and trying to establish a beachhead.

Futurologists like to talk about paradigms, those useful models for perceiving life. In the early 1980s, the model for western Colorado and other energy-boom areas in the West was growth. It was: "You lucky rustic people! Exxon and other companies are coming to your town. The nation needs energy and it's patriotic to rip into your hills to get it." Growth meant jobs, more people, a bigger tax base, a sure thing for young people, who would not be exported in such large quantities. In 1980, in one of its scenarios, Exxon promised a new town of fifty thousand in tiny Parachute. Who can forget that in 1982 one Sunday, Exxon summarily fired twenty-one hundred people and shut down its oil-shale works forever?

For most of the West, as our freelancers in ten Western states tell us, the definition of reality is no longer that of a cargo cult. No large industry drops from the sky and puts people to work. In small towns in the rural West, we are told now to be entrepreneurial, service oriented. These days that means flexible and poor. The problem is that work is somewhere else for many people with high school skills. We export maids to Snowmass and Aspen, coal miners to Carbondale. People in Carbondale, in turn, move to Paonia where they can afford a house. What's in the middle is McClure Pass, not a fun place in a whiteout.

But battered as Paonia and other small Western towns have been, the new world we're in, and presumably the future, feels very different from 1974, when my husband, Ed, and I arrived in Paonia with our two young children. We were to be dropouts from New York for a year. Those twelve months lasted fifteen years. Paonia, like many small Western towns then, was hostile to newcomers, labeled them as hippies and feared them because they were tainted by urban values. Worse, they weren't born there. Why, their parents weren't even born there! They weren't local. They were alien.

Fifteen years later, through boom, bust, and what *High Country News* has called a reopened Western frontier, hostility and suspicion have been replaced in 1990 by the welcome mat. New, schmoo. "We want you" is the motto. Small towns need kids in the too-large schools, they want families in vacant homes and businesses downtown. Cottage industries are identified and welcomed. The chamber of commerce can see that people are going where they want their job to be, not necessarily where their jobs are. There seems to be an understanding, or a movement toward understanding, in places like Moab, Utah, and the Paonias of the West, that the environment is the economy. The greening of the West is the new economic development engine.

The old ways still hang on, though, with a rush to dam the few places left in the West to dam, the rush to cut trees in inappropriate places. It seems *High Country News* freelancers are always reporting on yet another last-ditch effort by a small underfunded group that says one big-buck economic activity or another wants to destroy their community. And Paonia, a town that sees in the swing toward tourism and recreation the major ingredients of its future, probably still has a yen for a great big company.

Old paradigms die hard, just like a shot-up bad guy in a bar who turns three times, then twitches on the floor in the old Western movies. He just won't lie down and die. The yearning for a fat corporate payroll isn't surprising. For the new world that is coming into focus offers a generous amount of uncertainty along with hope. An entrepreneur usually means someone using fax machines, modems, Fed Ex, doing something for someone in some city somewhere. It's a sketchy present and a sketchy future, not filled in yet. But if you care about the West that might have lured you to turn one year here into fifteen, it is the future to work for and to believe in.

Journalists are notorious for depending on hunches, turning three stories on a subject into a trend, and leaning on intuition rather than statistics. But I see dedicated environmentalists whose ranks are growing, and they are getting tougher. They are willing to fight for a West that exists not just for humans, but for its ancient inhabitants: bears, aspen, wild rivers, tundra, hummingbirds, sandstone cliffs — you fill in the blank for that "best place."

Betsy Marston

THE ELUSIVE QUALITY OF THE WEST

My own initial contact with the West came when I was in a seventh-grade U.S. history class in, of all places, Miami, Florida, about thirty years ago. I found at that time that the West was really a strange place, a remote place. We studied it in the context of regionalism, because we Southerners thought that Westerners had something akin to our own interest at that time, and at other times in the past.

The West was presented as a place that was peopled by individuals who lived in a barren and arid climate, people who mostly spent their time either shooting at each other or riding around the countryside looking for people to shoot at. It was presented as a place where one could look as far as the eye could see and not see anything except a stray cactus and the happy clouds in the sky. Its remoteness is the largest memory that I have from that first introduction. I remember thinking, my goodness, what an isolated place. The image we were then receiving in the schools was of white cowboys, very few Indians, fewer women, no blacks, no Hispanics. The image was of a place that was rural, which I knew about, but a rural place without trees and where the largest city was Dodge. In short, from that adolescent perspective, it was not a place one would like to go, much less to live.

The most powerful aspect of that recollection was that the West was a place that had been, that it wasn't a place that really was anymore, that by the 1950s it had essentially disappeared, or what we Floridians really knew, it had turned into California. My own experience reminds me, and I hope you, of the power of the Turner thesis about the American frontier, at least as we were then taught about it. Although we have come to understand — at least I have after reading Patty Limerick's book *Legacy of Conquest* — that this is really a misinterpretation and a misunderstanding of the Turner thesis, the power of that misinterpretation stretched down even into the seventh grade and even as far away from the American West as Miami.

Thirty years later, in the fall of 1987, I found that I was a professor of history at the principal university in that region. I was situated exactly in the midst of the place that I had thought was beyond the pale. I'm a British historian, and thirty years later I also found that I was president of the Western Conference on British Studies. That reminds me of the view of the West, or of Westness, that we British historians hold. Our West begins sometime around the Norman Conquest. Our first outpost, as British historians, is the city of Westminster, which has a great abbey church, and in that abbey church is buried the penultimate Saxon king and the last royal saint to sit on the throne of England.

Be that as it may, the president of the Western Conference on British Studies has the obligation to nominate his or her successor and to select the site of the next meeting. And so, being a wicked person living in the West, I decided to make a statement about Westness, and we nominated and selected as my successor as president of the Western Conference on British Studies a professor at Georgia Southern College, which is about thirty-five miles inland from the Atlantic Ocean. This is west only if you live in Savannah. Under his leadership we were to meet in New Orleans, which at least has the merit of being west of the Appalachian watershed, beyond which George Grenville tried to stop the colonists from going in 1763 without success — the same lack of success as other governments have had in trying to stop westward expansion both physical and intellectual in other places at other times.

My point is that the concept of the West seems to be a constant in European history, and certainly in the Anglo-American experience. But it's an elusive one, in that at various times the concept can be found to apply to different places. By that, I mean it could be that the West is Springfield, Massachusetts, or Springfield, Illinois, or Denver, Colorado. It may turn out that where you stand on where the American West is as a geographical concept, depends largely, if not exclusively, upon where you sit.

In fact, we all know that it's more than a geographical concept. It's more than that, much more than that. At this symposium we're going to think through a variety of themes and issues, which will only whet our appetites for more study and invite us in a variety of different contexts to further consideration and reflection on these topics and related concerns that will grow out of this conference into future conferences in the years ahead.

Charles R. Middleton

THE LAST BEST PLACE:
HOW HARDSHIP AND LIMITS BUILD
COMMUNITY

While the spirit of democracy sweeps eastward across Europe, over the Urals, whistling through the cracks in the Great Wall, America stands bemused, with no hint of any awareness, at least in official policy, of what all this might mean. Schiller's words and Beethoven's music resound in Berlin and will again, I believe, in Beijing. But in Boston or Boise a self-satisfied smugness resembling a hypnotic slumber holds the world spirit at bay.

Watching all of this, I can't help but recall certain words of Hegel, whose articulation of the idea of a spirit of history seems indispensable to capturing what is happening to the world. In 1820 Hegel set out to write his *Philosophy of History*, seeking to identify those forces that had made and would make real human history. Hegel paused for a moment at the starting gate to dispose of one nagging question, namely whether America had any prospect of contributing anything worthwhile to the history of human civilization. His answer, delivered without hesitation, was "no." His reason speaks still to America, and especially to the American West.

In a nutshell, Hegel predicted that America would not begin to contribute to civilization until it had confronted its own limits. Specifically, he argued that the safety valve of the frontier had prevented and would continue to prevent the development of a truly civil society. In making his case, Hegel took a position diametrically the opposite of Jefferson's. Jefferson had argued that civic culture was essentially rooted in agriculture and threatened by the growth of cities. He therefore assigned to the Western frontier a crucial and at the same time foredoomed role, which he repeated over and over in a standard Jeffersonian formula that went like this: Civic culture would remain strong in America as long as agriculture expanded faster than cities grew, which would happen as long as there was "vacant" Western land into which agriculture could expand. That this pattern could not recur indefinitely — that there had to be an end, sometime, to the filling in of what white Americans called vacant land — was a reality that Jefferson chose to suppress. In doing so, he contributed very substantially to the Myth of the West — specifically, to the myth that it was somehow a place without limits.

Hegel, as I have said, argued that civic culture, far from depending on the existence of the frontier, could only be achieved once the frontier was closed. More specifically, he turned Jefferson on his head by assuming that civic culture was an essentially urban phenomenon — something that really only occurred when significant numbers of people were forced to stop farming and to gather in cities. He agreed with Jefferson that the Western frontier allowed agriculture to outpace urbanization. His conclusion was simply the exact opposite of Jefferson's; he wrote that until Americans began facing each other in cities, they would not become a truly civil society and would not make a substantial contribution to the history of civilization.

Now, one hundred years after the 1890 census, which led the Census Bureau and then Frederick Jackson Turner to declare the frontier closed, we stand, here in the West, at a cross-wiring of historical currents that almost forces us to ask who we are and where we are going. We mark the centennial of the closing of the frontier just as world history turns Karl Marx on his head, which presumably might mean that Hegel has again landed on his feet. If Hegel were here at this conference, along with Thomas Jefferson, what would he say now about the West and about the possibility of its contributing to the history of civilization?

I'm going to use the challenge of this occasion to propose an answer to that question. I believe the world spirit is alive in Western valleys and to the leeward side of Western cutbanks where people claimed by this landscape have gathered to carry out the business of living well in hard country. I believe that there is, native to this soil, a politics of truly human proportions. It is a politics that we have not yet been bold enough to propose to ourselves. But the hour of its being proposed is drawing near. When that proposition is articulated in a genuinely Western voice, the West will respond, and its response will make its mark on the course of history.

Now, predictions like these deserve to be subjected to a variety of tests, the chief one being, of course, the test of time. Beyond that, anyone making such predictions might be asked to warrant in some way his or her standing to make predictions. In America, we can always make the grand claim of citizenship; we can remind our listeners that it is, after all, a free country, and I can predict anything I want to. Since I hope to deal with a more meaningful form of citizenship, I had better pass up that way of backing my claim. Others can warrant predictions by their training in the discipline of history, but while I deeply admire the discipline, I am certainly not trained in it. It is, rather, as a politician that I make my predictions about the near future of the West. And I think that is fitting enough, since my predictions are about the political future of the region.

I have long believed that places select people. Portland selects people who like rain. Having grown up in Montana in a pioneer family that settled four generations ago in eastern Montana, I have observed over the years how frequently recurring the pattern of my own ancestors was in the settlement of the high plains of the state. My great-grandparents tried Oregon in the early 1880s, but the rain and the overcrowding finally drove them away, and they moved east, back across the Rockies, to the open country that could be cursed in an almost infinite variety of ways but could never be accused of being too wet. Over time, the place of my upbringing came to be peopled by folks whose words were as sparse as rain and whose humor was as dry as the hills out of which they eked a living.

The shaping of a people by the land they inhabit takes time, and in America it has taken longer, simply because we have never been quite sure that we were here to stay. Wendell Berry begins his book *The Unsettling of America* by observing that Americans have never quite intended to be where they were — that they have always thought more in terms of where they would go, rather than of where they actually were. But Berry also identifies a second strain in the pattern of settlement — what he calls a tendency to stay put, to say, "No further — this is the place." One peculiarity of the settlement of the West is that it attracted — it selected — people who were more given than others to escape settlement. Only they would be willing to put up with the harshness, the inhospitality of the land, which grew more inhospitable the nearer they came to inhabiting the last of the frontier.

So the West drew to itself more than its share of unsettlers, of people whose essential relation to place was the denial of place. And yet the places that they came to, being the last place to go, finally took hold of them, drew them down into their flinty soils, rooted them, claimed them, shaped them the way they shaped sagebrush. Over the generations, these people increasingly came to recognize themselves and to recognize their neighbors in the forms the land produced. And the selection process did not stop at some point; it goes on still. People still are drawn here not just in spite of but because of the hardness of the land.

Gradually, a culture grew out of the land, a group of storytellers and imagemakers capable of holding this people up to itself. In Montana we relied on people like Joseph Kinsey Howard and K. Ross Toole to show us who we were, and in each locality there were similar voices. But there have been regional voices as well, not least that of Wallace Stegner, and now a new generation including voices like Bill Kittredge's. Bill and Annick Smith have proven, dramatically, how deep and powerful the common culture of place is by producing for Montana's centennial an exceptional and exceptionally popular collection of voices entitled *The Last Best Place.*

Let me touch now for just a moment on democracy — about what, at least from the perspective of a practicing politician, democracy is or might be. There is an unsettling premonition, as we watch East Berliners pouring through the breached wall to go shopping in West Berlin, that democracy may in the end not reach very far beyond some notion of equal access to all good things, especially blue jeans and cheeseburgers. As a politician, I have had my fair share of exposure to the behavior, and the fundamental insatiability, of the citizen as consumer. I am convinced that democracy is steadily diminished, just as the earth's capital is steadily diminished, by this version of democracy. It is a democracy that cannot endure, and all true democrats must warn against its dangers.

In the age of fast food and pervasive fingertip convenience, we have come to believe that democracy is a birthright that is as easy to practice as a precooked microwave dinner is to heat and serve. But it has never been so, and it will not be so for the coming generation of world democrats. Here, at least, Frederick Jackson Turner still speaks in a voice of Jeffersonian democracy to which we need to attend if we are to understand what makes democracy possible. Turner speaks of how the frontier created democrats; he writes that the rigors of the frontier instilled (and I would argue selected for) what Turner called a "competency" — a capacity to get done what needed doing — which translated into a truly democratic confidence. Hard country breeds capable people — capable, among other things, of genuine democracy.

But let's take a little closer look at this competence. It is, has always been, and must necessarily be the competence, not simply of individuals, but of a *demos*, of a people. To have this kind of competence, a people must be bound together in ways that enable them to work together. What the project of inhabiting hard country does, above all, is to create these bonds. And when I speak of bonds here, I do not mean to evoke anything particularly soft or mushy. These are practical bonds, although they do often lead to a kind of affection among those so bonded. But they are in the first instance practical. They are the kinds of bonds that made of barn-building and similar acts of cooperation something that must be understood as a culture. It is a culture bred of hard places, nurtured by the practice of inhabiting those places.

I want to draw attention to two words I have just used. The first is "practice" (and its derivative "practical"). The second is "inhabitation." These words are rooted — quite literally rooted — in the same quite literal soil. Inhabitation depends upon habits; to inhabit is to dwell in a place in an habituated way. To do this requires practice. This practice revolves around certain practical necessities of living in hard country, necessities like a good barn. But to say a "good barn" is not to speak lightly, for not just any barn will do, and this is true of a great range of such practical necessities. What was done must be done well or it would not survive — it would not enable survival. Thus, the practices that lie at the root of all true inhabitation — especially of the inhabitation of hard country — are always practices that carry within themselves demanding standards of excellence.

It is these standards of excellence, arising out of the soil itself, bodied forth in certain habituated and deeply shared patterns of behavior — it is these lived standards of excellence that alone give meaning to the concept of "value." Over the past decade or so, more and more people have engaged in a vague recognition of the fact that "values" are somehow an important political factor. This has been a rather astonishing realization for liberals, instructed as we all have been in the liberal dogma that values are private concerns, and no business of the state. But as politics has increasingly become a game of "values, values, who's got the values?", even liberals have had to pay lip service to this new political icon.

But we have not yet understood that values are not something that simply come out of a black box in the individual soul, as the liberal dogma would have it, or from a deep voice on a mountaintop, as the fundamentalists think. What makes values shared and what makes them politically powerful is that they arise out of the challenge of living well together in hard country. When people do that long enough to develop a pattern of shared values, those values acquire a political potency.

It is here that the West has the capacity to contribute something deep and important and lasting to the history of politics and civilization. Simply because we have for so many generations worked on the project of living together in hard country, we have, although we don't recognize it, developed among ourselves certain patterns of behavior, which amount to shared values. The question is whether we will recognize this Western fact of life. The question is whether those of us who call ourselves liberals and those of us who call ourselves conservatives, all of whom are inhabitants of the West, can begin to turn to each other and begin to recognize what it is we have built together in terms of shared patterns of inhabitation and therefore of shared values. That is the challenge of the West. If we can begin to understand how we have been shaped by this country, shaped in similar ways, not so that we think alike all the time, not so that we believe alike, but so that we in fact have developed some shared values that give us the capacity to do difficult and important work together, then on this basis we can begin to contribute to democracy and to the history of civilization.

I say this as a politician who is willing to bet his career on the fact that this is a possibility. I am absolutely convinced that people will respond to being appealed to as inhabitants of a common place. They are willing to respond to anyone who will speak to their weariness with the kind of deadlock that our politics all too often creates. They will respond to a politics that speaks directly to their deep desire to be respected and to be treated as people — people who are capable of treating other people with respect. They will respond to a politics that speaks to their commonly shaped patterns of doing good work, to a politics that says to people on the right and on the left, "You are one people; you understand each other better than you think you do and you are capable of treating each other as if you do understand each other." And finally, they will respond to a politics that addresses their sense of what a good city or a good community might be, and how we would have to treat each other if we were going to go about the task of creating it.

It is said of Athens that in spite of its deep social divisions, it sustained its experiment in democracy and developed an outstanding culture because, in the end, each of the contestants in each divisive issue cared more about Athens that they cared about winning. I am convinced that in communities across the West, a majority of the people care more about their communities than they care about winning. But they have not been given a politics that encourages them to behave in that way. They have been given a politics that only encourages them to care about winning.

Are we capable of real politics in the West? I believe we are if we are willing to face ourselves and our neighbors in a way that we have never done. We need to be willing in the first instance to face the implications of our historical unwillingness to face ourselves. Jefferson, democrat that he was, believer that he was in the idea that democracy could only exist when it was practiced on a small scale, was yet willing through the Louisiana Purchase to engage in the building of an empire. He did that because in the long run he believed that democracy could only survive if it was rooted on the farm and that it could be rooted on the farm only if agriculture could expand endlessly. So he bought into an empire, and our ancestors bought into an empire, and we, by inheritance, bought into an empire. Part of the reason for this is because we, like Jefferson, have been unwilling to image the possibility of a good city. Jefferson could not image a city being good. All too often, I think, we are guilty of the same way of thinking. Robinson Jeffers, in his poem "Shine Perishing Republic," talks about the republic "heavily thickening into empire," and he ends the poem by writing:

> But for my children, I would have them keep their distance
>   from the thickening center; corruption
> Never has been compulsory, when the cities lie at the
>   monster's feet, there are left the mountains.[13]

That has been too much the Western attitude. We believed — we still believe — that we can somehow escape ourselves by slipping into the mountains, avoiding the hard task of facing up to ourselves in cities. Our mistake has always been that we have let empire shape our cities, rather than letting cities shape themselves and, above all, demanding of people that they shape their cities.

But the complicity goes beyond that. Once Thomas Jefferson bought the Louisiana Purchase, we had no choice but to buy both the military and the bureaucratic superstructure that went with it. We can take the attitude of saying all of that has been forced on the West. Or we can say that we have been complicit in it and that we have the capacity to do something about it. The way we will do something about it is to claim our homeland — to say this is our home, and to be able to say "our" and mean it, not only of the people that think and dress and behave like us, but of the other inhabitants of the region who are equally rooted here. When the West is ready to do that, then it will be ready for a real politics of inhabitation.

I will make one final prediction: that when that time comes, we will understand that, like every other region of the country, we are going to have to be in control of our homeland. That means that 90 percent of it can't be owned someplace else. The imperial presence would have to be removed from the ownership of Western lands. The West will not be ready for its own politics until it is ready to claim its own land. The real test of that will be whether we ever understand that the U.S. Senate was created in order that land-dominated regions like the West might assert their own land-based ways of life. When the time comes, when we are ready to develop a history and politics of the West, we will begin to elect a cadre of U.S. senators who will go to Washington to assert sovereignty over this country that we inhabit. Will we do it? Are we serious? Or are we just playing games?

In 1636 John Winthrop, soon to become governor of the Massachusetts Bay Colony, sailed with a shipload of Pilgrims from England toward the land to the west. As they sailed, he prepared for his shipmates a sermon on how they should expect to go about the task of inhabiting the fiercely inhospitable land that they hoped to make their home. He knew how hard it would be. And he knew how, out of that hardship, they might create what he called "the city on a hill." This is what he said to them: "We must delight in each other. We must labor together, suffer together, rejoice and mourn together, keeping always before our eyes our condition as members of one body."[14]

In our time, Wendell Berry, in a poem called "Work Song," sought to capture once again the essence of the enterprise of winning a good living from a hard piece of land. "This is no paradisal dream," he wrote. But in a land-rooted voice of hope that is the true voice of the West, he concluded, "Its hardship is its possibility."[15]

Daniel Kemmis

PART FOUR

The Limits

WHEN DID WE KNOW

When did we know
the rapist cutting into the tender flesh
of his shivering victim
was a drag line slashing into Elk Mountain?

When did we *
the bloody child lying limp
in a rotting heap in the dumpster
was a waste pit of poison chemicals
seeping into the water   in   that   glass?

When did * *
the crack shooting up that ruddy nostril —
cocaine crack riding into your child's room on an Army
                chopper —
was a jet of napalm crashing into a family working
                a field of rice?

When * * *
that the 10 pounds of carbon dioxide I aim at your
                lung each drive of the week
is a cannon of acid rain shot at the cedars
                on Wolf Creek Pass?

* * * *
that the tons of styrofoam clogging Big Hole River are
a bomb of plutonium slicing the soil at Rocky Flats?

* * * *

the multinational bribes of rainforest keepers — those
military thugs who bask on your taxes — are federal
contracts for Star Wars research in this state?

When did I know that MY shortcut trampling across
                    the buffalo grass
is U.S./S.R. assaults on the moon, Mars, and cosmos?

        When did we   When do I

        do something about it?

Cordelia Candelaria

THE HISTORY OF FUTURES

(for my students at Kent State, Spring 1973)

The long horn was an automotive
package of hide & bones, a few hundred
pounds of dope which delivered itself
entirely free of moral inconvenience
known otherwise as fat
yet with a memory fresh enough to market

The Bloody Red Meat Habit
dates from about 1870
Before that we were a Sowbelly Nation
feeding off the wisest of the omnivores
Beef is the earliest element
of the crisis, a typical Texas imbalance

Importations, trash beef from Argentina
are meant to satisfy
the Bloody Red Meat Habits
of our best friends, and in fact
as pet lovers secretly understand
you Can fool fido

With Foodstamps we have pure script
the agricultural subsidy farmers have enjoyed
under every name but socialismo
since World War II

Which brings us
to a truly giant dog named Ronald
the most immense friend conceivable

a Fenrir created by beef heat
and there you have your bullshit apocalysis

One morning, in his mythological greed
He swallows the Sunne

Edward Dorn

FREE MARKET CHINOISERIE

There will never be enough BMWs
for the stated Billion, there will never
even be enough paper towels
or gas barbecues or ever enough ribs
or sauce for those short ribs. There will never
be enough coupons to clip or scissors
to clip them with — and there will never be
enough accountants to count it all
or paper to keep the accounts on
or discs to store the accounts
for which there will never be entries enough.
Someone should tell them.

Edward Dorn

AGRICULTURE

1

Water birds were a metaphor for abundance beyond measure in my childhood. On a November afternoon my father sat on a wooden case for shotgun shells in the deep tules by Pelican Lake like a crown prince of shotgunning, and dropped 123 ducks for an Elks Club feed. The birds were coming north to water from the grain fields and fighting a stiff headwind. They flared and started to settle, just over him, and they would not stop coming into the long red flame from his shotgun as darkness came down from the east. The dead birds fell, collapsed to the water, and washed back to shore in the wind. Eventually it was too dark to shoot, and the dead birds were heaped in the back of his pickup and he hauled them to town; he dumped them off to the woman he had hired to do the picking and went on to a good clear-hearted night at the poker table, having discharged a civic duty.

2

In 1826 a Dr. William Kittredge took himself and his new bride west from Massachusetts to Michigan, where he practiced medicine in Ypsilanti and Grand Rapids. My great-grandfather, Benjamin Franklin Kittredge, was born in 1828, the eldest of eight children. In 1850, aged twenty-two, Benjamin Franklin took his younger brother Harrison and headed west for the gold fields of California. You have to wonder about the intensity that drove those boys, really not much more than children. Imagine the stories they were telling themselves.

So many travelers, and not just young men with an itch, were driven by a simple desire to go *out*, away to the world with hope of discovering some interesting fate. Families sold good farms in Ohio and rolled west in their wagons, and were so often destroyed before they were done, driven to ruin by the thrust of what came down to nothing more profound than a pure yearning for excitement, a thing simple as one chance at a life that was not boring, paradise over the mountains, some fine blend of all that.

Benjamin Franklin was a single man. It is easy to imagine his leave-taking might have been simple. Goodbye to your sweetheart, and father and mother, and a kiss to the younger children. You and your brother can just walk away. What will you be?

Benjamin Franklin and Harrison made their passage down the Mississippi and across the Gulf of Mexico to the narrows at Panama, long before there was any canal, where they set off and just walked to the Pacific. Then another boat ride, this time to San Francisco. But gold didn't come easy. There was winter, mud, and snow in the camps. Harrison was killed in a dispute over a mining claim.

There are no details. I imagine some showdown over a hundred yards of creek-bed or a shovel. Ben Franklin went home. Back in Michigan, he married, and he came west again, this time in a wagon, with the goods of his marriage, again to the gold camps, where he had no more luck than before.

A first son, Herbert, was born in a settlement known as Jackass Flats outside Redding, California, on June 8, 1863. After some seasons in the foothills around Mount Shasta, panning little streams for trace, Benjamin Franklin moved his family north, always moving, as if to examine the promise of things. He owned acreages in the Willamette Valley of Oregon, literally some of the finest Class A agricultural land in the world, but nothing worked (family lore has one of those farms in the heart of what is now downtown Portland; there is a Kittredge Street).

My grandfather and namesake, William Kittredge, was born in 1875 (the seventh child of nine) while Benjamin Franklin was school-teacher at old Fort Simcoe, near Yakima in the state of Washington. Then Benjamin Franklin moved south beyond the gorge of the Columbia River, to a ranch in the hillslope country near Antelope in Oregon (where the Rajneesh set up his freeloading version of paradise in the early 1980s), and then to some fringes of mostly salt-grass meadowland in the far outback around Silver Lake, Oregon. There he ended his life in 1897, flat out of possibilities.

My grandfather was twenty-three, and poor, and his father was dead. I wish I knew what my grandfather thought as he lifted his eyes to study the scrub-brush flats around Silver Lake; I wish I knew how resolve came to him, and how he named it; I wish I knew what he saw as the gifts life might give him; I wish I knew what he thought they were worth.

3

The northern quarter of the Great Basin, southeastern Oregon and northern Nevada, is a great drift of barren sagebrush country the size of France. The landforms confront us incessantly with news of geologic time and our own fragility. The rims were built over eons, we can see the layers, lava flow on lava flow. The shadows of clouds travel like phantoms across the white playas of the alkaline wet-weather lakes.

That landlocked country is not all desert; there are great mountains where the winter snows accumulate: the Warner Range, Bidwell Mountain, Winter Rim, the Ochocos, and fault-block upliftings that rise from the distances like islands: the ten-thousand-foot escarpment, which is Steens Mountain, Hart Mountain, the Ruby Mountains of Nevada.

The most significant geography, so far as settlement is concerned, lies below those mountains in the meadowlands of the waterfowl valleys, like Warner Valley, where we lived. The snows melted and ran off in great floods, the landlocked lakes filled and dried up and filled, the sedges and tules grew and died and grew and died and rotted away into peat soil.

Before the white men came in the latter half of the nineteenth century, that country was inhabited by a scattering of Northern Paiute and traveling bands from the timbered country to the west, Klamaths and Modocs who came to the swamplands for the water-bird hunting.

The Northern Paiute did not have much in the way of what are called "cultural items," which are everything from spoons to ideas of magic. They lived sparse and traveled light. The country did not reward them for owning things.

The clan that lived in my home territory around Warner Valley was known as "The Groundhog Eaters," a name wonderful in its inelegance. You wonder what it meant to them as they managed lives that no doubt did not seem either splendid or numbing or even simple.

Some of us envy what we think of as their existence in a communal life as they moved through their so-called hunting and gathering in an endless sway of time, in which the world was alive and their true companion. But the content of their days is difficult for us to imagine.

It is country that can be imagined as a kind of hideout geographical enclave. Sensible routes of travel, wagon trails and railroads, went around to the north (the Oregon Trail) or to the south (the California

Trail). Settlement by white men with families, who were intent on setting up ranches, did not begin until the 1870s, and that huge drift of country, Lake County and Harney County and Malhuer County in Oregon, Washoe County and Humboldt County in Nevada, each large as some states in the East, is still populated by no more than a few thousand people.

After the Mexican-American War, in 1848, drovers began trailing herds from Missouri to the central valley of California. One of the men who was in on those drives from the beginning was Dr. Hugh Glenn, a young Virginian whose ambitions influenced a considerable part of history in southeastern Oregon. Before a decade had passed he owned one of the great Spanish ranches in the Sacramento Valley.

In 1859 the miners around Virginia City in Nevada found that the black rock they had been discarding was silver, and the Comstock boom began. The miners didn't want much but a place to dig; but they had to eat, and the people who fed them felt they had a right to run livestock anywhere that was handy, including the creekside meadowlands where the Truckee River emptied into Pyramid Lake.

The Indians traditionally camped there in early spring. The bands came for hundreds of miles to work the great cutthroat trout fishery. Winter was over, there was food for all; the leaders talked; by 1859 they were tired of being driven from their hunting grounds.

Two Paiute girls were kidnapped and abused by two brothers at Williams Station, a whiskey stop on the Carson River. A party of warriors killed the brothers and burned the station. There began a series of battles across northern Nevada, initially called the Pyramid Lake War, which never really ended until the natives were effectively broken and driven to the reservations.

Six years later, in March of 1866, the *Humboldt Register* described a battle:

> At half past nine the order was given to charge. Right merrily the men obeyed. The Indians stood up bravely, fighting sullenly to the last — asking no quarter; but the charge was irresistible. The boys rode through the Indian ranks, scattering and shooting down everything that wore paint. . . . 80 warriors, 35 squaws. The latter were dressed the same as the bucks, and were fighting — and had to be killed to ascertain their sex. . . . [1]

The U.S. Army was seriously into subduing the natives and protecting settlers, and establishing forts and encampments as a foundation for governing the wilderness. In the best book on the subject of prewhite storytelling in Oregon, *Coyote Was Going There: Indian Literature of the Oregon Country*, Jarold Ramsey writes:

> The white response, organized during the Civil War, was brutally simple: extermination. The unpublished "Field Journals" of Lt. William McKay (a medical doctor who was himself part Indian) make it vividly clear that Army detachments like McKay's, aided by Indian scouts from Warm Springs and elsewhere, went through the upper reaches of the Great Basin country hunting Paiutes and other Shoshoneans down like deer, killing for the sake of what in the Viet Nam era became known as "body-count."[2]

By the summer of 1868 the Indians in northern Nevada and southeastern Oregon were being rounded onto desolate reservations. An educated Paiute woman named Sara Winnemucca, employed as a liaison for the army, found starving bands of her people collected at Camp C. F. Smith in far southeastern Oregon. She sent fifteen wagons for the children, and some eight hundred Paiutes were moved to the Reserve at Fort McDermit, on the Oregon-Nevada border, where they were issued daily dole-food rations.

Sara Winnemucca helped hand out the food, and hated what she saw. She wrote to Major Henry Douglass, Indian superintendent of Nevada: "If this is the kind of civilization awaiting us on the Reserves, God grant that we may never be compelled to go on one, as it is much prefferrable [sic] to live in the mountains and drag out an existence in our native manner."[3]

The open range was pretty much taken up in California. Stock growers who wanted to expand were driving herds over the Sierras into the Great Basin. A man named John Devine brought his blooded horses to Camp Smith (already abandoned by the army), built a quarter-mile race track, and settled alongside the all-season creek. Devine set a weather vane with a white horse atop the cupola on his barn, and named his new empire The White Horse Ranch.

You wonder what drove John Devine. The ranch was vastly isolated in those days; it still is. Far out to the west there is the Alvord Desert, a great playa in the rain shadow on the eastern side of the long ridge that is Steens Mountain; there is not much else to see; nobody lives nearby. But maybe John Devine knew what he was doing; he became a prince of the country; the history of settlement was started in that part of the world where my imagination still lives.

In 1872 Dr. Hugh Glenn put a twenty-three-year-old man named Peter French in charge of driving twelve hundred head of his Sacramento

Valley cows north to the deserts of Oregon. French found the swamp-lands in the Blitzen Valley and the high summer range on Steens Mountain, and he claimed them, hauled saw-lumber fifty miles from a mill in the mountains to the north, built a white house, and began assembling the enormous P Ranch, which was arguably the finest natural set of livestock properties in the American West. Simple as that: This is mine. Soon the country was filling with settlers, white men and their families.

Late in the same year that French drove his cows to the Blitzen Valley, 1872, the Modoc War broke out south of Tule Lake on the Oregon-California border. A native man named Captain Jack and around 175 of his Modoc followers holed up in a labyrinthine fortress of natural tunnels through the lava beds and fought off the U.S. military until June 1 of 1873. It was a little war, but it was an embarrassment to the military. Captain Jack was hanged at Fort Klamath, and after-wards his body was dug up and embalmed and shown in carnivals all over the East Coast.

In the early part of 1873 a Lt. Col. Frank Wheaton, commander in the District of the Lakes in southeastern Oregon, reported that a stock ranch in Warner Lakes Valley owned by D. R. Jones, eighteen miles from the post, was the nearest residence or settlement to Camp Warner. Which makes D. R. Jones the first settler I know about in the valley where I grew up.

Sara Winnemucca was reported to be living with Mister Jones. Connections begin to accumulate.

In 1878 various native groups across the northern desert country left the Reserves and rose up in an outbreak called the Bannock War; they killed Charlie On Long, a Chinese cook who worked for Peter French, and after that they lost and lost. By the end of 1878 the war was over, and a considerable number of natives had been herded together at old Fort Harney, east of Burns. Sara Winnemucca was among them.

On January 6, 1879, the women and old people and children were loaded into some fifty wagons, the men following on horseback, and escorted north through the terrible cold and the snows. A woman gave birth and the child died; the woman died a day later. Their bodies were left by the trail. Three children died of exposure as they traveled over two mountain ranges and the Columbia River to Fort Simcoe, just south of Yakima in the state of Washington, where my great-grandfather, Benjamin Franklin Kittredge, was a schoolteacher.

It was a Trail of Tears, and yet I never heard it talked about in southeastern Oregon; I learned of it from books. It was not part of our common mythology. In that country we grew up without stories; we knew a history filled with omissions, which can be thought of as lies.

I wonder if people imagined those stories were too shameful to be told, or if they just didn't care, if they were not very interested, and forgot. I wonder what Benjamin Franklin Kittredge thought as those ruined Indians came to Fort Simcoe. I wonder if he saw them; I wonder if the children who survived ever entered his schoolroom; I wonder what he did for them.

Sara Winnemucca was the foremost woman of her time, among her people. In 1880 she was invited to visit Secretary of the Interior Carl Schurtz in Washington, D.C., and she went. Sara wrote and published a book, *Life Among the Paiutes: Their Wrongs and Claims,* and she lectured in New York and Boston and Cambridge and Philadelphia, all on behalf of her tribe, but nothing worked, the government was finally not interested. So Sara went home, and at least in some metaphoric sense she went back to sleeping in blankets on the ground with the traditional people. In October of 1891 she ate a big meal, she took to bed, she died. The official cause was too much wine; nothing about heartbreak.

Dr. Hugh Glenn ran for governor of California and was defeated, and then he was shot to death by a drunken bookkeeper. Peter French married Glenn's daughter, Ella, who never lived with him, accumulated a great empire, and was shot dead by a nester. Glenn and French and Sara Winnemucca were people of vast energies and vivid intelligence; they died with their purposes in disarray; they wanted to move the world but it would not go.

My great-grandfather died the same year as Peter French, 1897, impoverished in Silver Lake.

There was gold but he never found it. And anyway such riches were to have been only the beginning. The real treasures lay no doubt in some vision of wholeness and easy fields greening up in spring, croplands flowing across the rolling plow-ground out back of the white-painted home place, and the gleeful crying of grandchildren at play on the lawns sloping to the mossy spring-creek — some particularly American version of perfect promised-land solace. All this we promise you.

"Americans," wrote D. H. Lawrence,

> will not stand for the pioneer stuff, except in small, sentimentalized doses. They know too well the grimness of it, the savage fight and the savage failure which broke the back of the country but also broke something in the human soul. The spirit and the will survived, but something in the soul perished: the softness, the floweriness, the

natural tenderness. How could it survive the sheer brutality of the
fight with that American wilderness, which is so big, vast, and
obdurate!

The savage America was conquered and subdued at the expense
of the instinctive and intuitive sympathy of the human soul. The fight
was too brutal.[4]

Lawrence goes on to talk of "an inward individual retraction, an
isolation, an amorphous separateness like grains of sand, each grain
isolated upon its own will," and he laments "the breaking of the heart,
the collapse of the flow of spontaneous warmth between a man and his
fellows . . ."[5] He might have been writing directly about my people.

4

In 1936 my grandfather bought the MC Ranch in Warner Valley.
The deal represented an enormous change in our fortunes. He signed the
legal papers and took possession of those fields and distances as his own
with no money down when he was sixty-two years old. He pledged
everything he had worked for all his life, unable to resist such a
kingdom.

Warner Valley, when I was prime in my readiness to witness
paradise, was in what I think of as its prelapsarian stage; it was clear my
people had stumbled onto a mostly untouched place, and rare good
fortune.

My grandparents were imperious and heedless; they came from
hard poverty on those high deserts around Silver Lake: My grandmother dried her wash on a barbed-wire fence around an unpainted
house until her children were mostly grown. My grandfather had
brought the family up from poverty. For decades he summered alone in
the empty country east of Silver Lake, isolated and tending his cattle.
His years were devoted to a brutal horseback notion of life; he felt he
had earned what he had, and he was right. But the earning hardened
him; he was absorbed with ambition. Running his properties on borrowed money, he wanted more.

It was his theory that we, in our family, should put work ahead of
every other thing, including compassion, for the common good, and for
a long time we tried to live by his theory. If you paid the bills, in the
philosophy my grandfather taught, you got to call the shots.

Accumulation was my grandfather's game. If we took enough care,
in his story, and sacrificed enough (and here the story goes sideways) we

would eventually get to live in town most of the year, as he did, in a big rock-walled house, with linens and painted china and silver tableware: Correct was part of secure, and at the heart of actual. It was a story he wanted to believe, a story he used to manipulate everyone, and he got away with it for most of his life. He was not so much cruel as indifferent to purposes other than his own, and mainly interested in his cattle and how they were doing, beef on the hoof, for sale.

For my grandfather, in that beginning, Warner must have been the ultimate answer to a lifetime of yearning, thousands of acres of meadow on the high side of the valley, cut with sloughs and willows for shelter, where he could winter his stock on native hay stacked with the beaver slides. Never mistake it: The MC was a great ranch.

Those people, so long as they had any choice, were never going back to the high deserts. They clearly knew that they were living in a dream that had come to them at least partway through luck: Right then they were having good luck in the Great Depression (cheap land), and later on they would have good luck during the Great War (terrific grain prices). But they also understood that most of their luck had come as a result of their own invention and sharp dealing, and they were pretty much justified in thinking they had made their own way. My grandfather had early on come to understand that a reputation for hard work and a kind of calculated recklessness, along with an absolute willingness to pursue litigation, could get you a long way with certain bankers.

So long as my people trusted one another inside the family, which wasn't even a couple of decades, their luck ran to aces for all of us. An ancient world was changing, and my people were on the leading edge of the conversion. They knew it; they gloried in it. The idea that they were connected to great doings and improvements in the world inhabited them and drove them.

Thirty-six miles of washboard-gravel county road twisted over the Warner Mountains to end with us; beyond to the east there were wagon roads traced down over the rimrocks and across the fringes of alkaline flats, but essentially the way into our valley was the way out. There was no electricity but that generated for house lights by the Delco power plant with its rows of glass batteries. There was no functioning telephone, although there had been some time in the past; up in the Adel Store there was an old hand-crank instrument on the wall, and there was telephone wire hanging loose from a line of spindly home-cut jack-pine poles along the road to town.

In February and early March the creeks draining out of the Warner Mountains — Deep Creek and Twenty Mile Creek — would flood and fill the vast tule-beds until at sunset the swamps on the far east side of the valley would shimmer with water like a lake. The unbroken peat soil under those miles of swamp was eight feet deep in places; experts estimate more than a quarter million water birds came through the valley each year.

The point here is abundance and great hunting, an overwhelming property thronging with natural life, and what my family did with it. At the end we had over twenty-one thousand irrigated acres in Warner Valley, something beyond a million acres of leased BLM rangeland. We ran more than six thousand mother cows. It could have been paradise; probably it was, maybe it still is.

My grandfather wondered how such a place could be best used. My father tried to show him. My father saw that valley as a great possibility; my father had been to school at the College of Agriculture in Corvallis; he was an engineer; Oscar Kittredge was one of the new men, a visionary. He bought a cable-drum Caterpillar RD-6 track-layer fitted out with a dozer blade, which he used to start building a seventeen-mile diversion levee to carry the spring floodwaters of Twenty Mile Creek north along the east side of the valley to drain our swamplands. Seventeen miles. In those times such a project was considered insanely ambitious, literally.

My father was the joke of the country, but not for long. He jerry-rigged a generator and battery system to run off the diesel engine of that RD-6, mounted it with lights, and ran it at the levee building twenty-four hours a day, summer and winter, except for fuel stops and maintenance. Then he bought an RD-7 and used it to build his levee while he started plowing the tule beds with the RD-6, also twenty-four hours a day.

By the end of World War II my father was making a lot of money farming grain off those plow-grounds. And he proved, as my mother said, to be ahead of his time in finding ways to spend it, money he didn't have to split with my grandfather or anybody, a fact that came to cause heavy grief in our family.

For a few years during World War II, as the catskinners brought more and more of the swampland under drainage and the plow, economics in my family swung heavily on the spectacular profits from my father's farming operations. And my father was running with his luck. There was an airplane, movie people, even a couple of race horses. But mostly, even ahead of the game, in my family, we worked.

My father bought two more D-7 Caterpillar tractors; the seventeen-mile diversion canal was finished; he bought four John Deere 36 combines with sixteen-foot headers; inside the diversion canal he built an enormous intricate network of drainage ditches and redwood headgates;

the shallow lakes were pumped dry, huge fields were ditched off, 750 acres in Huston Swamp, 800 acres in Dodson Lake. The headgates were opened when the spring runoff waters came. Those fields were flooded, and pumped dry. We were reinventing the land and the water-flow patterns of the valley on a model copied from industry, and irrevocably altering the ecology of everything, including our own lives, moving into that monied technology, which is agribusiness.

In the spring of 1946, with the war ended, came a simple and enormous change. We started putting up the loose hay on our fifteen thousand or so acres of wild meadow with tractors. Our work teams were sold for chicken feed. A great splendor and attachment to seven or eight thousand years of human experimentation and tradition went from our lives with those horses. I recall the dust and the slow drumlike clomping of their hooves on the dry sod of the late July fields as they snorted and trotted amiably toward the hay camp corrals before sunup; their harness hung on pegs in the barns and rotted.

In the haying we had traditionally worked crews of nearly a hundred men through the months of summer, thirty mowing machines and twenty dump rakes, which translates into a lot more than fifty men, some working, some coming, some going, and maybe two hundred head of work horses. Two stacking crews followed the mowing after a week or so of letting the hay cure, a one-hundred-ton stack every half a day through July and some of August when they were up to speed.

From hay camp to hay camp, the valley was a place filled with human life. You could look out over Warner valley in the morning and see the strings of dust rising to clean sky over those hay camps' corrals, stirred up by the circling horses as those crews caught their teams. You could think this was the right dream of ourselves as we were supposed to be before everything went to tractors.

We thought we were working toward a perfection of fields, and for a long time I loved it. We thought we doing the great good work, remaking the world on an image borrowed from efficiency experts. We had paved roads and electricity and television, and the old animal-centered agricultural world I had grown up in was mostly gone, that quickly. I congratulate myself on having lived in it for a little while. The ranch was being turned into a machine for feeding livestock. The swamps were drained, and the thronging flocks of water birds were diminishing, clearly, year by year; the hunting was still fine if you had never seen anything else, but we knew.

Our irrigation system was a masterpiece of complexity with over five thousand water-control devices, headgates, valves, eighteen-inch pumps. We could run the water around and around in a dry year, pumping it back up to irrigate with again — until it wore out, was the joke. The main part of my work in the spring of the year was that system, a twenty-four-hour-a-day job called "balancing water."

We had leveled a couple of thousand acres for alfalfa, and kept leveling more. For eight years after the death of my grandfather I was the farming boss at the MC, in my father's footsteps, running an operation we had always, since my father's early days, called "The Grain Camp." Those crops and that irrigation system were the finest playthings of my life. We were making something perfect as it could be in our notion of the world, inscribing our vision on the earth like artists, and the making was an art.

Do not mistake it, the impulse that drove us to work was a vision of artistry. We were doing God's work, and thought we were making a sacred place on the earth.

But it didn't work. We cut our alfalfa and tame hay with swathers, followed by five-wire balers, and Harrow-Beds to pick up the bales from the field and stack them mechanically. We sprayed 2-4-D Ethyl and Malathion, and the World War II German nerve gas called Parathion, for clover mite in the barley, and we shortened our own lives. We baited the coyotes with 1080, and field mice destroyed our alfalfa. We irrigated and reirrigated, pumped and drained, and our rich peat soil started to go saline.

We couldn't hire anybody who cared enough about our mechanical work to do it right. The old men were dying, and not many young men were coming to the work with much beyond disdain. Men who hired out for ranch work in the 1960s were missing the boat, and they knew it. They despised themselves for it. And they despised the work.

Up on the hill above the old buckaroo camp we built an industrial plant called "The Feed Mill," a collection of steel buildings with rollers and grinders and blowers and chain drives and augers and hundred-horsepower electric motors, a huge grain-storage bunker, and an endlessness of lots for fattening cattle. By the end we had built lots enough to hold most of our cow herd; every year we shipped toward five thousand fat animals to slaughter.

The mill was designed to chop hay and roll grains and mix in additives from molasses to growth-inducing chemicals like stilbestrol. It was a howling, stinking place where the work proceeded at the pace of the machinery.

Those thousands of animals, penned into those lots, waiting for the feed truck, were regarded as the ultimate step in a mechanical progression. We raised barley, we ground it up and mixed it with chemicals, they ate it, they fattened, they were butchered, they were food. In spring we cleaned the manure from the lots with D-7 Cats and scrapers. Our dream had led us to these processes. The work seemed distanced and unnatural, and thus demonic and hateful as we did it, and I think that hatefulness fueled our inability to cherish ourselves and each other; it fueled the family trouble that was already started, trouble I didn't really understand.

I had been boss at the Grain Camp for four or five years, and I had come to understand myself as a young man doing good work. We were farming twenty-four hours a day through early May while the Canada honkers hatched their downy young and the tulips pushed up through the crusted flower beds and the Lombardy poplar broke their buds and the forsythia bloomed lurid yellow against the cookhouse wall. But I don't think of such glories when I remember those spring mornings. I remember the odor of dank peat turning up behind those disc Cats as we went on farming twenty-four hours a day, and how much I loved breaking ground.

Before sunrise on those mornings I would come awake and go piss, then stand in my undershorts on the screened-in veranda porch attached to the house where I lived with my wife and young children. I would shiver with chill and happiness as I smelled the world coming awake. Far out across our valley the lights on our D-7 disc Cats would flicker as lights do when seen through a screen, moving almost imperceptibly. I would take my binoculars and open the screen door and gaze out to those lights as if I might catch one of my night-shift catskinners at some dog-fuckery, but really all I wanted to see was the machinery moving. Those track-layers would clank along all through the hours of darkness at two or three miles an hour, turning a thirty-six-foot swath, a hundred acres every night and another hundred acres on the day shift. The upturned soil would mellow in the air for a day, and then we would harrow and seal it with dust, and drill it to barley. In ten days or so the seedlings would break earth, and those orderly drill-rows undulating over the tilled ground toward the sundown light were softly yellow-green and something alive I had seen to completion.

It came to a couple hundred acres of barley every day for fifteen days, three thousand–some-odd acres in all. By the end of harvest in late September, at roughly a ton per acre, that came to three thousand tons of barley at $50 a ton, or $150,000 in the early 1960s. Which was some real money in our end of the world.

We drained the wetlands and thought that made them ours. We believed the world was made to be useful; we ditched and named the intersections of our ditches: Four Corners, the Big Pump, Center

Bridge, Beatty Bridge. We thought such naming made the valley ours; we thought the men who worked for us were ours.

5

Every so often, when I was a child, one of the women in my family would organize get-togethers, usually at one of the cookhouses. At precisely six o'clock, summer or winter, the cook would clang the dinner bell and we would troop in and seat ourselves down both sides of a long table with the workingmen. My grandfather was always at the head of the table, with my grandmother beside him, unless we were at the Grain Camp, where my father was the boss (we didn't go there but a couple of times). And there was me and my mother and my brother and my sister, and a mix of aunts and uncles and cousins.

I try to imagine what we looked like, the owners of the property and their wives and children, there in the late 1930s, at the heart of the Great Depression, laughing and confident as we passed the platters of boiled beef and the bowls of mashed potatoes and gray milk gravy.

Some of the workingmen would be too shy to talk, eyeing the women like they were creatures who had just come from another planet. I wonder how many of those men despised us, and if they understood that they did, or why. There was a kind of complaint you would hear at that table in the days afterwards, something like this: "Goddamn a woman. All that goddamned talk. You got to sit there and listen. You might say shit so you can't say a goddamned thing."

Blame it on women. But it was not women, they weren't the real complaint. It was what those women represented to those men, power and civility and the possibility of love, or at least affection and family. Those were the things we were supposed to be sharing when we went to eat in the cookhouses.

Some of those men must have sensed that those meals were a fraud. Nobody was actually sharing anything. Times were poor, the men in my family were capable of supporting women and children, they owned a great ranch; those were the trappings of power, and they were on exhibition.

It must have been my grandfather's idea that we should sit down with the men who worked for us, and eat what they ate, off tin plates. No doubt he passed it off as a way of staying in touch with our beginnings, another way of taking care.

Jake O'Rourke died in the bunkhouse. Jake didn't show for

breakfast, and I sent a man to wake him, but Jake was dead in his bed. I want to say his eyes were like mirrors in which I could see myself. It was my first confrontation with the notion that major promises were being broken. Jake's eyes were dry as river stones.

Vance Beebe came to crippling emphysema from a lifetime of smoking and running the hay baler in the deep summertime chaff and dust. When he couldn't work in the fields he would idle off his time doing things like building chairs for the bunkhouse bullpen on a design from upstate New York–rich-man resorts. Vance took his emphysema to town and died alone in a motel, and I thought maybe he had killed himself. I still do. Vance believed strongly in doing your own dirty work.

In retrospect those family meals in the cookhouses look like self-serving political bullshit designed to reveal my people as common and decent, designed to breed loyalty among the working men. And to feed the family ego: We were poor people who had risen; we were naming ourselves.

It is an old story: The ruling class observes certain decencies; if they do, everything might last forever. In some way my people may have believed such things. Maybe they believed in magic. We lived in a dream of machinelike, industrial perfection we had been given, a Corps of Engineers/Ag School mirage of remaking the world in our own image, and it didn't work, not at all, for both practical and spiritual reasons.

6

The ecology of our valley was complex beyond our understanding, and it began to die as we went on manipulating it in ever more frantic ways. As it went dead and empty of the old natural life it became a place where no one wanted to live; we found ourselves distanced from everything we might have loved, like each other, and the place where we lived. No wonder so many of us (like myself) thought it would be easy to leave. I find myself scabbing history out of books, and trying to fit it together in strings that reach from generation to generation, trying to loop myself and the people I care for into lines of significance.

In a family as unchurched as ours there was only one sacred story, and that was the one about work and property and ownership, which is sad. It seems to mean we had lost track of stories like the one that tells us the world is to be cherished as if it exists inside our own skin. We were new people in a new country; we came and went in a couple of generations. By the time I was grown my father had stopped speaking to his father, and my mother had left them both behind.

The poet C. K. Williams came to Missoula and talked about "narrative dysfunction" as a prime part of mental illness. Many of us, he seemed to be saying, lose track of the story of themselves, the story of who we are supposed to be, and how we are supposed to act. Stories are places to live, he seemed to be saying. Inside the imagination we know a lot of them, and we're in big trouble when we don't know which one is ours.

We want the world to be a sacred part of that long invention that is the story of our life, the most important character after ourselves. We yearn to live in a coherent place we can name, where we can feel safe inside our invention, and we want that place to exist like a friend, somebody we can know.

What we must understand is that we already inhabit such a place; it is alive. We must understand that the world cannot take care of itself anymore. The specific danger is us; this earth is our only friend, and we are destroying it increment by increment at a horrific rate.

We need to define a new and liveable story; it will be a story about staying put and taking care of what we've got, in which our home is named as sacred, a story that encourages us to take serious care, a story about making use of the place where we live without killing it.

It will be a story in which we come to understand that the complexity of the living world cannot be replicated no matter how much science fiction we hear about cities in space. We will understand that there will never be another setup like the one we have evolved to live in; ruin it and we will have lost ourselves, which is craziness.

William Kittredge

HOW WILL OUR GRANDCHILDREN
JUDGE US?

Bill Kittredge and I have something in common: We both were shaped by our grandfathers.

I remember how, as my grandfather's oldest grandchild, I was taken everywhere he went. My grandfather was, for some twenty years, president and chairman of the board of the Great Western Sugar Company.

I grew up to understand more about the sugar company and subsequently came to know that my grandfather — I didn't just love him, I adored him — was one of the authors of the wetback system. I was ashamed and embarrassed for so terribly long. Then, with greater maturity, I got to a point where I realized that you have to take it in context. Our grandparents were doing the best they knew how, and you have to respect that. They produced Bill, who cares a great deal, and me. I care a great deal. They housed us, they fed us, and they educated us, and that's not such a bad job to have done. I hope that when my granddaughters sit around and talk about what grandma was like, they won't judge me for the things that I didn't know I should have been trying to conquer.

Our families differed, Bill's and mine; mine came to the city. My Pennsylvania grandfather had come out here to the Union Colony and started in the fields in Eaton, Colorado. Then he made it big and he came to Denver, and as a result I come from a very urbane background. I am very much a citified person, and as state historic preservation officer, I deal not only with the cultural landscape, which is a great deal of what Bill has brought us, but also with the city landscape. Talk about rape and pillage in the nineteenth century — we have it right now. Not only our landscape but our cities are being raped and pillaged, and that is a damage about which our grandchildren are going to say, "Why didn't grandma do something about that?"

In the Western vernacular, it is time to say to ourselves: Don't look for another tree. This is not the last best place, this is the only place.

Barbara Sudler

DEFINING THE CARRYING CAPACITY
OF THE WEST

If we ask, "Are we exceeding the carrying capacity of the West?" in physical terms, the answer, with possibly one or two exceptions, is clearly no. But the physical limits are only one measure of the perceived carrying capacity and probably aren't what will determine when we feel we've reached the limit.

To illustrate what I'm talking about, let me use a personal example. Twenty-five years ago, shortly after my family and I had moved to the West, we took our first vacation in the newly created Canyonlands National Park. We spent ten days without ever seeing anyone else — only one or two sets of distant car lights high on the mesa across the river. We fell in love with the canyon country and went back every year for twenty years. We went for a variety of reasons — the fun, the beauty, the adventure. But mostly we went for the solitude and for the spiritual recharging we received from realizing that we were no more significant in that country than the lizards, or the deer that roamed the canyons. I found it somehow comforting to know that if mankind ever blew it, this magnificent country would continue its evolution.

Twenty years later we entered the park, stopped alongside the road, and had a ranger pull up next to us and tell us that we had to put our dog on a leash. I felt like we had seen the end of an era. My sense of loss was acute. At that moment, if someone had asked me whether we had exceeded our carrying capacity, my answer would have been a resounding yes. The regulations put in place to protect the park for others symbolized the ruin of it for me. I recognize that environmentally my dog did do damage. As he ran around, he broke up fragile crypto-gamic soil. When he ran on the rocks, he knocked off layers of lichen. And I'm sure that every time he took a leap into a water hole, he shortened the lives of the startled toads.

I also know that southeastern Utah was in deep economic trouble.

Grazing was prohibited in the park, the energy bust hit, and local people were hoping for a large influx of tourists. What I want to show by this example is that decisions regarding carrying capacity are very complex — and usually subjective calls. For decision makers, the pressures can be painful. In Boulder we're a supposedly enlightened lot who put growth controls in place years ago. We also have a whole raft of regulations to protect quality of life. But in less economically fortunate areas, doing the right thing may be almost impossible.

Let me give you a couple of examples from George Sinner, the governor of North Dakota. North Dakota, since 1980, has experienced a bust in both energy production and agriculture, its two biggest revenue generators. When ag prices finally started back up, the state had back-to-back years of the most severe drought in the nation. As North Dakota's revenues went down, the budget was slashed and taxes went up. In 1989 taxpayers revolted and in a December referendum defeated several taxes that provided about 10 percent of the state's already meager general fund. The day after the referendum, Governor Sinner took part in lighting the state Christmas tree. He was exhausted from campaigning to save the taxes and deeply distressed at what he knew the drop in revenues would mean. He tells about watching a class of second-graders wearing matching blue T-shirts singing Christmas carols, thinking how beautiful they were, and realizing that North Dakota probably would have to drop to last in its support of public education. He burst out crying, in front of everyone.

About six weeks later he called again, again in real anguish. His dilemma: he had received a call from the chairman of the Turtle Mountain Chippewas asking the state to sign a certificate of need for a home for the elderly on the reservation. Signing the certificate would obligate the state to pay the Medicare share of the costs for a population that doesn't pay state taxes. North Dakota has a disproportionately elderly population and already supports many nursing-home beds. His comment to me: "I can't approve a new obligation when I'm having to cut so many programs, but how can I deny a population which I know is probably the neediest in the state?" Most officials, elected or appointed, who have found themselves in those positions are reluctant to take actions that could hamstring the economy, lock up resources, or impose unnecessary regulatory or financial burdens.

Discussions about carrying capacity quickly become a clash in values — economic values, environmental values, spiritual and emotional values. It's also about governmental values, or at least about governmental responses to conflicting values. To return to my dog-on-a-leash story, those of you who have hiked sandy canyon bottoms or clambered over slick rock formations know that telling someone they have to attach themselves to a one-hundred-pound German shepherd on a six-foot leash is both ridiculous and dangerous. In this case, government action doesn't appropriately protect any of the values at issue, and because it doesn't, it invites scorn for governmental solutions.

And that's really my point. Whether we can avoid exceeding the carrying capacity — whether that capacity is real or only perceived — depends on how effectively government and our political system can accommodate the values coming into play. Physically, the West has a great deal of land, but we need to respect its integrity — avoid urban sprawl, desertification, exploitation without reclamation, and pollution. Economically, the potential is here for almost unending growth if we want it. But we need to ask ourselves at what cost, and we need to help ensure that it's fair. Socially, we have clear challenges because of the wide variety of cultures in the West. As Patricia Limerick said earlier, we need to learn how to talk to each other better. Environmentally, we're pushing our luck. We're making progress, but it's not enough and it's after the fact. Technologically, we may be able to find answers to most of the problems, but can we do it soon enough? Can we live with the results?

And that brings me to the *spiritual* carrying capacity. Most Westerners believe they live in a very special place. We feel nurtured by many factors that are more than economic. If public- and private-sector policies disregard them, we may hit capacity thresholds before we need to, simply because cantankerous Westerners dig in their heels.

To return to governmental carrying capacities: Here I'm perhaps least sanguine. Fragmented entities, lack of visionary leadership, unending litigation, unresponsive agencies, inflexible regulations, outdated laws — what Charles Wilkinson calls the "lords of yesterday" — all force a depressing and debilitating gridlock. More government is not the answer. Better government is. There are encouraging experiments going on. Hawaii has a legislative mandate to define its carrying capacity. The need and the limits may be clearer in an island economy, but much that is relevant to others should come out. The concept of sustainable development shows promise of moving from an emotionally useful concept to an operationally useful one.

Finally, more and more government agencies are starting to realize the potential return from dispute-resolution and consensus-building processes. The more we can get away from winners and losers, adversarial processes, and crippling prescriptive regulations, the better our chances of not just realizing, but acting, as though we're in this together and that what's good for one also benefits others.

We need to do more. Stewart Udall, in the introductory chapter to *Beyond the Mythic West*, a book the Western Governors' Association is producing for its annual meeting, quotes geographer Dennis Brownridge, who points out that few parts of the world have experienced such explosive growth. The West has grown from 250,000 people to 50 million in 150 years — or 20,000 percent growth. If the rest of the world had done the same, we'd have 200 billion people. Udall goes on to state, quoting former EPA administrator William Ruckelshaus: "Developing a sustainable economy will be 'a modification of society comparable in scale to the Industrial Revolution. The undertaking will be absolutely unique in humanity's stay on earth.' "[6]

We need to get on with it.

Jo Clark

RECOGNIZING THE WEST AS AN
URBAN PLACE

I was born in Kalispell, in the northwest corner of Montana, in 1923, to a lumber family. They were not then known as extractors. Just good citizens and lumber people. However, my father was the superintendent of the local national forest. So I was raised amid considerable argument between the federal land managers and the private-enterprise resource developers.

I went to high school in the Montana college town of Missoula, and then to Stanford. Then, after several newspaper ventures on the Pacific Coast and a few chapters outside of the West, I went back to Montana, where I was in the lumber business myself in a small town for a few years. After that I worked on the Great Falls paper, and came to *The Denver Post* thirty years ago. In the course of this, in addition to the Montana mountains, I spent time on the Plains, up in Wyoming, and, of course, in Colorado and New Mexico.

So I consider myself a Westerner. And yet, as I reflect on that experience, it was all what I call urban. This doesn't mean that I didn't learn how to fish. It doesn't mean I didn't spend time in the woods for my family's lumber company. It doesn't mean that I haven't been out in a wheat field, or I haven't done a number of other things that you do as you grow up and spend your business life in the mountain West. But practically the whole time, my natural habitat was in towns and cities; that is, it was urban.

Most Westerners are urban people. A much higher percentage of our population lives in units that the Census Bureau describes as urban than any other region of the United States. And yet, in our discussions about the West, so often our historical approach — the way we shape our ideas about the future — is to handle the city or the town as if it were the exception. The city is the place most Western historians don't want to think about. Let's talk about the mountains, the resources, the water. We really can't work in the cities when we're talking about the West. Yet the West has to be shaped, has to be preserved, has to be protected in such a way that it serves the places most of its people live, the towns and cities, as well as the beautiful empty places where they don't.

It is a convenient way to think about what we want to do with the West — to pretend to ourselves that we have a way of making a great number of people go away. I notice that in his latest work, Wallace Stegner — I revere no man more that he — concludes that one of the great hopes of the West is that its overpopulation will recede. I cannot find anywhere in any serious discussion of demography any basis for this hope. People will keep coming to the West. They will come at varying rates. They will come in varying places and different times. But they will come. One figure the American Planning Association offers, and I guess it is as good as any other, is that by the year 2000 the population of the West will have grown 20 percent. You can get any kind of figure, but all the figures seem to agree that we are going to have to think about more people.

Why do people come west? People come west because of their dreams. They dream that they will do better financially. They dream that they can find more space. They dream that they can find a better quality of life. And the fact of the matter is that one of the reasons they come west is that it is better than east: it always has been, in terms of people dreaming that if they went west they could make a new start. The dream isn't just of people coming west. The dream is still alive for the people in Mexico who are coming north. The dream is still alive for the people along the Pacific Rim who are coming east. They dream of the American West, although their compass direction, their label of direction, is different.

When you dream about going somewhere, by and large you don't stop to analyze whether there are enough schools or enough roads or enough water or what the economic situation is. People do not think about infrastructure first. They come on. That's the lesson of how people have come into the American West in the past. The miners that came in the mining rush didn't stop to think about what was here. They heard there was gold and they came. The immigrants who came and filled up towns and cities around the turn of the century didn't think about what the conditions were. What they were going to find, they felt, could by no stretch of the imagination be worse than what they were leaving. So they came. The veterans who flooded in here at the end of

World War II came because they'd been out here and they liked it. They figured that they'd take their chances on the schools and the roads, and they would build schools and roads if they weren't here. And they came.

My point is that people are going to come west regardless of what we do. If we are going to protect our west — if we are going to protect our landscape properly, protect our communities — we have to see to it that the investment is made in the infrastructure we need to take care of this. If we don't do that, all of these people will be competing for too few support facilities. That competition can lead to great expense, to great inefficiency, and even to violence.

One of the ideas that has to shape our future is cultural pluralism. We must finally learn how the races and the ethnic groups and the subgroups of the West can live together in peace, harmony, and productivity. The melting pot is a dead thought. That will give no comfort to the people who want to make English our official language. (I happen to think that English will always be our dominant language, just as it is now in world commerce.) The idea that one culture, one race, one group in the West, in this new era that we're entering, is ever going to be able to label itself as "superior" is passé.

The other point I'd like to address is this sense I have that we think that if we could plan better, if we could manage better, somehow we could solve all of these problems in a clean, efficient fashion. I don't think that is true. We are a politically free and mobile people. The whole history of the West gives no comfort to those who believe they are going to solve the problems of the West by some superior form of planning. Our problems in the past have been solved by political action through legislation as adjudicated by the courts. We are going to have to continue to work out problems through that mechanism, because that mechanism is not going to change.

Charles Wilkinson, an expert on law in the West, has observed that a lot of our problems of balancing resources are settled using the basis of nineteenth-century laws based on the principle of first come, first served. He argues that gradually, through the workings of our political process and through our courts, we're going to develop a new "ethic of place." An ethic of place would hold that the needs of people extracting resources are going to have to be balanced with the needs of community. An ethic of place would say that People are here and have rights, but Place also is here and has rights, and the law must balance the two.

That, after all, is what we're talking about when we talk about shaping the future of the West. We are talking about trying to find a better sense of balance between people and resources. At the moment our legal system is teetering. Our political system is teetering. But place, and protection of resources, are coming into fuller balance with people.

Those who are arguing for protection of place these days are polarized to the point where, in general, they are excluding the part of the equation that looks out for people. But in our political system, you cannot exclude the majority of the people in the long run. It does not work. You just can't draw lines that keep them out. You can't draw lines that keep them away. You have to hope you can instill in the majority attitudes that will protect place. Then those attitudes will lead to appropriate law.

William H. Hornby

THE DISPOSABLE WEST

Envisioning "A Society to Match the Scenery," one issue we might think about is preservation. We have a long tradition in the West of "get and get out," of devastating a place and then moving on, of moving away when times get tough.

But I think there has been a turnaround in the last decade, exemplified by the renewal of core cities. The Pearl Street Mall in Boulder is an example, as is the sixteenth Street Mall in Denver and Main Street Mall in Durango. We are seeing a trend toward historic preservation and an interest in not just trashing a place and moving on but in returning to the cities and beautifying them.

Another key issue is affluence. If you are interested in economic history or Marxist interpretation of Western history, this is going to be a key issue. The United States, particularly the West, cannot continue to produce a very small fraction of the world's wealth while consuming a much greater fraction of that wealth. We are not going to have single-family, detached houses — the ranch houses on 1.2 acres — in the future. There is going to be a severe economic crisis here — recycling resources will become much more important.

Another key issue that's so obvious that we may overlook it, except when we're reminded by wonderful books such as *Beyond the Hundredth Meridian,* is the geography of the West, the aridity. This has tremendous and very subtle implications, such as Colorado's unbelievably low tax on firewaters. Both liquor containers and water are now treated as disposables not worth recapturing.

The ghost towns are a great popular phenomenon in Western history, and here it seems to me is a place for historians to do some serious work. There are plenty of histories of places such as Aspen and Telluride. One comes out every year. But what about the Leadvilles and the Cripple Creeks — the really tragic and sad and dying towns? The focus should not be on the Horace Tabors and the Baby Does and the millionaires but on the twentieth-century heros — the people who hung on in those towns and continued to pay taxes, who tried to keep schools and libraries open, the people who waited until the 1950s, for instance, to put sewers in Leadville, a town where millions' worth of minerals had been taken out and moved on to New York (in the form of Guggenheim's and others' fortunes). The extracted millions that were not spent, obviously, in Leadville.

Kenneth Jackson of Columbia University spent ten years producing a book that I think is wonderful for Western historians called *Crabgrass Frontier: The Suburbanization of the United States*. He introduces that book by saying that the greatest single physical achievement of the United States in the twentieth century is suburbia. Suburbanization is the future of the West. We shouldn't be talking about ranches, but about ranch houses. The suburb is considered an enclave, an escape from racial tension, from crime, from problems that many people prefer to leave behind in the inner city.

Another negative factor is wastefulness — the idea of a disposable society, that whole towns are disposable, that you go in and mine a town and then leave it. In Denver even a billion-dollar airport — Stapleton — is disposable. You don't put any money into permanent improvements or upkeep. You don't care about the next generation. Here I'd like to make a special plea for historic preservation, which I think historians often regard as an elitist movement or something that's just cosmetic. But I submit to you that historic preservation is part of a larger ethic, an idea of preserving, of saving, of fixing things up rather that having disposable cities, disposable office buildings, disposable shopping centers, and a disposable past.

Thomas J. Noel

MYTHS OF VIOLENCE
IN *OWNING IT ALL*

In preparation for working with William Kittredge in this symposium, I read the chapter "Owning It All" from the book by the same title, and selections in *Montana Spaces*. In the former he writes about having had "the luck to grow up at the tail end of a way of existing in which people lived in everyday proximity to animals on territory they knew more precisely than the patterns in the palms of their hands."[7] In *Montana Spaces* he writes about the storytelling adventurers who were drawn to the West, people like Osbourne Russell, Samuel Clemens, and especially Charlie Russell, the cowboy painter "who got it right and traded his famous paintings for drinks and told it like it was." Kittredge tells about a celebration in Great Falls, Montana, where booster citizens were celebrating themselves until Charlie Russell spoke up. He said: "In my book a pioneer is a man who turned all the grass upside down, strung bob-wire over the dust that was left, poisoned the water and cut down the trees, killed the Indian who owned the land, and called it progress. If I had my way, the land here would be here like God made it, and none of you sons of bitches would be here at all."[8]

I begin with this story to introduce the idea that William Kittredge is as deeply concerned about stories and myths as he is about literature. He is *as* concerned about inhabiting a new story and a new myth as he is concerned about inhabiting "the last best place." I want to respond to two themes in his writings relevant to this conference: 1) the myth of ownership and 2) the rituals of violence against the land.

Kittredge gives us clues about what the "myth of ownership" means when he writes about the dream of power over nature or of making, in his words, "a perfect agricultural place," a kind of sacred place for humans to dwell in. As you read on in his powerful prose, you see that this myth of ownership is really a mask for another myth, a myth of war against nature. This war is carried out through the second theme, the theme of ritual or "participating in our agriculture," where humans turn a "home place" into a "machine for agriculture." This ritual is really an act of terrible violence, conscious and unconscious violence against nature. The result of this strategy of sacralizing nature so it could be owned and violated was the creation of a "howling, stinking place." At the end of this essay, I want to take us to a faraway place, a city of his ancestors, where myths and rituals of violence were created.

In *Owning It All* and throughout his work, we see a double consciousness in Kittredge. On the one hand he grows up enclosed in a topography of spirit, a landscape of neighborhoods that were sacred and demonic, some habitable, some not. Then he went to school and discovered that this landscape was only a fertile oasis in a vast featureless sagebrush desert. He struggles with these two images and with what he learns in the fields and in school. He is drawn throughout his life to images of enclosures. He feels their power in Oregon and Guam where he lives in compounds, Quonset huts, enclaves. Later, stories become enclosures that he strives to live within. In his stories he tells us that he came back to Oregon to participate in agriculture in order to "construct a great good place," a perfect agricultural place that was sacred. He describes the place this way: "The majority of agricultural people, if you press them hard enough, even though most of them despise sentimental abstractions, will admit that they are trying to create a good place, and to live as part of that goodness, in the kind of connection, which with fine reason we call *rootedness*."[9]

But as you read on in Kittredge you find that the good agricultural place was rooted in two tremendous forces, one obvious and one more obscure; namely, violence and cities. We see the presence of violence when he tells us that he grew up in a place where people were scared and the one sure defense against the outside world was property. The yeoman dream, the pastoral image, was not only a fortification against threatening humans, it was also a dream of power over nature, a war whose central instrument was the machine.

This dimension of Kittredge's work led me to reflect upon Rene Girard's *Violence and the Sacred*, where the author argues that "violence is the heart and secret soul of the sacred."[10] He argues that violence is endemic in human society, ingrained in our relationships. Violence is not to be denied, though it can be diverted onto other objects. Girard argues that humans have no braking mechanism for violence but they can steer it onto convenient enemies, scapegoats, so that violence will not destroy the "home place." The important insight of Kittredge is that violence is not only diverted onto other peoples but onto the land itself. The relationship between humans and landscape is a violent one. This pattern won't be changed by a few new laws or a blue line or two, but by a shift in the nature of the human, the "son of a bitch" Charlie Russell roared against.

Further, Kittredge shows that the myths of Americans against the land are enormously violent. In fact, he sometimes states that the myth of violence has been prodding us on for so long that it is too late, the violence has accomplished its work — "it all went dead, over the years, but swiftly. You can imagine our surprise and despair, our sense of having been profoundly cheated."[11]

Perhaps we are meeting in Boulder after the fact, disguising the funeral as a symposium. Maybe we have "owned" our own violence and it is now filtering back through our atmosphere and bodies.

His point made me think about a Native American case, the case of the collapse of the Classic Maya in the tenth century A.D. Archaeologists show us a frightening record of a magnificent culture falling to the ground, destroying its fields, killing its inhabitants at an astonishing rate between A.D. 830 and 930. It appears that these native peoples forgot their sense of limits in farming, celebrating, building, controlling, and expressing violence to such a degree that the whirlwind of deterioration they set in motion could not be stopped. The key here is that the Maya built early forms of cities, and cities own and destroy the landscape. This is the second force in Kittredge's vision, though it is infrequently drawn in his prose. He writes that when he returned to Warner Valley and saw paved roads and power lines and a TV translator beaming "fluttering pictures from New York and Los Angeles direct to us," he knew something terrible had come upon the land.[12]

Cities are the greatest forces of ecological transformation in the history of culture. As one scholar has written, "Cities are the style centers of the world, controlling life in the countryside and disseminating political, social, economic, aesthetic and sacred values to all who come under their sway."[13] Even though people in the West think they live in rural America, on the edge of the wilderness or in Montana spaces, they actually live in a world determined more and more by cities. A terrible feature of cities in terms of the landscape is their control by elites. From the origin of cities until the rise of new experimental cities, social order has been controlled by social privilege. The needs of the elites saturate space and make extraordinary demands on all the places of the globe. This is what Charlie Russell sensed, and we can rephrase him by asking, "Who turned the grass upside down? Who provided the barbed wire to mark off the slices of land that became towns and eventually city blocks? Who cut down the trees and poisoned the water and killed the Indians and called it progress?" The business in and of the city!

As a means of capturing the ferocious power and influence of cities on the landscape, let me read about a faraway place, a place far from Kittredge's Montana, but a place where, ironically, his ancestors came from. Consider this imagery of the violence of the city, the machine incarnate, a place that knows no limits and has all the possibilities of ownership of our future. Thomas Wolfe in *Of Time and the River* wrote:

> And the image of the city, written in his heart, was so unbelievable that it seemed to be a fiction, a fable, some huge dream of his own dreaming, so unbelievable that he did not think that he should find it when he returned; yet it was just the same as he had remembered it. He found it, the instant he came out of the station: the tidal swarm of faces, the brutal stupefaction of the street, the immense and arrogant blaze and sweep of the great buildings.
>
> It was fabulous and incredible, but there it was. He saw again the million faces — the faces dark, dingy, driven, harried, and corrupt, the faces stamped with all the familiar markings of suspicion and mistrust, cunning, contriving, and a hard and stupid cynicism. . . . the faces cunning, sly, and furtive, the hard twisted mouths and rasping voices, the eyes glittering and toxic with unnatural fires . . . menaces of privilege and power . . . moving in tune to that vast central energy, filled with the city's life, as with a general and dynamic fluid. . . .
>
> And as he saw them, as he heard them, as he listened to their words again, . . . it seemed that speech had been given to them by some demon of everlasting hatred only in order that they might express the infamy and vileness of men, or the falseness of women . . . it seemed incredible . . . that they could live, breathe, move at all among the huge encrusted taint, the poisonous congestion of their lives.
>
> And yet live, breathe, move they did with a savage and indubitable violence, an unfathomed energy. . . . like a single animal, with the sinuous and baleful convolutions of an enormous reptile. And the magical and shining air — the strange, subtle and enchanted weather, was above them, and the buried men were strewn through the earth on which they trod, and a bracelet of great tides was flashing round them, and the enfabled rock on which they swarmed swung eastward in the marches of the sun into eternity, and was masted like a ship with its terrific towers, and was flung with a lion's port between its tides into the very maw of the infinite, all-taking ocean. And exultancy and joy rose with a cry of triumph in his throat, because he found it wonderful.[14]

This is of the myth of the "all-taking ocean" of cities that Kittredge warns us about. This is the story we must hear and evict ourselves from before the last best place for ourselves and our children becomes saturated with indubitable violence.

David L. Carrasco

THE COLLISION OF WILDERNESS
AND CULTURE

For the first three years in my job as regional reporter for *The Denver Post*, I had a white jeep with my name on the door in cursive. (Thank God it wasn't rope script.) Below that, thanks to the marketing geniuses of the *Post*, were the words "Rocky Mountain Ranger," written large enough to be seen through the window of a 7-Eleven when I'd stop in for coffee. Just when I was afraid she'd recognize the name Carrier, the clerk would say, "Did you bring our Sunday papers?" When I arrived at national parks, I'd have to idle in line and pay the entrance fees just like anybody else. The real ranger inside the window would slowly count the change into my hand, all the while reading my door and wondering, "Who is this yahoo?"

But I still feel an exhilaration when I get into the jeep and drive out of Denver into the landscape that, for me, continues to hold the magic and meaning of the West. Maybe it is because I spend so much time getting there that I find the vistas so important. Whether it's descending the San Juans, kicking up dust on the switchbacks of the Sunlight Basin, or racing at what seems a snail's pace across the floor of Monument Valley, I can still feel what the pioneers did, what William Kittredge calls "owning it all." Ironically, it is private ownership by the West's growing leisure class, the Ralph Laurens and the Robert Redfords, that is preserving some of the look of the West. But it is still largely the public agencies that hold open lands with vistas that preserve those feelings of freedom and frontier.

As you may know, national parks in the West were preserved for those vistas, or for curios like Old Faithful. They were our first cathedrals. Congress approved the parks when they were convinced the land had no other useful purpose. And only recently has Yellowstone come to stand for wilderness. The battle between natural regulation and the leisure class of the RVs is less than twenty years old.

Now, before I go on, let me say that I hug as many trees as anybody. The green revolution is mine. I have come to accept intellectually that natural is good. The grizzly needs more space. The wolves are missing. Natural is good. We even hear it in our cereal ads.

But the fires of Yellowstone confused me. And if you were to visit Yellowstone as I did — and I was there all summer — under the beautiful blue skies of Indian summer, you'd wonder what all the fuss was about. The park is still there, the animals are still there. But there is a new attraction, a fire scape, widespread and black.

It is one thing, however, to stand in Colorado and bravely assert the rights of natural regulation, and quite another to spend the summer watching Yellowstone burn; to eat and work and sleep there, in the smoke, and to watch one crisis evacuation after another; to stand behind the Old Faithful Inn on September 7 (George Bush was right, that day will live in infamy) and watch boiling gobs of flame roll at you; to watch through squinched, watered eyes, air the color of soot swirl around you; to flinch when red embers the size of your fist bang against your helmet; to watch flames from burning buildings roar parallel to the ground in a fifty-mile-an-hour wind — and the water aimed at it blowing away, too. At that moment, natural regulation sounded as hollow as the fire extinguishers at the cabins that exploded in the heat. I was sad. I was angry. I was sick to my stomach. My emotions were speaking, and I think a lot of people watching television felt the same way.

In the weeks since then, I've searched for an intellectual answer for those feelings. The best I've heard so far comes from Steven Pine, who is a fire historian at Arizona State in Tempe. What happened at Yellowstone, he thinks, is a collision of two hybrids — wilderness, which is a concept, an idea, a hybrid of nature and culture; and fire, which is another hybrid of nature and culture. It is naive, he argues, to think that we can view fire as a wholly natural process or wilderness as a completely natural environment. It is naive to think that when you combine them you won't get the kind of anguished exercise we went though that summer.

Yellowstone is alive and well as a landscape, but I'm not sure it is as an ideal. I think that these fires have forced us, perhaps for the first time since the 1960s, to question things natural and those who preach it. I have written in the *Post* that the tragedy of that summer may be that Yellowstone, the last best place in the lower forty-eight for things wild, cannot be without the human hand.

The park is beginning a public relations campaign to convince the world that "black is beautiful." It is a campaign aimed largely at mending the economic fences. But the park needs philosophic PR as well. The wolf issue is dead for now as a result of the fires. The debate over whether to open campgrounds in the Fishing Bridge grizzly habitat may be renewed. The Forest Service wants to log the burned areas. And a haylift for dying elk is not out of the question.

I see, as I drive around the Rockies, a growing leisure class, interested less in backpacking than in golfing. The mountains are being carved into enclaves with security gates and lawns. People take their living rooms with them when they travel now. A woman I know who took one of those guided trips through the Grand Canyon for the first time said it best: "It's like something out of Disneyland." Control. Our dominion. That is what is going on at Yellowstone.

The time I spent in Yellowstone convinced me that the park is less a biosphere than an environmental proving ground. It's a very democratic place, subject to all the pressures of a public institution, including greed. I'm optimistic, as I think I have to be in a democracy. Yellowstone is a place not just for wildlife but for people, too. It's a place to learn about the environment. Most important, it is a place where the use of that park mirrors our country's attitude toward the wild. Like the miraculous serotinous lodgepole pinecones that open under heat, the polls are open again in Yellowstone, I think. And I also think you should be asking yourselves how you will vote.

James A. Carrier

EXCEEDING THE CARRYING CAPACITY
OF THE WEST: AN ARTIST'S PERSPECTIVE

The brilliant French thinker Jean Baudrillard has introduced a
concept that has had a powerful impact on the world of high culture.
The concept is "simulacra." In short, he suggests that the experiences of
life have been so thoroughly mediated by photography, advertising, and
film that we no longer have a genuine primary experience.

Our understanding of the West is no different. We know the West
from Hollywood films, TV Westerns, and Ansel Adams's photographs.
Our visions are of white, rugged cowboys roaming vast open places or
the uninhabited landscape spectacles of Monument Valley, Death Valley,
or the Grand Canyon. When one thinks of the American West, one does
not usually think of irrigation projects gone amuck, plutonium-contam-
inated landscapes, chemical-weapons storage dumps, forty acres of
grapefruit trees on fire, tens of thousands of swimming pools, and
millions of people.

For the last ten years I have been working on a project called
"Desert Cantos." The term canto is simply an old word that indicates the
subsection of a long song. It functions like a chapter in a novel. These
cantos are independent groupings — independent chapters about my
discoveries in the American landscape, particularly the American desert. Each of these groups is independent, but once you put them
together, you get a much greater whole.

Richard Misrach brought an artist's perspective to the concept of limits with a half-hour
slide show and commentary of his work. The flow of images during the commentary was
continuous. Presented here are representative images illustrating each of the sections of
his talk.

The first canto is called "The Terrain." Most of the work in this canto is based on a movement in photography in the 1970s called the "new topographics." The attempt was to redefine the landscape. Ansel Adams had become famous for his beautiful landscapes, and built upon the nineteenth-century ideal of pure wilderness, unsullied wilderness. The fact of the matter is that in the twentieth century you just do not have that kind of land anymore. A number of practitioners in the 1970s made a remarkable group of photographs while trying to look at the West in a more honest light. They were looking at what we call the cultural landscape. This movement was my departure point.

Downed Saguaro, Arizona, 1983
Richard Misrach, *Richard Misrach: Photographs 1985–1987* (Tokyo: Gallery MIN, 1988).

The second canto is called "The Event." It has to do with the space shuttle landing at Edwards Air Force Base in the Mojave desert. This is where about two hundred thousand people arrived in their Winnebagos and campers to witness the space shuttle fall from the sky like a stone. They were supposed to park on the outside of the fence. I asked people what the snow fence was supposed to do, and they said, "Well, it's to keep the people from running onto the field toward the space shuttle." And I thought that was sort of absurd — for two hundred thousand people, it didn't seem like it would do the job. And then somebody else said, "No, no, no, that's not it at all, it's to keep the space shuttle from running into all the people."

After the first shuttle landing there was such a traffic jam after the shuttle finally landed that, according to one journalist, it took the two hundred thousand people and their campers twice as long to get out of the parking lot as it did for the shuttle to go around the Earth twice. So this next time around, the military decided to lay down tar lines so that everybody could line up.

Campers and Restraining Fence, Edwards Air Force Base, California, 1983
Richard Misrach, *Desert Cantos* (Albuquerque: University of New Mexico Press, 1987),
p. 18.

The next canto is called "The Flood." This involves the Salton Sea. It is in the southern California desert, a fact that is wrought with irony. It actually was Salton Sink in the early 1900s. But an irrigation project along the Colorado River went awry, and this area flooded. Eventually they decided to keep the water and build a whole economy around it. So hotels, motels, and recreational areas were introduced. Water skiing was promoted. They stocked fish. Later on, they worked out a system whereby water was taken from the Colorado to support agriculture in the Coachella and Imperial valleys. That's where California gets all its great grapefruits and dates. The water would go through these farms and then leach into the Salton Sink.

In the 1970s the irrigation districts negligently pumped a lot of water into the sink, and all the businesses, ranches, and homes that had built up along the shore over the years were flooded out. So what we have now is a flood museum. It's been in a state of permanent flood now for ten years. It's starting to get better. A few years ago the residents finally won a class-action suit for millions of dollars against the irrigation companies. The irony here is that you have this exquisite body of water and light, unlike anything I've seen, and yet it is an environmental horror.

Flooded Marina (gas pumps), Salton Sea, California, 1983
Richard Misrach, *Desert Cantos* (Albuquerque: University of New Mexico Press, 1987),
p. 33.

The next canto is called "The Fires." This canto has an anecdote that I think is an important parable. For the two years I was photographing — between 1983 and 1985 — there was an engineer from the fire department who set more than two hundred fires. In his briefcase he had a couple of hundred match books, with cigarettes among them, tied around a rock. What he would do is light the cigarettes and throw the rock out of a moving car, and thus have a delayed fuse. He'd set up to six fires in a day. Finally he was caught and he's in prison.

All the fires were human caused — they were either accidents, arson, agricultural controlled-burns, or agricultural controlled-burns that got out of control.

Desert Fire #17, 1983
Richard Misrach, *Desert Cantos* (Albuquerque: University of New Mexico Press, 1987),
p. 50.

This is from a series about nuclear fallout in America:

Snow Canyon is part of the area around St. George, Utah, which was exposed to fallout from early atomic testing. It also was the site of the 1954 Hollywood production *The Conqueror,* directed by Dick Powell. Despite concerns expressed by Powell and the RKO scouts, government experts reassured the filmmakers of their safety. Dick Powell died of lung cancer in 1963, Agnes Moorehead died of uterine cancer in 1974, Susan Hayward died of skin, breast, and uterine cancer in 1975, and John Wayne died of lung cancer in 1979. At the time of Wayne's death, 91 of the 220 remaining cast and crew members had developed cancer.

Today Snow Canyon is a breathtakingly beautiful state park enjoyed by thousands of campers and visitors each year. There are many who believe that the dunes are still contaminated by plutonium (half-life, 235,000 years).[15]

Snow Canyon State Park, Utah, 1987
Richard Misrach, *Richard Misrach: Photographs 1985–1987* (Tokyo: Gallery MIN, 1988).

This is from a project called *Bravo 20: The Bombing of the American West*. It's a book that my wife, Myriam, and I worked on together. The book is divided into three parts and it opens with the military abuse of the West.

Bravo 20 is a bombing range. It is public land used by the United States Navy for thirty-three years without authorization. The navy literally bombed this place every day. It was the location of an important Northern Paiute puberty-ritual site called Lone Rock. The recent history of Lone Rock, in the Carson Sink, is an incredible story. It involves two men who lived in Nevada who took the navy to task. These men went onto the bombing range when it was active and announced to the press and the military that they were going out on this land because the navy was bombing it illegally.

The first part of the book is the historical background of this bombing range. Part two comprises the photographs documenting the post-apocalyptic landscape — the landscape that has been showered with bombs and craters and shrapnel.

In 1986, when the navy was caught by these two civilians, Doc Bargin and Richard Holmes, they had to stop bombing, so they went before Congress and said, "Look, there are thousands of unexploded live bombs that have been buried beneath the sands over the years and we can't decontaminate them. It would cost millions of dollars and would be only 95 percent effective." And so, given that the navy could not clean it up, Congress passed the Military Lands Withdrawal Act of 1986, which gave the navy authorization to resume bombing for fifteen years, until the year 2001. Part two of the book is a photographic documentation of what that bombing has done to the land.

Unexploded Bomb, Bravo 20 Bombing Range, Nevada, 1986
Richard Misrach, *Bravo 20: The Bombing of the American West* (Baltimore: Johns
Hopkins University Press, 1990), p. 53.

Part three of the book is a formal proposal I designed to convert this bombing range into a national park, the first environmental memorial. I think it would be a useful memorial. You would have "Devastation Drive" — a driving tour around the bombing range. You would have a walking tour of the craters and the bombs called "Boardwalk of the Bombs." The boardwalk would lead to a number of different site exhibits. There would be craters and active eagles' nests and the sand-dune biota and, as in any conventional national park, there would be site plaques and displays to educate the public. A picture window would continue down to a subterranean floor, giving park visitors the chance to view the bombs that were buried beneath the surface. I found out in talking to a military detonation expert that the place can be decontaminated and cleaned up and that the navy has the ability to clean up the site. So we could just replace live bombs with dummy bombs so it would be safe. And of course you've got to have a walk-in crater. It's the only way people can get the real sense of the nature of the devastation.

The project would cost about seven or eight million dollars — about one-fourth the price of one F-A-18 jet bomber. We figure that, as compensation for forty years of illegal use and contamination, the money should come out of the navy's budget.

Boardwalk of the Bombs, illustration by Rico Solinas
Richard Misrach, *Bravo 20: The Bombing of the American West* (Baltimore: Johns
Hopkins University Press, 1990), p. 107.

The last canto is more somber. It's called "The Pit." This is in Nevada. It is one of three dead-animal pits that are like trash dumps. It is about eight miles from Naval Air Station Fallon, which is about an hour east of Reno. Fallon was the site of one atomic test in 1963 — Operation Shoal. Some people still believe the area is hot with plutonium and that the leukemia rates are higher than the state and national averages. All of this is speculation that needs to be researched. In our research for the Bravo 20 book, Myriam and I discovered an internal navy document that is now coming to light documenting the navy's own research into twenty toxic-pit sites. Every military station in the country probably has terrible toxic sites. Chemicals such as napalm, Agent Orange, jet fuel, and so on are being leaked into the groundwater, possibly (according to the navy) affecting the agriculture nearby, in this case Fallon.

I should say — because there's always confusion about this — that if your pet died, you would bring it to this dump. If an animal of yours died of old age, if there was a road kill, if animals for whatever reason died, they would be brought to one of these pit sites.

On March 24, 1953, the Bullek brothers were trailing 2,000 head of sheep across the Sand Springs Valley when they were exposed to extensive fallout from a dirty atomic test. Within a week the first ewes began dropping their lambs prematurely. The lambs were stunted, woolless, legless, and pot-bellied. Soon, full-grown sheep started dying in large numbers. They had running sores, large pustules, and hardened hooves. Horses and cattle were found dead with beta burns. At final count, 4,390 animals were killed. Initial investigations by government experts indicated that radiation was the cause. However, when the Atomic Energy Commission recognized the potential economic and political liability, all reports and findings were immediately classified. The AEC did provide a public explanation. A dry year and malnutrition were blamed. Today designated dead-animal pits can be found throughout the West. They function much like trash dumps. Locals are encouraged to deposit animals that die suddenly. The causes of the animals' deaths are often unknown.[16]

Dead Animals #86, Nevada, 1986
Richard Misrach (forthcoming).

This work is not meant to be a literal journalistic exposé. It is a protest, if you will, a scream against this practice of the military and the government, of conducting incredible experiments in the desert, of screwing up constantly and then covering it up. You have it in Denver with Rocky Flats. You have it with the Nevada Nuclear Test Site. You have it with the Yucca Mountain nuclear-waste dump, where the nation's high-level nuclear waste will be buried. They still are going to try to shove it in Nevada on top of an earthquake fault, which is an unsound place to put it. It is totally dangerous, but nobody else will take it. Contaminants from these dumps get into the groundwater. After the tests from the early 1950s, the stuff would get in the air and it would end up in Buffalo, New York. It ended up all over the world. It's not something that you can put in the desert and be done with.

Richard Misrach

THE PRESS IN THE WEST:
CO-OPTED INTO A CELEBRATION OF
TECHNOLOGY

I would like to add a third theme to the themes that, first, the government and the military are always screwing up and, second, always covering up. I want to add a third theme, because I am somewhat guilty: that when the government screws up, and then there is a cover-up, often the press ignores it.

I, too, have been to the land of the motor homes, the landing of the space shuttle Discovery STS 26. I was struck not only by the image of the motor homes and the way they are lined up, all to pay homage to technology, but also by the rows behind the motor homes. There are rows and rows of cotton candy, hot dogs — anything you need to buy is available, including insignias from soldiers of fortune. You can get the latest badge that was worn in whatever war you are looking for. One Australian man whom I interviewed told me that coming to the landing of the space shuttle was a near-religious experience, and he had been to the Mecca twice.

When the space shuttle actually hits the ground, the NASA folks increase the celebration by playing "The Star Spangled Banner." And, of course, a lot of people have tears in their eyes. The way journalists fit into this is interesting.

We begin the process of covering an STS landing a few days earlier in a desert motel, where we get our press credentials. This is how they put you in the system. First of all, they give you these fancy badges. They give you a giant vehicle pass that says "STS 26" and has a little shuttle on the bottom. It is great to give to any kids in your family. Second, they give you an ID badge labeled "STS 26" in bright red letters, which you get to wear around your neck. Third, they give you stacks and stacks of models and technical diagrams that are so technical you will never understand them, but that allow you to become part of the system and become an insider. You are then co-opted into the celebration of technology. During the coverage of a shuttle, most of the journalists there don't question whether the technology is valid, only whether it works.

Another of the ways that journalists get co-opted is perhaps more serious than the shuttle, and that is by the military technology in the West. If you are covering anything for the Department of Energy, the process is essentially the same as it would be for NASA. You get credentials, you get a fancy badge, you get access to places that other people don't, and you get co-opted. I have been to the "national nuclear bomb park." It is open only to the press at this point — the Nevada Test Site. Not only do you get the fancy badges, you also get a fancy device that tells you if you get too hot. You never get to keep that, though, they always take that back. So you never get to know how close you really were.

In the West, we still are living with two places at which the United States has decided we can bury our most deadly inventions. The things we have engineered as a human race that have lasted the longest are the pyramids, which are about four thousand years old. Yet our nuclear high priests tell us they are fairly certain that they can bury our waste in New Mexico and Nevada in containers that will last *ten* thousand years.

I am reminded of an image that sticks with me from Yucca Mountain, Nevada. Yucca Mountain is far away from the test site. There is nothing much around there other than beautiful country. One of the first things the scientists did there when they decided that this is where we can bury the high-level wastes — the waste that will be a problem for ten thousand years — was to put in two pipes that go down about 250 feet. The rock is supposed to be so solid that there won't be any problem with leaking of water, leaking of anything else. Yet when they put these two pipes into the ground, they found an interesting phenomenon. In the wintertime, warm air flows out of the pipes. In the summertime, warm air is sucked into the pipes, the reverse process. In short, the earth breathes. They still don't know why this happens, and the geologists tend to say that they don't think it would affect the radionuclides that would be buried underneath it. But nonetheless, the earth breathes.

A final point I would like to make is that these are places we think of as somewhere "out there." When you think of the West as a nuclear place, you should remember that it is all right here.

Recently I had a chance to take a look at the transportation of nuclear items on our public highways. And the interstate highway system is about the busiest place there is for things nuclear. If you want to see a nuclear bomb, for example, you are almost guaranteed to see one if you sit along I-40 between Albuquerque and the Texas border. Bombs roll through there roughly two times a day, sometimes just once a day. Right now we are transporting on public highways 2.8 million tons of radioactive material, including H-bombs, high-level waste, transuranic waste, low-level waste, and other things nuclear. I was going through some court records for this transportation story and I was amazed to find that last year near the Colorado-Nebraska border, a truck trailer was hauling Cobalt 60 from Canada to Denver, and it was stopped at a state truck-inspection station simply because it had a broken axle. The Cobalt 60 inside was just a side problem.

When I was researching this story, I thought a lot about this problem of journalists becoming co-opted and becoming part of the celebration of technology. I decided that for this story I did not want to become part of the system. So we decided to see what we could follow, a photographer and I, without telling the Department of Energy, and to be outsiders like everyone else. This put us in a whole different camp. We went to Pantex, Texas, which is the final assembly point for nuclear bombs, and we set up in a car outside. We thought we would be somewhat obvious. We put our big long lenses on top of the car and put notepads out to try to make it look like we were reporters so they wouldn't shoot us. We sat there all that day and no trucks rolled out. We knew that they had a shipment scheduled, so we began to wonder. We decided, well, we work for a large newspaper, we have lots of resources, let's rent another car and park it on the other side of the base in case they are going out the back door. We did that and we decided they were still sneaking out, so we bought portable radios to keep track of where they were moving the bombs. After we did that, we looked into the sky and saw a helicopter flying back and forth keeping track of where we were. At that point we realized that the Department of Energy had more resources than we did. Fortunately we were able to get pictures of the bombs. The amazing thing is that they travel at speeds you wouldn't believe. We were chasing one between Albuquerque and Amarillo and we were averaging 75 miles an hour and we couldn't keep up with it. But if you want to see it, all you have to do is sit along an interstate. Another one would be I-70, or I-15 in Idaho. Most of the roads are already nuclear.

With the West becoming so nuclear, and the military constantly covering up, finding these things out is becoming more and more difficult, because the whole system is set up to keep these things secret. We can hope that we in the press will start reacting more and finding these things out.

Mark Trahant

PART FIVE

The Future

KOKOPELLI'S RETURN

One night, beneath the ruins of Keet Seel, we heard flute music — music so sweet it could have split the seeds of corn. Earlier we had wandered through the rooms of Keet Seel, admiring the redrock construction dabbed into the sandstone alcove like swallows' nests, but there had been no music then — only the silence pressing against us in the cool Anasazi air.

Above the ruins, clouds covered the full face of the moon like gauze. The land seemed to bow with the melody of the flute. I reached for my husband's arm and he reached for our friend. We kept hold of one another like children, and we listened, holding our breaths between the intervals of our own heartbeats. The flute music flowed out from the cliff dwelling like an ancient breath.

The next morning we sat around camp, drinking rose hip tea. We were tired and stiff from the cold, still half stunned from the night before. Our friend, who was Hopi, looked down at the cup he held in both hands, and told a story.

A man traveled this country with a bag of corn seed over one shoulder. His shadow against the desert looked like a deformity. He would stop at every village and teach the people how to plant corn. And then when the sun slipped behind the mesa and the village was asleep, he would walk through the corn fields playing his flute. The seeds would flower, pushing themselves up through the red, sandy soil and follow the high-pitched notes upward. The sun would rise and the man would be gone, with cornstalks the height of a young girl shimmering in the morning light. Many of the young women would complain of a fullness in their bellies. The elders would smile, knowing they were pregnant. They would look to the southwest and call him "Kokopelli."

We finished our tea, broke up our camp, and organized our packs for the trail. Before leaving, I walked back to the base of Keet Seel. The ruins appeared darker than usual, full of shadows that moved from room to room. My eyes followed the tall timbers from floor to ceiling as I imagined macaws perched on top. Kivas held darkness below, and I wondered if old men's bones might be buried there. Just then, in a stream of light, a pictograph on the ceiling of the alcove jumped out. It was a buglike creature, but as I focused more clearly I recognized it as the humpbacked flute player.

"Kokopelli," I whispered to myself. "It must be Kokopelli."

The light shifted and he seemed to be rocking on his back. I had missed him the day before, noticing only the pictographs of bighorn sheep and spirals. At that moment, I recalled the flute music that flooded the canyon the night before and the clouds like gossamer hands with long, long fingers that pulled me into an abyss of sleep. I placed my hand over my stomach, turned away from the ruins, and walked back toward my fellow campers. Halfway down the canyon, I felt stirrings in my belly. Sweet corn was sprouting all along the river.

Terry Tempest Williams

SOMETHING STARTING OVER

You don't see buffalo skulls very much any more
On the Chugwater buttes or down the Cheyenne plains,
And when you roll at twilight over a draw,
With ages in your heart and hills in your eyes,
You can get about as much from a Model-T,
Stripped and forgotten in a sage arroyo,
As you can from asking the blue peaks over and over:
    "Will something old come back again tonight?
    Send something back to tell me what I want."

I do not know how long forever is,
But today is going to be long long ago,
There will be flint to find, and chariot wheels,
And silver saxophones the angels played,
So I ask myself if I can still remember
How a myth began this morning and how the people
Seemed hardly to know that something was starting over.

Oh, I get along all right with the old old times,
I've seen them sifting the ages in Nebraska
On Signal Butte at the head of Kiowa Creek.
    (You can drink from the spring where old man
        Roubadeau
    Had his forge and anvil up in Cedar Valley,
    You can look back down the valley toward Scotts
        Bluff
    And still see dust clouds on the Oregon Trail.)
I entered the trench they cut through Signal Butte,

And I pulled a buffalo bone from the eight-foot layer,
And I watched the jasper shards and arrowheads
Bounce in the jigging screen through which fell dust
Of antelope and pieces of the world
Too small to have a meaning to the sifters.

One of them said, when I held the bone in my hand:
    "This may turn out to be the oldest bison
In North America," and I could have added:
    "How strange, for this is one of the youngest hands
That ever squeezed a rubber bulb to show
How helium particles shoot through water vapor."
And the dry wind out of Wyoming might have
        whispered:
    "Today is going to be long long ago."

I know how it smells and feels to sift the ages,
But something starting over and I say
It's just as beautiful to see the yucca
And cactus blossoms rising out of a Ford
In a sage arroyo on the Chugwater flats,
And pretend you see the carbon dioxide slipping
Into the poverty weed, and pretend you see
The root hairs of the buffalo grass beginning
To suck the vanadium steel of an axle to pieces,
An axle that took somebody somewhere,
To moving picture theaters and banks,
Over the ranges, over the cattle-guards,
Took people to dance-halls and cemeteries —
I like to think of them that way together:
Dance-halls and cemeteries, bodies beginning
To come together in dance-halls where the people
Seem hardly to know that hymns are beginning too;
Then bodies separating and going alone
Into the tilting uphill cemeteries,
Under the mesas, under the rimrock shadows.

I can look at an axle in sage arroyo,
And hear them whispering, the back seat lovers,
The old myth-makers, starting something over.

Thomas Hornsby Ferril

PUBLIC USE AND THE FUTURE OF
THE FEDERAL LANDS

The public lands of the American West are both a historical anomaly and a continuing political paradox. Given our individualistic culture, preference for private property, antipathy toward government, and recurrent movements to privatize anything public, one could reasonably assume that the public lands had long since been sold, auctioned off or given away simply to get government out of the land business. Yet in the twentieth century the public lands have remained largely intact, and the consensus for public ownership seems to grow with each generation.

If there is a solid consensus for public ownership, there is as yet no such agreement about how our Western lands should be used and administered. The century-old debate between the disciples of John Muir, preaching wilderness for its own sake, and the followers of Gifford Pinchot, advocating utilitarian doctrines of resource use, rages on unresolved and growing ever more intense as the once-empty spaces of the West begin to fill up. Likewise, there is still no settled consensus on where land-use decisions should be made — at the federal, state, or local level — or by whom — the public, elected officials, judges, or professional administrators. Given the unique history of public lands, proposals for reform require some discussion of what has happened in the past.

As the American frontier advanced from Atlantic shores across the Mississippi and onto the Great Plains, lands were routinely transferred into private ownership through land sales and the operation of the various preemption and homestead laws. As a result, public lands east of the Mississippi River have almost disappeared; they are now limited to a few small forests and parks and some larger tracts in New England and the Appalachians.

In the second half of the nineteenth century, as the line of settlement moved off the Great Plains into the front ranges of the Rocky Mountains and beyond, the historical process of privatization began to slow, eventually coming to a halt. As homesteaders, conditioned by their experience on the rich agricultural frontiers of Iowa and Nebraska, began trekking into the empty spaces of the West, they expected to plow the soil into a checkerboard extension of the Middle West. But for the most part it would not happen, for the climate was too cold in the high mountains and too hot in the desert bottoms, soils were often unproductive, and almost everywhere there was too little rainfall.

Out of the failure of the homestead experience, two opposing concepts of land tenure gradually emerged. One, rooted in the traditional urge to privatize, advocated that the public land be sold or given away in whatever quantities necessary to stimulate development. If small homestead grants were not a sufficient inducement to settlement, then large grants surely would be. In the nineteenth century Congress gave 58 million acres of land to Northern Pacific Railroad, just the first of many huge grants to railroad companies. As Congress enacted laws authorizing expanded mineral, timber and grazing grants, land monopolies began to develop as individuals and corporations manipulated and stepped over the edge of new land laws.

Even as Western lands were sold, granted, and otherwise concentrated into huge private landholdings, a new concept — that public lands should be retained in permanent ownership and managed for public purposes — gradually emerged. It began with a traditional concept — public parks — implemented on a grand scale. In 1872 Congress set aside 2 million acres in Yellowstone "as a public park or pleasuring ground for the benefit and enjoyment of the people."[1] Yosemite National Park followed in 1890 after a long and acrimonious fight led by John Muir.

After parks came a less familiar concept — public forest reserves. In 1891 the Congress, in response to accelerating destruction of Western forests, authorized the President to "set apart and reserve, in any State or Territory having public land bearing forests, . . . any part of the public lands wholly or in part covered with timber or undergrowth, whether of commercial value or not, as public reservations."[2] As Presidents Harrison, Cleveland, and then Theodore Roosevelt invoked this law to create a national forest system, Congress began backtracking, but by the time the executive authority was rescinded in 1907, the modern forest system was largely in place.

If one president gave shape to the public-land system that we enjoy today, it was Theodore Roosevelt. In seven years in the White House, he expanded the national forests fourfold to 172 million acres, established seventy-two wildlife refuges and eighteen national monuments, a new category of public reservations intended to preserve areas of scenic, scientific, and archaeological interest. He initiated the first mineral and reclamation withdrawals. Most importantly for the future of the public lands, it was T. R.'s enthusiastic evangelizing and instinctive love of the outdoors that once and for all established the concept of public lands as a permanent part of the American heritage.

After Theodore Roosevelt left office, the debate over public-land policy drifted off to the shadowy corners of American politics. Timber, oil, and mining companies, aided by the connivance or plain indifference of public officials, discovered they could exploit lands without bothering to own them. The Teapot Dome scandal came and went, yet in the easy atmosphere of the 1920s, the public seemed uninterested in demanding meaningful reforms.

The conservation movement revived with the coming of Franklin Roosevelt and the New Deal. Still, at heart, the New Dealers were social planners rather than environmentalists. To them, conservation meant building dams for flood control, public power, and reclamation; replanting forests to increase the timber harvest; and conserving soil to increase agricultural production.

The Tennessee Valley Authority became the model for Western lands; F. D. R. told the nation that TVA "leads logically to national planning for a complete river watershed involving many [States] and the future lives and welfare of millions."[3] The Bureau of Reclamation was the Western TVA, and during the New Deal it geared up development programs that would eventually run amok, causing more environmental destruction than any other public-lands program.

If the New Deal emphasized the utilitarian aspects of conservation, implicitly exalting humans over nature everywhere in the West, it nonetheless clinched the idea of national ownership of Western lands as a permanent part of the national heritage. The Taylor Grazing Act effectively closed the public domain to homesteading and established federal management responsibility for the nonforest lands administered by the Bureau of Land Management. Public power legislation further strengthened the concept of public ownership of Western natural resources, even as it compromised environmental values.

The concept of public ownership is now so firmly established that it is no longer seriously in question, notwithstanding an occasional horse opera like the Sagebrush Rebellion. And in several Western states the Forest Service and, notably, the Bureau of Land Management have undertaken innovative land-exchange programs to consolidate inholdings and protect critical environmental areas. From this point forward, however, the public-land debate will shift to the task of reconciling the growing conflicts over the use of public lands.

Just as the struggle for public ownership began on Western forest lands in the last century, it was excessive timber cutting in this century that ignited the present use controversy. Congress reacted in 1960 by enacting the Multiple-Use Sustained-Yield Act, which formally introduced the concept of "multiple use," stating, "It is the policy of Congress that the national forests are established and shall be administered for outdoor recreation, range, timber, watershed, and wildlife and fish purposes."[4]

For its time, multiple use was a forward-looking, progressive concept that at last awarded recreation, wildlife and watershed uses official parity with timber cutting. The act reflected the views of many, including the leadership of the Forest Service, that the agency was in danger of becoming little more than a government-owned timber company.

Whatever its original promise, multiple use is a concept that has proven unworkable in practice. Political pressure to increase timber cuts has caused the Forest Service to commit to doubling timber production from public lands. The service has accelerated road-building programs, increased clear-cutting, and put virgin old-growth forest to the saw. The federal courts have been largely unwilling to control forest abuse because the phrase "multiple use" is so vague that judges seem powerless to set priorities or otherwise limit the discretion of the Forest Service officials. Meanwhile, in Oregon, the heirs of John Muir are taking protest and civil disobedience directly into the old-growth forests.

The controversy persists; Congress, responding halfheartedly to public pressure, has enacted still more planning statutes, notably the National Forest Management Act of 1976 (NFMA). Yet without congressionally set priorities, expanded multiple-use planning has resulted in little more than interminable hearings and administrative reviews, which do little to restrain an agency determined to elevate timber cutting above all other values.

A similar multiple-use controversy is unfolding on lands administered by the Bureau of Land Management. Just as the Organic Act of 1960 brought multiple use to the Forest Service, so the Federal Land Policy and Management Act of 1976 (FLPMA) established a similar mandate for the Bureau of Land Management. However, the bureau, lacking the professional esprit of the Forest Service, tainted by politics and incompetence in upper management and heavily influenced by mining and livestock constituencies, has been even slower to change.

No public-land policy can be complete without accounting for the waters that originate on and flow through the public lands, nourishing diverse communities of plants and wildlife. Unlike the land over which it flows, Western water has not remained under public stewardship.

Beginning with the Desert Act of 1871, Congress ceded control over Western water to the states, which in turn allocated public waters to settlers on a first-come, first-served basis.

Given the scarcity of water and its essential role in development, it was perhaps inevitable that a large share of Western water would quickly be diverted into private use and ownership. But after yielding control of Western water in the nineteenth century, the federal government reentered the field in the twentieth century by means of a 1902 congressional enactment, the Newlands Act, which created the Bureau of Reclamation, and a 1908 court decision, *Winters v. United States*, which established the doctrine of federal reserved water rights.

In due course, the Bureau of Reclamation became the most formidable of all the federal agencies operating in the West. With a mandate to open desert lands to small farmers and with huge budgets financed by hydropower from federal dams, the bureau changed the course of western development. Its practices have been the most environmentally destructive of all the public land agencies, and to this day the bureau has been scarcely touched by the reform movements that have begun, however slowly, to change the Forest Service and the Bureau of Land Management.

The reform agenda for western land and water must start by recognizing that multiple-use planning has, for the most part, been a failure. Multiple use skirts the central reality that in the new urbanizing West, there is no longer enough space to accommodate every competing use on every section of the public domain. Commodity production, whether of timber, minerals, or livestock, is increasingly infringing on the broader public values of open space, wildlife, wilderness and recreation. Choices will have to be made, and those choices are too important to be left to district land managers imposing their own preferences camouflaged in the jargon of land-use planning.

To some degree, the environmental legislation of the last thirty years, notably the Wilderness Act, the Endangered Species Act, the National Environmental Protection Act, and the various clean-air and clean-water laws, has nudged the federal agencies toward administering their lands for public values. Wilderness classification represents a decision for wilderness and water and against mining and timber cutting, yet it applies to less than 5 percent of the public lands. And the listing of a threatened or endangered species can trigger strong measures against habitat destruction. Yet, as we are learning in the old-growth controversy in the Pacific Northwest, the presence of a threatened or endangered species such as the spotted owl is not an adequate substitute for an outright policy against cutting the remaining old-growth forests.

And the fact remains that the vast majority of public lands are still administered free of the restraints imposed by generic environmental legislation.

The next step in the evolution of public land-use policy is to replace multiple-use management with a new concept — dominant public use — that gives priority to recreation, wildlife and watershed uses. Dominant public use would be a mandate to reconsider destructive resource exploitation that is of marginal economic importance.

Many areas of the West, especially in the southern Rocky Mountains, produce small amounts of timber whose harvest would not be economically justified without federal subsidies. In the Tongass and in Oregon and Washington the values of old-growth forest far outweigh the profits from exporting raw logs to Japan. The canyonlands of southern Utah, unique in the world, should be off-limits to prospectors. The introduction of heap-leach gold mining, a technique that allows on-site gold recovery by leaching with sulfuric acid, permits recovery of the microscopic amounts of gold present in the landscape all over the West. As one mountain ledge after another is blasted apart, crushed up and drenched in sulfuric acid, it is none too soon to ask why the mining of gold for monetary speculation, rings and necklaces, should be allowed everywhere on the public domain.

The battle for Western water reform will require changes in both the big land agencies and the Bureau of Reclamation. The Forest Service and the Bureau of Land Management still retain powers to protect streams and other riparian areas by asserting federal rights to instream flows. Federal agencies can also protect federal waters by petitioning for instream flow rights under state laws; yet with just an occasional exception they have failed to do so.

Court decisions and the hostility of the Reagan and Bush administrations to water protection have made the task all the more difficult. Conceivably, the Congress could step into the void by both asserting and creating reserved rights for wilderness and other public lands. Hamstrung by opposition from Western senators and representatives and the indifference of most others, it has so far refused to do so.

Now that streams and rivers are virtually exhausted, thirsty water users are flocking to the last water holes in the West, the huge groundwater reserves hidden beneath remote desert basins. While groundwater may be out of sight and of little direct use to humans or beasts, it does support the marshes, springs, and intermittent streams that maintain life in arid desert lands. Once the hydrologic connection is broken by pumping, the surface waters will disappear, altering desert ecosystems on an unprecedented scale.

The big test of federal resolve to protect the interconnected ground-water and surface waters on public lands will probably occur in Nevada, where the city of Las Vegas, asserting rights under state law, is preparing to pump groundwater from twenty thousand square miles of federal land in the remote desert basins of eastern Nevada. The project threatens the Pahranagat Wildlife Refuge in eastern Nevada, the Ash Meadows Wildlife Refuge and Devil's Hole National Monument in western Nevada, and even springwaters emerging across the state line in Death Valley National Monument.

The Fish and Wildlife Service, the National Park Service, and the Bureau of Land Management have filed protests before the Nevada State Water Engineer. The Secretary of the Interior and the Congress have remained silent. Ultimately, a federal groundwater-protection law may be the only way to avoid a repetition of the environmental tragedy of Owens Valley and Mono Lake from recurring in Nevada and throughout the West.

The Bureau of Reclamation presents a special challenge to public water reform. With its cultivated image as champion of the small farmer (although it is a longtime ally of corporate agriculture) and a long record of delivering water projects and public power to eager Western members of Congress, the bureau has never attracted the public scrutiny routinely accorded most other federal agencies. Even the great controversies of the past — Glen Canyon, Echo Park, Bridge Canyon, and Marble Canyon — and present — Glen Canyon again — do not seem to slow down the bureau juggernaut.

Remarkably, no member of Congress has, at least in modern times, ever come up with a comprehensive plan to reform the bureau. For non-Westerners, picking a quarrel with such a gargantuan bureaucracy is an all-consuming task of no interest to constituents. For a Westerner, taking on the bureau would amount to an assault on many venerable Western institutions, including the political power centers that have grown and intertwined around local reclamation projects.

In environmental terms, the case for taking on and reforming the bureau is simple. Growing Western cities must have more water, and they will either get that water from agriculture (which consumes more than 80 percent of the water used in the West) or they will continue to raid and destroy the remaining waters located on the public lands.

Meanwhile, the bureau remains locked in a tight embrace with the apparatchiks of Western agriculture, who are dedicated to protecting the political power of their organizations by blocking water transfers, even when individual farmers may want the option of selling their water. The reform task is to break the link between the bureau and the agricultural bureaucracies and redirect the bureau toward a policy of facilitating market water-transfers. Doing so will be about as easy as transitioning the Kremlin to a market economy.

One reform alternative is to abolish the bureau and transfer its river-management functions to interstate river-basin councils modeled on the Northwest Power Planning Council. A less drastic alternative is to abolish the bureau's construction budget and authority for new project starts, take hydropower revenues from the basin accounts that feed bureau projects, transfer them to the general fund, and enact a new reclamation law that eliminates all federal barriers to voluntary market water transfers.

Even a decade ago, talk of fundamental reclamation reform would have seemed utopian. Now a four-year drought in California is beginning to expose the institutional inadequacies of the present system. As California moves ever closer to crisis, there will be pressure to relax environmental standards in the Sacramento River delta, to dam more wild rivers in the Sierra Nevada, and to increase groundwater pumping in the Owens Valley and Mono Lake basins. None of these alternatives will be necessary in California or elsewhere if Congress will use the drought crisis as a springboard to redesign the bureau from the ground up.

One hundred years ago Congress authorized the first forest reserves, putting a new concept of perpetual ownership of public lands on the path toward public acceptance and support. Now, at the start of the coming century, the American public and its leaders must accelerate and complete the step of dedicating public land and public waters unequivocally to the highest and best public use.

Bruce Babbitt

ECO-POLITICS AND ECONOMIC
DEVELOPMENT: WEALTH, HOPE, AND
CHOICE

A recurring theme in science fiction is the earthling lost in space in his clunker spacecraft. All of a sudden he lands on the lost planet of Omega. It turns out that Omega is inhabited by these incredibly intelligent people — did you ever notice how in science fiction the other people are always more intelligent than we are? The earthling travels around Omega for several months looking at things, but finally he decides he wants to go back to Earth. So he tells his Omegan friend, "It is time for me to go home. It will take me many years to get there, so can we get started?" The Omegan says, "Oh, it is not going to take very long at all. It is only 17.5 minutes to Earth." The earthling says, "Now wait a minute, our theories tell us that nothing in the universe can exceed the speed of light." And the Omegan looks at the earthling and says, somewhat patronizingly, "I know. But we have different theories."

That is the point of view I would like to express. At the Center for the New West we have different theories about the future for the West, the United States, and the world, and for the course of events on a global scale; events that are driven by increasing wealth, expanding choices for people and communities, and expanding choices in politics. Expanding choices in politics is what democracy is all about, and expanding choices in economics is what capitalism is all about. Capitalism and democracy have been expressing themselves dramatically over the last twenty-five years and in a revolutionary way in the last fifteen months. In fact, the other day when I pulled off my bookshelf Robert Heilbroner's book *The Future As History*, written about thirty years ago, I was struck by Heilbroner's discussion of how collectivist ideologies had finally won out. It was in the wake of the Cuban Revolution, and Heilbroner said that communal ways of organizing societies, economies, and political systems were the wave of the future. It is amazing how wrong he was.

The other change, on a global scale, is the higher standard of stewardship that we are finding everyplace: increasing concern for the family and its role in nurturing children, and increasing concern for communities — not nation-states, but communities and the roles they play. In fact, one of the most remarkable developments of our time is the decentralization of power and authority in nation-states, including France, where Charlemagne would turn over in his grave if he could see the extent to which central power has decayed in the society that invented modern centralized government.

An increasing sense of stewardship also exists about the environment — not only among those who classify themselves as Greens. Maybe another way to say it is that more and more people consider themselves Greens. Three out of four Americans call themselves environmentalists, and four out of five say they would pay higher prices to preserve environmental values.

Let me begin with the big picture. Contrary to popular view, we think that the world is on the edge of a major global economic expansion. We also believe the United States is well positioned to benefit from this expansion. This is a minority point of view, but it has an increasing number of adherents. The first expression of this perspective in a popular medium was an October 1989 article in *The Atlantic* called "The Coming Global Boom." This article expressed the viewpoint we have at the Center for the New West. It is also a viewpoint expressed by others, including Ed Guay, the chief economist at Cigna, Ed Yardine, the chief economist at PruBach, and a number of other economists and observers.

Why is this going to happen?

One of the reasons is new technology. The explosion in new technologies is incredible. Innovation and economic expansion in the last decade was driven by the computer — and not just in this society. However, the United States is number one in computers. In 1989 the United States had 50 percent of the world's installed computer capacity. The next-highest country was Japan, with 10 percent. The impact of computers has been unprecedented, and as we look into the next decade we will see an even greater expansion of power in smaller packages, and new levels of capability.

Biotechnology is another area that will drive new economic activity, an area where Colorado has a great investment and a great deal to offer. We are seeing major new changes in transportation technology. The Japanese now have a prototype of a seagoing cargo vessel that can reach fifty knots — 60 miles an hour — which makes the Pacific the same size as the Atlantic measured by transit time. The changes this will make in how industries relate to each other will be enormous. About a year ago I was in Nebraska, and I visited the Kawasaki plant. They use a just-in-time inventory system there, in which parts come in from Japan almost nine thousand miles away. They have a three-day warehousing period. Think what will happen as these high-speed ships come into play. And think what that will mean for the western part of the United States as we are able to be more closely integrated with the expanding markets and modern societies emerging in Asia.

Another example is telecommunications, where back-office operations today are creating tremendous opportunities, as well as some challenges, for remote areas like we find in much of the West. Today 17 percent of Citicorp's profits comes from Sioux Falls, South Dakota, where it located its credit card–processing and service activities. "Telework" and other communications-based activities will make it possible for more people to work at home and on their own time and under their own conditions. We will have more job-sharing and flex time — once again, more choices for people and for families on how to integrate their work life with their family life, and greater possibilities for technical projects that are telecommunication-based, such as traffic management. Highway engineers want to lay more concrete. They want to build more light rail, they want to do more of the things they have done in the past. But new technologies offer new approaches. Look at Los Angeles. During the Olympics in 1984, everyone predicted the city would come to a grinding halt. It didn't. On the San Diego Freeway, the average speed actually increased about 25 percent during the Olympics. Why? Because there was a concerted effort to use modern telecommunications and information technology to make full use of the tremendous surface capacity that exists in that city to move people around in cars. This was a primitive application of what we now call "smart cars" and "smart highways," and we are going to see challenges from these new technologies to those who want to lay more concrete on our cities and tear down neighborhoods and divide communities with railroad tracks.

We have a major global expansion coming because of new markets. In Europe, we have twelve nations with a gross national product of $4.3 trillion and a population of 325 million. The eleven free-market nations of the Asia-Pacific region — including the United States and Canada (remember, the United States is also a Pacific nation, not just an Atlantic nation), Japan, South Korea, the Philippines, Thailand, Indonesia, Malaysia, Singapore, Australia, and New Zealand — represent 800 million people, as opposed to 325 million in Europe. These Asian-

Pacific countries have a gross national product of $3.4 trillion (not counting the United States), as opposed to $4.3 trillion in Europe. But the Asian-Pacific economies are growing at the rate of $3 billion a week — not a month or a year, but a *week*. The growth in that area is enormous, and that is another reason there will be a major global expansion.

Then there are the changes in demography. Everybody talks about the aging "boomer" generation in this country — that baby-boom pig moving through the demographic snake. It is a huge bulge, an unprecedented discontinuity in population. In this country it represents more than 78 million people — more than one-third of the U.S. population. The baby-boom phenomenon also exists in almost every other industrialized country. But the baby-boomers in this country are from twenty-four to forty-five years old, while in Japan they are about ten years older, because the baby boom started there in the mid-1930s. Furthermore, the Japanese have mandatory retirement at fifty-five. So baby-boomers in Japan are now retiring, while in this country most of our baby-boomers are between twenty-eight and thirty-five. Therein is a noteworthy point. Most of the United States' boomers are in their high-consumption and low wage-earning years. Those are the years when you buy your first house, your first car, your first television, your first radio, and your first bassinet. So it is no wonder that we have a low savings rate in the United States. But those of us who see that we are on the edge of a major global boom will argue, as Ed Yardine argues, that we are going to see a huge increase in the United States' savings rate over the next six years — as high as 8 to 10 percent by 1996. Savings rates at this level would generate savings surpluses as high as $500 billion per year. If we can get the budget deficit under control so that money is not sucked up by a profligate Congress and a federal government that is out of touch with grassroots concerns and priorities, then we are going to see interest rates go down and the United States' emergence as the major exporter of capital for a capital-hungry world.

A fourth factor driving global expansion is the worldwide environmental cleanup. We have serious environmental problems in this country — air, water, nuclear-waste disposal — of which we are all aware. But nobody can spend any time in Eastern Europe or in Asia, as I have during the last year, and not be stunned by the scope and magnitude — and in some cases the tragedy — of environmental pollution that exists in those countries. In Taiwan, South Korea, Thailand, and even in Japan — the problems in those countries are much worse than they are here, yet they are nothing compared to the environmental tragedies that are imminent in Eastern Europe, not in the next century, but in the next several years, if drastic action is not taken. In the Eastern European countries — in Poland, Czechoslovakia, East Germany, and Bulgaria — we are finding one serious problem after another. Not only do communist-command economies fail to increase wealth and expand choices for people, command economies also destroy the environment in ways that capitalism never has. For example, Poland may not have potable water by the end of this decade unless extreme remedial actions are taken in the next three to five years.

So as we look out over the next decade, we see a major expansion in global economic activity along with a major shift in political and social activity from centralized forums to increasingly decentralized forums. The United States is in the catbird's seat to benefit from these changes and to provide leadership. But we can't make mistakes. We have got to be attentive to how we develop our responses.

Now, let's bring this back to Colorado. For the last 140 or so years, developments in Colorado have been driven by many different economic forces, as detailed in a report last year by Dean Coddington. From 1859 to about 1900 mining was the driving force. From 1901 to 1940 agriculture was the driving force. From 1941 to 1963 the Colorado economy was shaped by the growth of the federal government and especially by the defense industry. Then, contrary to conventional wisdom, from 1964 to 1973 (the year the first energy boom began) Colorado achieved a very diversified economy. IBM moved in, along with Hewlett-Packard, Kodak, Manville, Western Electric — many of what now constitute the high-technology industries on the Front Range of the Rockies came during that period. So when the energy boom came in 1973, it really masked a lot of solid, diversified and largely healthy economic activity that had already taken root in this area. But even the energy boom itself, from 1974 to 1983, was a misnomer, because there were four or five other things going on simultaneously. In addition to an energy boom, there was a mining boom — in coal and molybdenum. There was a real estate boom induced by misguided federal tax policies. There was a tourism boom; for example, the skier days doubled during that period. There was a regional air-transportation boom as Denver became a major national hub in the wake of airline deregulation in 1978. There was a business-services boom as legal, accounting, and other professional firms settled in Denver and the metropolitan area to provide services throughout the Rocky Mountain region. Since 1984 we have experienced an important economic restructuring. Foremost, the mining industry is transforming from a caterpillar to a butterfly right before our eyes. Today the mining industry is one of the most important industries in the state, not because it is digging things out of the ground on the Western Slope, but because of the brainpower and know-how that exist on the Front Range. The future of the mining industry in this state is not primarily in western Colorado; it is on Seventeenth Street, and at the Colorado School of Mines. And it is not just in mining; it is also in tunneling and other applications of geotechnology that are in increasing demand today.

Environmental management is another manifestation of economic restructuring in Colorado today. Colorado and the United States have been leaders in three important areas in environmental management. The first is innovative legislation, especially in the last several years, to help achieve a cleaner and greener environment. The second is new technologies of environmental cleanup and environmental preservation — for example, new ways to get water out of the ground and preserve what is there in a more effective way. And third, this country and this state have been leaders in the policy sciences in developing market-oriented solutions to environmental problems.

In Colorado we face one of the biggest challenges of the next decade, and that is balanced growth and economic development of the Colorado Plateau. The Colorado Plateau is a 132,000-square-mile area. It is not an issue on the front pages. It never has been. But it is one of the most important areas on the face of the globe. This 132,000-square-mile area has nine national parks, two national recreation areas, twelve national monuments, twenty-six national wilderness areas, eighteen national forests, and five national landmarks. It covers two-thirds of Colorado, almost one-half of Utah, the northern portions of New Mexico down to Santa Fe, and northern Arizona, including the Grand Canyon.

If you asked foreigners where they most want to come in the United States, Disneyland is almost always first. But of the next nine on their top ten list, six or seven, depending on whether you are talking to Asians or Europeans, will be in the Colorado Plateau. They will be the Grand Canyon, Canyonlands National Park, Aspen, Dinosaur National Monument, and other major tourist destinations in the Colorado Plateau. But that Colorado Plateau can be destroyed by piecemeal development. It is being destroyed today by piecemeal development. In the mining industry it is very well known that you can destroy an ore body by the way you mine it. That which is true of a natural resource is true of a tourism resource. A tourism resource can be destroyed by the way it is developed. For this reason we need to move with dispatch to put in place a comprehensive, multijurisdictional, public-private business plan to develop this area. It needs to be a process that involves environmentalists, political leaders, community and civic organizations, including Native

Americans along with the federal government. We need to avoid a process dominated by big business and big government making all the decisions in ways that haven't worked very well.

If we examine the postwar period, we can identify three important waves of economic development. In the first wave after World War II, there was an urge to develop at any cost. There was a rape, scrape, and run mentality. Communities competed to attract outside industry. That's what we call a "hunting" strategy.

But in the 1980s that began to change. We began to move to a "gardening" strategy — to build on our strengths, stick to our knitting, adding value to existing activities. We began to realize that in both the private and public sectors we had to nurture and cultivate what we had; we couldn't destroy what we were given. We couldn't foul the nest in the process of developing new choices for people and communities.

If increasing wealth and expanding choices, not simply growth, are the goals that drive economic development, and are the major purposes of a political culture, they have to be achieved in a way that preserves environmental and other values, because amenities are an increasingly important part of what people are seeking. In the 1980s the gardening that was done was monopoly gardening. Usually, large governmental institutions — but sometimes private institutions — became monopoly suppliers of what made the garden work: monopoly suppliers of education, monopoly suppliers of technology, and monopoly suppliers of job training, capital and other resources. People are increasingly turning their backs on that kind of approach.

It is interesting to look at education. No one would argue that postsecondary education in the United States, even with all of its problems, is the world's best, most productive, and most effective system of higher education. Nearly everyone agrees with that. Whether you talk to the Japanese or the British or the French, almost anyone — it is pretty easy to get a consensus on that point of view. But our kindergarten through twelfth grade system ranks very low by almost everyone's estimate and by almost any measure of performance. Think of the difference between higher education and K-12 in the United States. In K-12 you have to go to the school to which you are assigned. There is no choice. In higher education you shop three or four schools. In K-12 you take the teacher who has been certified by the certification process. In higher education you are exposed to all kinds of people. Some have Ph.D.'s. Some don't. Some have been in education all their lives. Others pop in and out. A variety of people with a variety of experiences and backgrounds are classroom teachers in U.S. higher education. Consumers are deeply involved in higher education, the people who pay the tuition: the parents and the students. In K-12 the consumer is almost never involved. Look at *Fortune* magazine's education reform meetings that have been going on for the past three years. I recently reviewed the list of participants in the latest meeting. There are a large number of business people and school administrators, but there are few teachers, parents, or students. The school boards aren't even on the map. How can we reform U.S. education if the primary consumers are not at the table and if the main publicly accountable institution for making school policy is left out of the loop?

Monopoly gardening as a way of trying to make the nest a better and more prosperous place with more choices for everyone is slowly giving way to incentive gardening. We are now moving to a new phase in which we are trying to provide competition and incentives in fields such as education and technology and capital and environment.

Today we have new clean-air legislation. In the "old days" in 1977, the Clean Air Act mandated the "best available control technology" for utilities. Today we are talking about having emission-reduction credits, whereby areas will be allocated a certain level of emissions and polluters there can decide among themselves how those credits will be apportioned. If, for example, the people or utilities undertake certain kinds of emission-reduction steps, they can earn credits and sell those credits to someone else who doesn't want to or feels it is inefficient to take those kinds of steps.

In this country, right after World War II and in the early 1950s, we built a lot of utilities. They have twenty-five to thirty-five-year life spans. Many will be decommissioned in the mid-1990s. We should have choices about whether we install very expensive emission controls or let those managing aging power plants buy emission credits. That is the smart way to regulate the environment. That is the smart way to get the kind of performance and improvements that we need.

Then there is nuclear-waste management. In Rocky Flats, right outside Denver, we have a prime example of what happens when you have monopoly gardening. Rocky Flats shows what a monopoly supplier, the federal government, will do when it is both a broker and a doer, when it is both in the business of taking care of nuclear waste on the one hand, and of enforcing standards on the other. At Rocky Flats the federal government "enforced" standards by exempting itself from nearly every single important safety and health measure.

The lessons of the past several years and the new directions that we are taking suggest that environmental policy can and should work through market forces, that the market can function very effectively to allocate environmental values, that the market can reconcile the

Industrial Revolution with the Green Revolution, and that leaders of business and government can bring grassroots organizations to the table because it is at the grassroots level that the impact is the greatest.

As we go forward, we can't let the dinosaur institutions call the shots. The federal government, the political action committees, big labor, big business — these are the institutions that have got us where we are today. We have to broaden the base. We have to change the way we intervene in the environment. We must do away with the monopoly suppliers and the regulation and micro-management of activities by far-off central authorities. We must move toward using government to specify standards and results and leave it to innovative individuals and institutions to achieve those results. Where they fail, we need to change our approach and the incentives we use in order to get the results that are needed.

In addition, we must assign more responsibility to individuals. Today individuals don't have much responsibility to reduce environmental pollution — not for auto pollution, not for disposable diapers, not for the waste they put out in front of their homes. We need to charge people for their waste by the volume they put in front of their homes. We need to charge people who want to drive a Mercedes diesel. We need to look hard at how we bring the individual and the individual's responsibilities into these matters. Our future is one that promises tremendous economic expansion and new prosperity that is more widely shared. It is a future that needs to be and will be constrained by environmental considerations. Those constraints should be market-driven. We have the knowledge to do that. We need to have the courage to reject "politically correct" regulatory approaches and substitute market approaches. Why? Because they work.

Philip M. Burgess

THE AMERICAN WEST:
WHAT IDEAS SHOULD DETERMINE
ITS FUTURE?

What ideas should determine the future of the American West? Before attempting an answer, I have confessions to make. First, my ideas will be not be the kind one can enumerate and list in order of importance. They are observations on the nature of rural Western society and conclusions drawn from those observations. Second, these ideas come from a newcomer in the rural West. I have lived here only since 1974 — a part of a winter, to use writer George Sibley's phrase.

In addition, I do not engage in work usually associated with the West. I had only been in what is now my hometown for a week or two back in 1974 when a rancher knocked at my door. He had come to load up logs left for him by my next-door neighbor, a logger, and he needed a hand. I was pleased to be the hand, pleased to be helping a real rancher and real logger so soon after arriving in the West. We worked for thirty minutes putting the newly cut logs — I didn't know what kind of trees they came from, and wouldn't know today — into a long stock trailer. By the time the heavy green logs were loaded, I was barely walking. The rancher, who was about my age and size, looked as if he had spent the last thirty minutes drinking coffee. I couldn't claim altitude or lack of condition. I had spent the summer at our mountain cabin, the structure that had drawn us west, chopping wood and climbing mountains. I was in the best shape of my life. In addition to paying me ten dollars, that rancher taught me that I couldn't earn a living in the West as a hand.

I was, of course, statistically safe from such a fate. The West is associated with cattle roundups and the felling of trees, but most Westerners work as real estate and insurance salesmen, teachers and hardware-store clerks. We turn "Western" only on weekends, when we climb into, not onto, our Broncos and create new roads and new verbs by four-wheeling into the backcountry.

We — Betsy Marston and myself — obeyed the statistics. Instead of felling or loading trees, we chose a typically Western way to earn a living: we sold advertising. To put it more romantically, we founded and then ran for six years a hometown weekly serving the 2,600 households in and around the towns of Paonia, Hotchkiss, and Crawford. Betsy and I — a former television producer and a former college professor from New York — were provoked to start a newspaper by a mischievous $4,000 loan from a bored country banker, and by our visceral reaction to the existing newspaper, which declared from every page: "Stop Gun Control! It's almost too late!!" When it had a news hole, which was every week, it plugged it with the John Birch Society Liberty Log and other far-right handouts. Thinking globally and acting locally, the publisher also inveighed against the "hippies" — former urbanites like ourselves who were settling and unsettling the socially conservative North Fork Valley. The valley's own children routinely left after high school, and the town folks weren't keen on the young newcomers who were replacing their children.

In retrospect, I can see that we must have been a figment of that publisher's worst nightmare: left-wing New Yorkers come to invade his survivalist retreat. He and his gun-nut friends were also ex-urbanites, but from a different background than us "hippies." The survivalists had retreated to small Western towns to await what they saw as the inevitable collapse of urban society. When the starving urban hordes came fleeing from the burning cities, the survivalists were going to load their rifles, climb into their Broncos and head the refugees off at the passes. (The trend continues today with the far-right groups settling in northern Idaho.)

The publisher was ready for the panicked urban exodus but he hadn't expected an economic invasion using the tools of free enterprise. Worst of all, from his perspective, was the fact that the residents of the North Fork Valley were more interested in subscribing to a newspaper that provided news than they were in his views on gun control. We, I can see now, were almost as doctrinaire as he was, but we wrote better and we did reporting.

So we thrived, and he found a new way to earn a living. For six years I learned about the lightly populated western half of Colorado from the ground up: town council meetings, school board meetings, ditch company meetings, county fairs, Jeep poker runs and slide shows at the Jehovah's Witnesses' Kingdom Hall. The slide show, especially, was a revelation. It revealed a movement I thought had died with the Scopes trial. The argument against evolution was one hundred color slides of birds, flowers, lovers walking hand in hand. Each slide was followed by the question: Could this beauty have come about by accident? No one in that Kingdom Hall, including myself, suggested that it could have.

So some of my Western education came from covering news events and selling advertising. But more came through our children. I was amazed at and gratified by the close attention the schools and community paid to kids. A typical event happened at the height of the Hunt brothers silver boom, when a roll of silver quarters was worth $70. I got a call at the newspaper office from the woman who ran the game room down the street. (In a town of 1,400, everything is down the street.) My eight-year old was there with a roll of silver quarters I'd accumulated. He was using them to play video games. I didn't know this woman — I still have not learned to recognize everyone I should or to engage in the rural pastime of waving at people who drive past me on the highway. But the woman knew my kid and me, and I went down and recovered the quarters.

The attention had its drawbacks. Some parents felt free to rebuke us for missing a school event. "Oh, you should have seen how well your daughter did at the band competition. But we gave her a big hand." The "we" were the good parents taking up the slack left by people who wouldn't drop work to watch their kid play a Souza march with fifty other kids. Not that I accepted the "bad parent" status — I simply had other standards. I was amazed at the lack of emphasis on education. Starting with the fourth grade, our children would ask why they should try to do well on the Iowa Basics test. Our son told us: "The other kids say the test doesn't matter. They say they're going into the mines when they're eighteen and make more money than the principal." When they reached high school, our boy told us his biology class had put evolution to a vote. By a large majority, the class voted for creationism; the majority included the biology teacher.

Events like this sent many urban parents into flight from traditional small towns. We didn't move. We believed we could supplement our children's education at the supper table. But what could we do about the other children, and therefore about the future of the valley? One doesn't publish a community weekly for the money or the prestige. We were doing it for ideological reasons, just as our competitor had. The paper was our instrument of change, a way to push social, economic, and physical evolution. The North Fork Valley was a wonderful place. We wanted to make it more wonderful — more like the city we had left, but without the bad aspects of urban life. I understand now that I saw the place in one-dimensional terms, still within my New York experience. The schools were producing youngsters who were led to see high school as an end rather than as preparation for a larger future. High school was often seen as the high point of life, a place where hero status could be earned on the football field or wrestling mat. I wanted to see the rural schools imbued with urban values both for the sake of my children and for what I assumed were the best interests of the town.

The schools reflected the priorities of the communities as a whole. I was struck by the quickness with which traditional small Western towns, including my own, would put their community and landscape and clear air at risk in order to host a mine, mill, or power plant. The issue of education was an undercurrent in our newspaper. We pushed our values by publicizing academic achievers, the local schools' rankings on national tests, and alumni who had succeeded in the outside world. By comparison, the issue of coal development was a pitched battle, with us newcomers generally lining up in opposition to new mines. Only gradually did I come to see the relationship between education and the hunger for mine or mill jobs. Those mine and mill jobs pay well, are local, and require little formal training. The kids who had ignored the Iowa Basic tests could indeed come out of high school, with or without a diploma, and start earning $30,000 a year. The statement made so often at public hearings — "We need the mining jobs for our children" — was unanswerable so long as the schools remained what they were.

I should say one other thing as part of laying my outsider cards on the table. When I realized a few years ago that I had lived in the same small town for a decade and had no thought of leaving, I began to worry about who would bury me in a community of twenty fundamentalist churches. Now I only worry that nothing will happen to force me to leave the rural West.

The concluding service is still a concern, but it is a concern submerged by my inability to imagine being a free person anywhere else in America. The rural West allows me to be free both physically, because of the vast space and the scarcity of people, and mentally. The sense of physical freedom is easy to explain. The sense of mental freedom is more difficult. It is made up, for me, of freedom from the social, economic and intellectual lockstep I associate with urban areas: their high degree of organization, their intense economic demands, and the large amount of time given over to such chores as commuting and shopping.

I believe the latest wave of immigrants to settle in the West's small towns are in search of the same freedom earlier settlers sought. I have a theory about western Colorado, based on nothing more than my reading of obituaries of old-timers. My guess is that western Colorado was settled by people fleeing the early twentieth-century industrialization of the Appalachian hill country, and that the ancestors of those people had, in their turn, fled Adam Smith's Europe. Western Colorado, I am convinced, is populated in part by people who have never been subject to the time clock or to that other yoke, the necktie. A city person's attraction to the Rocky Mountain West is much like a male's attraction to the woman he eventually marries. I was captured by snowcapped mountains and high, cold lakes. But after several years had passed, I was held by the sense of community, despite my outsider status, and by the more subtle beauty of the arid land below the mountains.

In the same way, after six years of publishing the hometown weekly, and now five years of publishing the regional *High Country News*, I am only beginning to get some feel for the larger West. In the first few years of doing *High Country News*, the map I carried in my head was of national forests and Bureau of Land Management domains. Laid over these political boundaries were issues — strip mining, wilderness, endangered species — and the courts, agencies, and local and national environmental groups that concerned themselves with those issues. Then came a sense of the vast, empty nature of the West. The land the paper pretends to cover includes the rural parts of ten states. If you exclude the three cities — Salt Lake, Denver, and Phoenix-Tucson — only a few million people live on the one million square miles that stretch from the Idaho-Montana-North Dakota border with Canada to the Arizona-New Mexico-Texas border with Mexico.

For one hundred years, the foundation of this region's economy has been farming and ranching, mining, milling, and drilling, and a special, lucrative relationship with the federal government, which has built dams, nuclear-bomb factories, military installations, power plants, and the like. It is true that the region has more salesmen and hardware clerks than ranchers or miners, but it is the latter who shape the place. A way of life — I call it an extractive culture — has grown up in step with the extractive and agricultural economies. We collided with that way of life when we tried to settle in the rural West. That extractive culture is, among other things, family centered, religious in a fundamentalist sense, and anchored in the region's small towns. It is characterized by its recreation — hunting, snowmobiling, jeeping; by its disinterest in or xenophobia toward the outside world; by its friendliness; and by its pride in the beauty of the place.

To a religious, family-centered community, formal education can appear a threat. The child who becomes interested in mathematics or literature will inevitably leave the community and probably the region. The geographic separation will be aggravated by the different values that accompany higher education, a home in an urban area, and a spouse who probably grew up in a suburb. It is not only Hispanics and Native Americans who worry about losing children to the larger America. Many small-town Anglo families have the same fear. The schools that seemed to me to foreclose a larger future can also be seen as ensuring that the town's children will want to remain at home and adhere to the family's and community's ways.

The schools illustrate the workings of a remarkably stable way of life, one based economically on the extraction of natural resources and culturally on the religious, recreational and social arrangements I've described. I could have made the same points using politics rather than education. The West's army of twenty U.S. senators has maintained the nineteenth-century laws that guarantee cheap, free or subsidized access to public land and water for miners, loggers and ranchers.

That tremendous political power — 6 percent of the nation's population controlling 20 percent of the Senate — could have been used in many ways. Instead, it has been used almost exclusively to defend the extractive culture by preserving the extractive economy, just as the South's senators for so long defended that region's racial arrangements, and thereby foreclosed other opportunities. The Western senators are the primary defenders of what Charles Wilkinson calls the Lords of Yesterday.

In addition to stealing from Charles, I have also appropriated historian Frederick Jackson Turner's metaphor on the closing of the Western frontier. Turner, following the U.S. Bureau of the Census, said the Western frontier closed in 1890. Turner's frontier was physical; I say that the frontier that closed was a social and economic one. I take the 1890s as the decade, more or less, in which the small-town Western way of life based on extraction was established. It limited who could live in the rural West, it determined the aspirations of the schools and other community bodies, it selected the kinds of churches that could attract parishioners, and it determined the candidates who could successfully run for public office.

The continued existence of this strong culture, one hundred years later, is demonstrated by the existence of its alter ego — towns such as Aspen, Telluride, Santa Fe, Jackson, et al. Why would people settle in these very expensive places if they could live in hundreds of equally scenic rural Western towns, most of them with higher physical qualities of life. Why, to take a Colorado example, is real estate in the ski town of Crested Butte a hot seller while land and homes in the nearby college town of Gunnison languish?

The answer is culture. Urban people instinctively shy away from the traditional communities and toward the ski and resort towns. It is easiest to see in Utah, where a Park City is a gentile island in a Mormon sea. But it is true everywhere. During the energy and minerals boom of the 1970s and early 1980s, the wives of corporate executives new to the region complained of the "lack of shopping." I am sure they missed large shopping malls. But "lack of shopping" was also a code for their dissatisfaction with traditional communities' schools, the lack of planning and zoning (which meant a lack of protection for invested money), and the lack of such social mechanisms as country clubs. It is these lacks — perhaps accompanied by the very high rate of violent death that afflicts young Anglo males in the West's small towns — that created a barrier between the rural West and the larger America. It was as if the small towns exuded an invisible chemical that kept urbanites out despite the beauty, the friendliness, the low real estate prices, and the high quality of life.

The dominance of extraction and the extractive way of life persevered into the early 1980s. Then a huge, pervasive bust occurred. Mines closed, power-plant projects were canceled, mills shut down, and the prices of land and water plummeted. There was an outflow of people from the region. Whole sections of small towns emptied, schools lost one-third of their students, churches lost chunks of their congregations, ambitious public administrators — school superintendents, hospital directors, town managers — went looking for yeastier places. The bust is interesting for the havoc and losses it caused, and for its revelation of just how wrong the Exxons and Amaxes of the world can be. But most interesting is this question: Why did a politically strong region (remember the twenty U.S. senators) open itself up to the inevitable devastation of the bust? One didn't have to be a seer in the 1970s to recognize that bust would follow boom. Former Colorado Governor Richard Lamm is best known for his prophetic warnings, but almost all of the West's governors saw that a bust was inevitable.

There are examples of communities and states that protected themselves against the boom. Meeker, Colorado, did what it could to damp down the effects of the oil-shale boom. Utah, despite the need for jobs created by an astronomical birth rate, said no to the federal racetrack-missile project, then estimated as a $100 billion construction job. But for the most part, the region went along with the boom.

It did so, I think, because the rural West lacks three important institutions. The lack of these institutions left the region open to the boom, because the West had no way to explore, analyze, and communicate what was happening to it. I list those missing elements in no particular order; they are intertwined and of equal importance.

Education. To the weaknesses of primary and high school education must be added the lack of a strong regional university. Some of the
West's universities, such as the University of Colorado, have depart-
ments or schools concerned with Western questions. But for the most
part, the West's universities are national- or international-looking institutions doing such things as seeking Superconducting Super Colliders.
When the West faces serious problems, such as the forest fires of 1988
or questions on grazing and public lands, there is no regional university,
no Western Harvard or Stanford or Berkeley, to turn to. Most new ideas
concerning Western questions come from nonuniversity sources: Allan
Savory's Holistic Resource Management Institute on grazing, Amory
Lovins' Rocky Mountain Institute on energy and economic development,
and the Greater Yellowstone Coalition on a new way of looking at the
Yellowstone region. So when the boom hit, there was no university to
help the region understand and cope with it.

Communications. The second missing element is a regionwide communications medium. The West lacks a newspaper or television station
or magazine that can talk to the rural West as a whole, the way *The New
York Times* talks to its region, the *Atlanta Constitution* talks to the
South, and the *Los Angeles Times* talks to the Southwest.

Reformers. Also missing is a citizens' reform movement. The West
lacks the kind of do-gooders who fought against child labor and slums in
the nation's cities at the turn of the century and against segregation in
the South in the 1960s. The closest the West has to reformers are those
in the environmental movement, and that movement until now has been
more concerned with the preservation of land than with the well-being
of people and communities.

What we have, then, is a region rooted in nineteenth-century
economies, ways of life, and laws. The economies and culture are both
in decline. So the West approaches the twenty-first century uprooted
from its traditional economies and way of life, and lacking the three
institutions that could help it meet the new century. The collapse,
symbolized by extremely low prices for homes, land and water, and by
an outflow of population, has resulted in a reopening of the Western
frontier — in the West being up for grabs.

What is likely to come of this reopening? Will the West build the
three missing institutions in response to this crisis? Will it be taken over
by urbanites enamored of its landscape and low real estate prices? Or
will the region both fail to reform from within and be rejected by the
larger, wealthier America, and thus have no choice but to decline into an
Appalachia-like dark night? The West is so thin in terms of economics
and population that conventional extrapolations of trends are useless.

Nothing could have seemed stronger than the land-energy-minerals boom of the 1970s, and yet a slackening of the global economy's appetite for commodities blew away that trend. The West's current trend to recreation- and lifestyle-based economies and cultures could be decimated even more easily.

Nevertheless, I have a prediction, or at least a guess, based on the staying power of small Western communities. I believe they will change in order to preserve their cohesiveness, their extended families, and their traditional, conservative values. The survival of those hundred-year-old values will require almost the opposite of what was required in the past. Now those values call for an emphasis on education and close contacts with the outside world. The new concern with marketing among farmers and ranchers recognizes the importance of links to the outside world. Of course, not everyone in agriculture has recognized the importance of marketing — only the survivors have.

In the same way, the surviving towns will turn to education and to links to the larger world. Those towns won't give up the pleasures of Friday night basketball and football games, but instead of being ends in themselves, as they are now, they will be seen as adjuncts to academic achievement. Rural Westerners will recognize that telecommunications, facsimile machines, satellite dishes, Federal Express, and computers have opened rural areas to the kinds of work that formerly could be done only in metropolitan areas. Education and technical skills, once a passport out of small towns, will now be seen as a way for a small community to keep some of its youngsters at home.

It is, of course, almost a cliché to predict an economic future for rural areas based on modern communications. But if the West is to survive as a rural region with a rural culture, there must be more than subdivisions of electronic cottages, tourist resorts, and retirement villages. Some extraction — hopefully less destructive extraction — will continue. But my hope and expectation is that the new rural economy will be based on reclamation and restoration. The damage or neglect of the past century will be healed by communities that sit among the ruins created by the last century of mining, milling, logging, and agriculture. My expectation, and prayer, is that over the next century, forests will be deroaded, dams will be dismantled or operated so as to preserve streams and rivers rather that destroy them, mine sites will be reclaimed, and acidic streams will be restored to health. Such work will do a great deal for the Western landscape. But it will do more for Western communities. Anyone can take a watch apart, as the history of the West shows. It takes very different individuals and a very different society to put a watch together. The latter requires patience, understanding, respect for the original watchmaker, and humility.

To accomplish reclamation and restoration will require deep changes in the West: different schools, different social institutions, different media. Those changes will not come automatically out of a wish list. But they will develop as the region changes and adapts to new times. I see the signs of change not in large events, but in the same kinds of small events I discussed in the first part of my talk. The major danger is that the commodities (coal, uranium, oil shale, et al.) will boom before the West has set itself firmly on the path to reclamation and restoration. If that happens, the West will again sacrifice its landscape and sky to provide jobs for the young people whose basic attitudes toward education were shaped during the boom. But each year that passes with low commodity prices, and with an economically straitened federal government unable to sprinkle dams and subsidized logging on the West, encourages change.

For its first century, European settlement in the rural West has transformed the scenery to match a society that had its strengths, but that was also weak and destructive in many ways. Now, thanks to global economic events over which the West has no control, the region is being encouraged to transform itself and create a society that will want to restore what has been damaged.

Edwin H. Marston

REGIONALISM AND THE WESTERN
UNIVERSITY

I want to speak briefly about regionalism and the western university — not in any parochial sense, but because I believe that weaving a strong regional thread into the curricular and research fabric of our universities is both intellectually appropriate and necessary to fulfill the university's role in society. I intend to focus on the West, but I think the principles I will address are applicable to higher education in other regions of the country as well.

This is a fascinating topic to me. I confess to being a water lawyer — a Colorado water lawyer, the most fervent of the species, at that — and I have spent the last twenty years of my academic life studying the allocation and use of the water resource. Arguably, there has been no greater influence on the development of the West than water, or the absence of it. Walter Prescott Webb, in defining *his* West, emphasized the cultural and institutional impact of crossing the geographic barrier from the humid to the semiarid, into the region where one feels, in Wallace Stegner's words, "[a] dryness in the nostrils, a cracking of the lips, a transparent crystalline quality of the light . . ."[5]

My own experience in the study of water-resource allocation, and the law in general, has led me to the conclusion that the law curriculum is one obvious area where emphasis on Western legal problems and principles is entirely appropriate. This subject has been capably discussed elsewhere and I don't want to dwell on it today. My colleague Charles Wilkinson has begun to explore in depth the law of the American West, and David Getches gave an excellent paper to the Mid-Continent Association of Law Schools in 1988 entitled "Putting a Western Brand on Legal Education." David suggested that courses dealing with distinctively Western issues — water law, federal public land law, Indian law, and mining law are notable examples — are appropriate to the curriculum and that cases dealing with Western issues can be used in more traditional courses. He noted that Western law "has an essential ingredient that lends it curricular legitimacy. The ingredient is a richness in its issues that calls for rigorous analysis and which demonstrates the synthesis and interaction of a variety of basic subjects." He also made the crucial point that emphasizing Western law "does not mean consciously leaving weaknesses in other areas but it does mean special concentration and institutional commitment that can spawn excellence, reputation and notable scholarship in a chosen field."[6]

I want to expand on that point today by observing that the fertility of Western regional subject matter does not cease with the law. It encompasses many subjects that cross the entire spectrum of the university curriculum.

Let me turn, as an example, to that much-maligned subject, historically suffering from the slights of regionalism, Western literature — the literature focusing on the West and its distinctive human characteristics: individualism, self-reliance, grit, the sense of oneness with the land. In fact, there have been numerous major Western writers, among them A. B. Guthrie Jr., Willa Cather, John Steinbeck, Frank Waters, and Wallace Stegner. Further, there is a whole new generation of Western writers hard at work today. This vigorous, multifaceted body of literature has been built by novelists such as Leslie Marmon Silko, Edward Abbey, John Nichols, James Welch, and Rudolpho Anaya, and by essayists such as John McPhee, Gretel Ehrlich, and Bruce Brown.

Professor Paul Bryant of Colorado State University, who himself has taught a course in Western literature, has observed that "the study of the West in American literature offers significant insights into the whole of American culture," and noted that Western ideas can be used to examine the viewpoints of society at large, as in the use of *The Ox-Bow Incident* to discuss the role played by the tests of masculinity in contemporary society.[7] The entire effect of Western ideas on modern American culture is an important area of inquiry.

In Western literature, at least in the Southwest, we have a bicultural literary tradition — Anglo and Hispanic. Universities need to celebrate that fact or we will, in the words of Professor Phillip Ortego, "deprive not only millions of Mexican Americans of their literary birthright but deprive millions of Anglo-Americans of a literary birthright that is naturally theirs too."[8]

We can also note the strong bond between Western writing and the physical environment — perhaps the West's most striking quality and a common thread throughout virtually all of Western writing. How often in Western literature we see the characters of the story adapting to, or succumbing to, the physical challenges, be they mountains, deserts, or the great distances and their corresponding solitudes. This has led Western writing to be a particularly apt vehicle for the embodiment of environmental issues, as Abbey's *The Monkey Wrench Gang* well illustrates. This point, incidentally, has been sensitively explored by Professor Fred Erisman of Texas Christian University in a 1979 paper before the annual meeting of the National Council of Teachers of English.[9]

Surely the accommodation of new ways of thinking by old culture patterns, characteristic of the development of the West, has application for much of what humankind faces today around the globe. If my friends in the literary world are correct in believing that the modern West is producing some of the world's best writing, then we ought to capitalize on it and infuse it into our curriculum.

The same comments could be made of Western art. Of particular interest is not only the way Western artists view other parts of the country, but the way these artists have taken forward historical forms, especially pottery, in a manner that celebrates traditional cultures yet is, in its very essence, contemporary. Rick Dillingham, the historian, collector, artist, and potter from Santa Fe, and the great contemporary Hopi potter Al Qöyawayma of Phoenix, exemplify this tradition. It is not narrow parochial thinking to focus on these developments in the world of art. Rather, a great Western university ought to celebrate the distinctive artistic achievements of Western artists by making the study of them a central part of the university's vision.

Let me also make reference to history. The history of the West has long been seen as a stepchild of American history. That is wrong. The history of the American West is rife with fascinating events and personalities and is jam-packed with intellectual content. This applies both to the historical and contemporary West, a point demonstrated by the scholarship of two of the nation's first-rate historians, the late Robert Athearn and Patricia Nelson Limerick. The University of Colorado has been proud to have both of them on its faculty, and our university has long been a leader in the study of this region's history. Nevertheless, we can do still better at the task of exploring the many aspects of this challenging body of thought.

Finally, we have the most dominant yet overlooked contributor to the American West — the Indian. One might comment not only on the Indians' contributions, but also on the distinctive relationship over time of the tribal cultures to the culture of the American West. Universities must play a special role not only in celebrating — as we should with all cultures in the region — but in illuminating for non-Indians the sovereign governmental status of Indian tribes, and the richness of the history, language, customs, and philosophy of the Indian. The university's role in exploring and articulating the wealth of American Indian culture, especially as it is seen by Indian people themselves, has gone unrealized for far too long.

In a recent issue of the *University of Colorado Law Review*, you can find a poetic and exciting article by Charles Wilkinson, "Law and the American West: The Search for an Ethic of Place" — an ethic Charles describes as "founded on the worth of the subcultures of the West and [which] thereby promotes the diversity that is the lifeblood of the region."[10] Surely the public universities should be major players in this search, and not just in those subjects that I have touched upon, but in all of the areas of the academic landscape where the human spirit, character, and experience are being examined — history, philosophy, sociology, art, psychology, law, journalism, geography. The list could go on and on; all of these topics are part and parcel of the university mission of research and teaching. It has always struck me as somewhat peculiar that "service to the community" is listed, along with teaching and scholarship, as a distinct category of institutional activity. In my view, these are not separate things. Rather, creative inquiry and teaching — the discovery and dissemination of the knowledge that guides the human condition — represent the fundamental "service" that universities provide: the enrichment of the societies that support them.

Our Western society calls out for a celebration of its distinctive contribution to American culture. By responding, the Western university will not, as some fear, diminish itself. Rather, the university community will seize the most promising chance of reaching its fullest potential.

James N. Corbridge, Jr.

FREEDOM COMES FROM PEOPLE,
NOT PLACE

In his essay, Mayor Kemmis has set out to find the source of America's moral and physical strength, and he locates it in the West. His argument is based on two assumptions and draws on the most powerful of our nation's myths. The first assumption is that America is democratic and serves as a beacon of democracy and freedom to the rest of the world. The second is that Americans share values and interests. To support these assumptions, Mayor Kemmis draws on a variety of national myths. He uses words with deep symbolic meaning to Americans.

First, there is the myth of the rugged individual going into the wilderness, the frontier — an empty wasteland waiting to be trained — and making a place for oneself. The image is essentially a male image. So the myth is of a rugged individual going into the frontier and in the process recreating democracy and becoming tougher and being made physically stronger by the environment. Second there is the myth that Americans have a divine mission to create a perfect society, a city on the hill. Phrases full of symbolism give power to these myths, phrases like "rugged individualism," "democracy," "freedom," and "liberty."

The West of Mayor Kemmis is not the West I know. Nor is it the West of my people — Hispanos, that is, mulattos, mestizos, African slaves, and European Spaniards, who settled in what is now New Mexico in 1598, before the Pilgrims landed at Plymouth. Nor is it the West of Indian peoples who were in the region twenty-five to fifty thousand years ago. Instead, it is a West unformed by the myth of a city on a hill, Anglo-Saxon, Protestant, and free — that is, free from government and church meddling in the pursuit of economic gain. The West I know, the United States I know, is where large groups of people have been and continue to be disenfranchised on the basis of their race, their gender, and their language. If a democracy is a government in which ultimate political authority is invested in the people, and which includes the concepts of individualism, liberty, equality, and fraternity, then we have some work to do before we can hold ourselves up as a beacon to anyone.

The changes taking place in Eastern Europe, namely the creation of a market economy under socialism, have more to do with the disruptive power of capitalism than they do with democracy as it is expressed in the United States. The momentous changes taking place in Eastern Europe also include a rise in anti-Semitism and a restriction of the rights of women and of minorities. While some Eastern European countries are extending greater freedoms to some groups, the U.S. government continues to support the repressive governments in El Salvador and Guatemala, and U.S. troops have killed civilians, most of whom are women and children, but also civilian men. In the United States, our concepts of democracy, freedom, and shared values of members of small communities tied to the land — from which they recreate themselves — obscure, hide, erase those who don't fit into this model, who don't fit into this myth. Athens, after all, was a democracy based on slavery. I argue that the danger to democracy is not consumerism but the continued use and legitimation of national myths that obscure and redescribe oppression of women, people of color, gays, and dissenters, so that this kind of oppression will fit into the mythical views and goals of those early English colonists. John Winthrop said "we shall be as a City upon a Hill, the eyes of all people are upon us."[11] But he also said that he knew a woman who had become mentally ill from reading too many books. For, he added, if she had attended to her household affairs and such things as belonged to women, and not gone out of her way to meddle in such things as are proper for men, she would have kept her wits. Apparently Winthrop believed that the last, best place for women was the kitchen.

I agree with Mayor Kemmis that the world spirit is alive in Western valleys, but it is alive in people, and not a place; in the white settlers, women, men, children, who created a life for themselves with hard work; in Mexicano, migrant farm-workers in the beet fields of Colorado; in Hispano and Eastern European miners; in Central Americans in the Los Angeles garment district; in Indian peoples throughout their land, struggling to survive European concepts of democracy and freedom; in Southeast Asian immigrants and in African-Spanish and African-American settlers. If hardship is possibility, then it is in these people and their continuing hardship, as Herbert Marcuse argued thirty years ago, where those powerful concepts of freedom and democracy might finally be realized.

Camille Guerin-Gonzalez

THE LANDS, NATURAL RESOURCES, AND ECONOMY OF THE WEST

This is about public lands. I do not believe in the assigned topic — the West as a discrete political or cultural entity. Public lands may be the only thing that makes the West coherent or distinctive. I'm going to make a few rather sparse arguments about process and participants in public-land policy decision making. Both are changing in ways that are interesting and, in my opinion, likely to endure.

I will paint a broad picture rather than try to prove a piddling little one. I also will not refuse to say something interesting and perhaps true just because I cannot find a footnote for it.

My first point is that public-lands management issues are likely to continue to be less and less important as national issues and as the focus of national attention and debate. Second, I will argue that this change will leave the field clear for increasingly effective participation and control by state and local officials. Finally, I argue that this will be especially important to watch when related to my third point about change in local participants: Key groups are changing in their priorities and importance in the process.

I will conclude with two thoughts, one about issues that will be caught in this changing maw and one about the importance for all this of continuing advocacy about public-lands decision making.

Before I start on that, however, I wish to express some general reservations about the assigned task. I am not sure that I believe in the American West. Surely it exists as a direction for travel. And clearly we learn something about ourselves that is important — or at least remarkable (in the sense of "worth remarking about") — when we say "out West" as opposed to "back East." It is fun and educational to explore what that might mean. However, it does not establish the legitimacy of the construct "West" as a source of visions to guide a shared future. In the brochure that described this symposium, we find that the disparate subgroups that make up the American West were challenged to "put aside their differences and pull together so that the region can build a society to match its scenery." This suggests that our scenery somehow translates into a common political agenda. That makes me very cranky.

As a political scientist, I am genuinely annoyed by people urging subgroups to give up their priorities to embrace somebody else's. At best, the exhortation is unrealistic. At worst, it makes me want to warn all subgroup members to keep their hands on their wallets. Differences are the essence of diversity. We cannot talk about the American West without recognizing the legitimacy of both. Period.

I also get grumpy about the "pull together" motif because I have spent a long time trying to ferret out or imagine a common agenda for the region. I do not find one. Even during the Sagebrush Rebellion, which was a period in which public assertion of an integrated Western strategy was at a peculiarly high pitch, it was not possible to find *any* issue that consistently or even suggestively united the West as a region *and/or* (both are important) consistently or even suggestively distinguished this alleged region from any other.

I am not going to throw a whole bunch of footnotes at you, but you might be interested in the literature of political regionalism. The data are full of anecdotes about local color but precious few indications that region matters to policy except for some slight hint in the deep South. Both the rule and the slight exception ought to interest us intellectually and morally — if that is the root of American regionalism, do we want to beef it up?

Finally, I should confess that I am not a Westerner. I have lived for extended periods of my life in New York City and environs, upper New York state, Boston, North Carolina, Michigan, and most recently Berkeley, California. Even if California is acceptable as a part of the Western region — and there has been considerable doubt expressed on that topic — one will probably not want to include Berkeley.

Given my questionable heritage, it is perhaps understandable that I do not find Western scenery to be a unique spiritual or political force. With the arguable exception of New York City, every place I have lived is surrounded by scenery. Characteristic scenery, wonderful scenery, which may be different from Western scenery, but which is cherished by the natives, including a significant number who define themselves and their lives, in part at least, in relation to their geo-emotional (or whatever) setting. I have just spent a week in Vermont and the week before that on the road between Socorro and Santa Fe, New Mexico. In many dimensions, there is less difference between the two regions than you might think. I do not deny that the concept of the American West is an important marketing device that can be used, inter alia, to sell high-heeled, pointy-toed shoes, not to women but to males from Los Angeles. That is not all bad. De Witt John, featured in the first of *High Country News*'s recent series on this general issue, has been convincing for as long as I have known him that selling cowboyness and scenery is a viable economic option. But it is not clearly a culture, it does not define or distinguish a society, and, most centrally, it does not define a basis for political unity or a common political action.

I am looking for the basis of a shared and/or distinctive political agenda and I do not see it. Hence, I am not sure that this conversation has a real subject. However, other equally insightful folks do not share my qualms, so let me speak my piece.

My point — that public-lands management issues are likely to continue to be less and less important as topics of national attention, and that state officials and evolving local groups will play a larger and more decisive role in decision making — is, you may readily observe, actually three points: one regarding the scope and intensity of attention to public-lands issues; one regarding the level of decision making; and one regarding local advocacy.

Regarding the first, I note that public lands have been receding from the center of the national stage for most of a century. Let me point at a few carefully selected generalizations from history to support that observation.

Public lands were, for much of our first century as a nation, the dominant, if not the only, national public issue. Those who have attended even briefly to the period in which the Articles of Confederation, the General Land Ordnance, and then the federal Constitution were drafted and acceded to know that title to and authority over the Western public lands — which at that time were basically confined to the area between the Appalachians and the Mississippi — were *the* major issues of nationhood and governance. It is probably only a slight overstatement to argue that virtually every issue of trade, fiscal policy, and industry, among others, was discussed in the context of the public lands. The public lands were everything, the cauldron in which all the major issues were manifest and fought out.

They are not any more.

This is true in spite of what may appear to have been two decades in which the public lands were major political issues. There is no doubt that they were issues. But we are, I am arguing, in the winding-down phase of a slight burst of national concern with the environment and, by a clear extension, the public lands. That burst was real and important. Indeed, I think that it is fair to say that the wilderness/aesthetic-preservation movement, which is directly related to the public lands, was a key wedge in opening the American consciousness to the environmental decade of the 1970s. Further, wilderness was and will likely continue to be an ideal entry-level issue of immense pedagogical value in arousing upper middle-class white kids to concern for "the environment."All of that is true. Further, it is to a large extent what we have done with our lives. But it costs us in perspective on the history of the public lands.

We who have lived through or come of age during the last twenty years are in a remarkably poor place for realizing that we are in fact experiencing the tail end of a peculiar blip, or for understanding that our blip is a rare and much-diminished period of nationwide attention to public lands.

To demonstrate the argument that national attention to the Western public lands manifest in the last several years has been a blip in what is clearly a long-term removal of the public lands from the center of the nation's political, economic, and psychic stage, I will point to the evolution of the revenue programs associated with those lands. I believe that in those programs you can clearly see a pattern evolve and then dissolve. At first, old states were willing to bribe new states to go along with meeting old states' priorities on public lands. As new states became more numerous, the bribes got bigger. But then, as the new states began to become old states, the configuration shifted to East versus West or public domain versus non–public domain states. Eastern demands clar-ified — in the form of land reservations — and the bribes became bigger still. Witness the 90 percent of gross revenues that were dedicated to the Western states in the Mineral Lands Leasing Act of 1920.

What I am leading up to here is that in the last several decades, Eastern states have been increasingly unwilling to bribe Western states with receipt-sharing programs. The 1976 PILTs (payments in lieu of taxes) Act is national in scope. All the states are defined as having public lands, which allows all the states to benefit. Current efforts to undo old decisions — to shift the basis of receipt-sharing payments to net rather than gross revenues, for example — can be understood, if I am correct, as a sign that the Eastern states are less interested than in times past in achieving their own goals on the public lands and want some of the money back to reconstruct their own deteriorating infrastructure. Hence, a small data point to support the argument that the Eastern states are no longer so interested in Eastern priorities for Western public lands that they are willing to pay to achieve them. Indeed, just the opposite. For all these reasons, I am arguing, the federal government will recede. It will not disappear overnight — or ever — from the management of Western federal lands. But it will leave greater and greater room for state and local decision making and priorities to be expressed on the land.

My point is that if and when the lands come up for discussion, they come up as lands and resources, not as the linchpin of American life. Thus, I am arguing, we as a nation care less and less even in that very diminished and constrained context. Having "proved" that point, let me make my second point, about the level of decision making regarding public lands.

Curiously, during most of the period when the interest in the lands was national in scope, much of what we now consider *the* key decisions, that is, the decisions about access to and "management of" the lands, were made at the state and local levels or by coalitions of states acting in Congress. For much of the nineteenth century and for a surprising extent in the twentieth century, it was not consistently clear that the federal government had authority to do much about the Western lands. Even if it had authority, it was perfectly clear that the central government had neither the will nor the wherewithal to act on it. Many major resource management and allocation programs were developed by and continue to be state undertakings (for example, oil and gas conservation, wildlife management, water allocation).

That position of state primacy has been concealed from current view by another trend that I am arguing is now ending: the centralization and domination of the decision making by federal agencies, instrumentalities, and priorities. That trend — which we usually relate to the New Deal but which, like everything that grows, has roots that are deep — is also ending, at least as regards the public lands. The reasons for what I am presenting as a decline in federal control over public lands are numerous, complex, and obviously related to decline in the nation's interest in the lands. They also are related to a decline in discretionary federal funds and a staggering growth in the efficacy of state and local government, in the West and elsewhere. These are generic points applicable to many familiar discussions. I will not bore you with the details. I will belabor two other points that may be more interesting in this setting.

First, if the West is not a myth, I want to try to convince you that "the federal lands" are. This will, I argue, contribute to increasing state control. My argument has two prongs. The first is a physical reality, what I have recently been calling "the myth of the green blob." Lots of people seem to have the idea that the federal public lands exist out there as contiguous entities about which the federal managers can make decisions. While occasionally that is true, the dominant and more problematic reality is that federal lands are chopped up, interspersed among a diverse mixture of state, private and other federal lands. Frequently, chopping is vertical — that is, the government may own only the surface or the subsurface values, while another owner owns the other. The federal government cannot make decisions about its little fiefdom without regard for what the other owners are doing. It is almost always true, for example, that an oil, gas, or coal lessee must laboriously assemble hundreds of property rights, including diverse federal leases, in order to operate. The myriad access problems are only the currently most apparent manifestation of this important but easy-to-overlook fact.

This green-blob myth also has a legal dimension. It is frequently assumed that the federal government has authority to manage absolutely where it owns the land. The facts are otherwise. I have already referred to water, oil, and gas conservation, and wildlife programs that are and always have been essentially state operations. The environmental programs of the 1970s add another dimension to this division of authority. The Forest Service, for example, is not authorized, funded, staffed, or sufficiently skilled to manage air, water, toxic clean-up and other environmental protection programs.

Discount my words if you must in light of the fact that I am a known *Granite Rock* fetishist — and one of the particularly dangerous California brand at that. Nevertheless, my position is that even if Supreme Court Justice Antonin Scalia and his merry band preempt the state environmental programs, they will not prevent the duplication in programs which so anguished Justice Lewis Powell; rather, they will create vacuums that the federal government will not be able to fill on the federal lands. This is because they have no specific authority to do so, and, understandably, no motivation to add staff to undertake the programs in these trying budgetary times.

Perhaps you believe in both the West and the green blob. My second point concerning the probable rise in state authority over public lands is one we can hopefully all agree on. The federal government's ability to dominate in land-management decisions is threatened by the fact that it does not know what it is doing. This does not distinguish it from anybody else — nobody has a sound technical basis for the kind of land-management decisions that the federal agencies glibly assure us they are qualified to make. But as that fact becomes more and more obvious in the planning process, the local interests will prevail in a more and more explicitly political arena. That is the argument I am making at any rate.

By saying the federal government does not know what it is doing, I do not mean that the agencies are dumb or have sold out to the cattle, minerals or timber industry. I see nothing that sinister. My point is

simply that we do not have the knowledge to do multiple-use land
management. Let me illustrate by referring to the Below Cost Timber
Sale issue. The contention was that the Forest Service spends more to
put together timber sales than it gets in receipts from those sales. That
ultimately turned out to be a dud intellectually as far as I am concerned.
At bottom it was an argument between two standard approaches to
accounting, with each side distorting different inadequacies in the data
to make its points.

What lingers in my mind as interesting about that dustup is that we
cannot express relationships between and among different land uses in
the language that is simplest, least exacting, and easiest to measure,
trade off, and express: money. We cannot even do the easiest, idiot part
of the multiple-use analysis. We surely do not now and likely never will
understand complex, diverse ecological interactions with sufficient acu-
ity to predict and manipulate those ecosystems and their responses to
different management regimes and uses. We cannot, in fact, even moni-
tor the diverse impacts of what we already did. Not to put too fine a
point on it, but we cannot even agree post hoc on the consequences of
clear-cutting.

It is not clear to me what kind of policy tilt, if any, will result from
the shift from federal to state and local primacy. However, it is important that we think about the shift for numerous reasons, not the least of
which is that the state and local scene as regards federal lands and land
management is changing rapidly. Here I move to my third point about
changing local groups.

To make this point I am not going to bore you here with any variant
on the urbanizing Western scene. I think it is interesting to wonder what
"the West" means if, as has been suggested, it does not include the cities.
Cities in fact contain most Westerners and most of the economic and
political values that drive the rural lands interspersed. Nevertheless, I
will let that argument drift, briefly I hope, and make four other
observations.

First, I think that the state and local political scene will be altered
by a radical shift in the range livestock industry and its political
priorities. The range livestock industry as we know and love it — or
know and hate it — is dead as a result of changes in taste and economics.
I am not one of those who believes that range chickens loom large in the
future economy of the nation, but range tourism and put-and-take
wildlife do. I have long believed that the range livestock industry, rather
than the timber industry has been by far the most controlling political
force in public-lands management. That group is in the process of
altering radically, and I think it matters and bears watching.

A second changed participant is the water crowd. One of the strange things about Bureau of Land Management and Forest Service politics is that since John Wesley Powell got shot down on his dam-site reservations in the late 1800s, the water folks have been noncentral players — and decreasingly important players — in the federal land-management agencies. That is changing dramatically. A hint of what is to come is found in the recent conjunction of reserved water rights and wilderness designations. I think we can all concede that this is a bit fluky and confined in its impact. However, when we start including water-related factors (such as water production and water drop) in the calculation of the value of alternate uses, and expressing the price of a tree in terms of the water it consumes while growing, the plot thickens. We can safely predict that water valuation promises some interesting alterations in management priorities.

Third, the economists are coming. This does not mean that economic or commodity uses are coming. It means that the notions and methods of economic analysis are finding unprecedented legitimacy in the public-lands field. Amenity advocates may protest, alleging that economics have always dominated. Perhaps so, but not economic analysis. The fact is that the economist is a new kid on the block and will alter the nature of the debate considerably.

Finally, I would like to point to changing demographics in the West. This leads in turn to changing definitions of efficiency and productivity. My perspective is narrow but perhaps useful. You can get your history on this point from the work of Pat West or Bill Dubuis or others who describe the Forest Service's preference for large, "efficient" producers of range livestock as opposed to the inefficient, communal production that characterizes the Hispanic community's use of the southwestern national forests. John Nichols's *The Milagro Beanfield War* is a less academic but equally valuable introduction to early years on this issue.

The current importance of the altering demographics for federal land management may be apparent now in litigation involving University of California agriculture programs. The University recently lost a suit to California Rural Legal Assistance (CRLA). The suit was premised on the assertion that the land-grant university has violated its authorizing statute by serving only one part of its potential constituency, to the exclusion and detriment of other California citizens. White, large-scale growers have been the exclusive target and beneficiary of Extension, Ag Experiment, and kindred programs. They are "efficient producers." Ostensibly less-efficient or less-important growers, farm workers, and a host of others are not part of the picture.

This whole structure is now subject to serious questioning and challenge. The CRLA suit has suggested that it is legally vulnerable. The whole movement around — here is another disgusting buzzword, this year's intellectual equivalent of the pasta machine — "sustainable agriculture" strongly suggests that it is technically vulnerable as well. Indeed, the whole notion of efficiency in production — even what constitutes productivity — is up for grabs. My point is that other people, other values, and other priorities have long existed at the margins of public-land management — which has been undeniably a festival of refreshment and upward mobility for whites, primarily of the male variety. This will change and may have profound effects in the direction I have tried to suggest.

Thus, we can readily see (as we say in academe) that my basic argument is correct: Public lands will be increasingly less important as a national issue, leaving the field to more effective state participants and altered interest groups.

Let me close with two only apparently unrelated points that I think ought to give you fuel for thinking about the policy tilt of these prognosticated changes.

First, what are the issues that will emerge in this new regime? I will point to three. First, to the extent that Congress pays attention to these questions at all, it will result in single-issue legislation. The 1990s, I am suggesting, will be more like the 1960s than the 1970s. There will be no mega-statutes like FLPMA and NFMA that seek to chart the future for the lands in their entirety. Rather, we will have, if anything, single-focus, one might say zoning, statutes. The Wilderness Act, the Trails Act, and the Wild and Scenic Rivers Act are appropriate reference points.

Second, I think that there will be intensified interest given to land consolidation and access. The state land managers' interest in this is obvious, critical, and long ignored. It will become dispositive, in my opinion. Finally, and this is more of an advocacy statement than a prediction of what will come based on what I have said, I hope that the Forest Service will finally gain authority to manage the minerals on National Forests. That they do not now have that authority is an historical anomaly that ought to be corrected.

My second closing observation is that I think advocacy regarding public-lands management will be and ought to be less central in decision making. It *ought to be* less important because the issues are basically resolved. I have a long paean that I occasionally deliver about the diminishing returns to advocacy. I will not bore you with the whole nine yards now. Basically, the argument is that we have accomplished so much of what needs to be done regarding balanced management of federal lands that I believe it is time to turn our attention to other issues that are less well defined and less adequately addressed.

I think this will happen whether we accede to the inevitable or not. Advocacy *will be* less important, in my opinion, because what will be central to outcomes is increasingly less likely to be subject to interest-group influence or preference.

I see myself focusing on major national and international trends rather than the specific preferences of groups or interests — demographics, institutional evolution at state and local levels, taste for beef, and so on. The most obvious one — which has not been referred to, so I will mention it here — is the weather. We allocated the Colorado River, as every schoolgirl knows, during the year of highest water flow since the birth of Christ. Similarly, I believe that we allocated water resources throughout the nation, and developed industrial, domestic, and agricultural consumption patterns, during a period of uncharacteristically mild, hospitable weather. With or without the greenhouse effect, any deviations back toward the meteorological mean will drive public resource management to a far greater degree than human will or purposeful activity. I think that is fine. Perhaps another blip of preoccupation will be necessary or appropriate in another lifetime. For now, we have more important things to do than bleat about the margins of public-lands policy and management. We have gotten quite good at that, but we are needed elsewhere.

Sally K. Fairfax

AN ETHIC OF PLACE:
THE ISSUE AT THE HEART OF ALL ELSE

I think there would be a certain amount of skepticism among tribes about the notion of disparate subcultures coming together and talking about our common future. It's been a lesson of American history and Western history that Indian tribes have been left out of that process. But in the last twenty years, particularly through the courts and through Congress, tribes have made tremendous strides in regaining their sovereignty and their resources and their cultures.

Whether people like it or not, tribal leaders and tribal issues have to be dealt with and have to be put on Western agendas. Tribal leaders, I think, enjoy this new status that they've found. But at the same time, they approach that still with a great amount of skepticism, realizing that it was barely thirty years ago that official policy in this country called for the termination of Indian tribes, elimination of Indian cultures and the assimilation of Indian people into the melting pot. That memory is very, very fresh in the minds of Native American people. I think that even though we may be at the table, we come there with a great deal of skepticism. At the same time, if we can survive that process, I have a great amount of optimism about what may be ahead of us. I think that the enlightened Western leaders, both Indian and non-Indian, foresee a future in the West that includes Indian people, that includes Indian tribes. Again, this is something that is fairly new. It wasn't very long ago that Indian people were seen as vanishing Americans, and there were no plans for us because we were not visible on the political landscape at all.

The tribes do come to the table with, I think, a lot to offer. We're talking about land, natural resources, and economies. Tribes control 3 percent of the land in this country still. They have substantial treaty rights to large amounts of fish, timber, and energy resources, among other things. Tribal leaders, now that their sovereignty has been recognized and fortified more and more, are taking on the responsibilities that political leaders have to shoulder in terms of developing tribal economies. Everybody knows that our people, as people who socially and economically are at the bottom of the heap, need that desperately.

As tribal leaders approach that challenge, the issue of public lands in the West is going to become increasingly important because it raises the same kinds of questions that tribal leaders face when they go about using their newly fortified governmental authority over resources that are now firmly in their control. What's to be done with these resources? What's to be done about the need for economic development, the need for jobs for people? The kinds of questions that tribal leaders face are the same kinds of questions that other Western governmental leaders are going to face. The basic question about public lands and the broader question for all of us that is epitomized by the environmental movement is: How much do we develop? How much of our resources do we use now, for us, for this generation, and how much do we save, and how do we preserve it for future generations? This battle is fought, for better or for worse, largely through the discussion and resolution of issues involving public lands.

These issues are very dear to tribal people because they go right to the questions of our very existence. There are religions that we have. Something that is central to all Indian religions is the basic relationship between man and the land, the environment. These are the same kinds of issues that, when we come down to it, encompass a big part of the dialogue that we are having in this symposium, because the West, more than any other place, is concerned with the ethic of place — the issue that is at the heart of everything.

John E. Echohawk

PART SIX

Creating a Geography of Hope

CENTENARY SEQUENCE FOR
THE DREAMERS

(selected passages)

Knowing depravity from Calvin
old Marc Whitman must have
died smiling, as a
jagged Cayuse hatchet jellied
his relentless brain . . . One
hundred years prove
he didn't smile
in vain. This happy
valley reeks with God's
inexorable plan, his
grace: here
Whitman came with
Calvin's god and small
pox malignantly in
hand; with Augustine's heart
burnt cork he smeared
alien stone
age souls, he
dipped their well
pocked bodies in this
valley's many waters — at
Walla Walla vestigial un-
elected savages atoned
grim souled Swiss or
rare Babylonian
sins . . .

Waiilatpu, place of
rye grass, once
ground for this
valley's native councils,
now it honors
Whitman, his
mission and his
kin. His hilltop
monument tapers to the
sky — a finger gesturing
abuse, enshrined, officiously
fenced in. Down
the hill, across
a road, beyond
the mission's old
foundations, a rutted creek
bed commends the Nez Perce,
Walla Walla and
Cayuse, drained long
since and dead . . .

It is the soul of things the thing's soul
whatever it may be the soul of
we must discover. And can. There are
arguments in history worth hearing.
We do what we can, though some say *must* and others
will. Nonetheless, we do. And poetry
among them is not much. We may agree
on that. Yet, as the Dr. said, every
day we die for lack of what is found
there. True, the state of gods is not what
it was . . . Likewise authority, and magicians
among us now are entertainers. Still
one quite lately says, "I am not
an entertainer," putting us on our mettle.
It is hard work for us, this talking . . . like
heavy lifting it buzzes in our heads . . .
too heavy lifting every day, said Yellow Wolf . . .

[Smoholla the Dreamers' Song]

My young men shall never work
For men who work can never dream
My young men shall never work
For men who work can never dream
And wisdom comes to us in dreams
And wisdom comes to us in dreams

Among us those who choose. As we step
up to the bar, the barkeep, resplendent in
his handlebar mustache, his sleeves bloused
by red silk garters, or sometimes sporting black
robes and judicial airs, the barkeep,
always affable and adroit, smiling
says, *All right, Gents, name your poison.*
And smiling back, we choose. Graciously
we toss the man a tip. *Buy yourself
a drink*, we say. He deftly scoops the spinning
coin from midair and tests its purity
against his teeth. His teeth indent the soft
rich gold. Smiling, he pockets the coin. The truth
is this: *he doesn't drink*, he only pours . . .
As if, said Joseph, *a man should come to me
and say, I like your horses, I want to buy them.
I say No, my horses suit me, I will
not sell. He goes to my neighbor and says, Joseph
has good horses . . . I want to buy them but
he will not sell. My neighbor answers, Pay me
the money, and I will sell you Joseph's horses.*
Affable and adroit the barkeep changes
guise . . . but, in whatever guise he goes
his sleeves are bloused for business. So, we choose.
And yet, we drink precisely what he pours.
Clever Lawyer, changes guise, and learns
to mix a drink. . . . He was a man, as one
might say, of exquisite understanding, one
who was a Christian, one who learned the laws . . .

Is the story, then, too simple
for our own exquisite tastes? We
speak not here of noble
savages nor of their romance. This
story, though often told, has been projected
so transpicuous its plot must thicken
into mush. And it is after all
the lucid soul of things the
thing's soul whatever
it may be the soul of
we must discover. And can.
For matters of art, like life, are
matters of execution, and if
we would have the cause we
must go back. There
are arguments in history worth hearing . . .

If after suffering we would not be purged
we must go back, declining
ancient draughts and bromides
we vulgarians who came to conquer
and stayed to learn, remember it? as we were taught
the critics of it, Gibbon even, smug
and securely . . . Mediterranean,
we must go back
       to?
       O Brave New World!
       Elizabeth and Isabella picking up the pieces
   of empire . . .
               •

handing them to the fathers . . . Adams, remember it?
praising Athens and Rome, *powers* he called them,
for having "honored our species
more than all the rest . . ." Meanwhile
George Washington, throwing a silver dollar west
across the Potomac, winked and said, shrewdly,
"Stay out of foreign wars . . ."
"By which he meant," said Quincy, a chip
off the old block any way you chisel,
"It seems the very will of *Providence*
that this entire continent be inhabited
by one people, but, since *Providence* (*God* wouldn't

melt in his empirical mouth) helps those
who help themselves, by all means stay
out of foreign wars . . . let's
keep our eye on the ball . . ."
> *I have done nothing*
> *for their teaching, these*
> *savages, they will not*
> *listen and prate of the land*
> *our mission tithes from them . . .*
> *and of the pox . . .*
> *They are diseased*
> *and the hand of Providence*
> *removes them to give place*
> *to a people more worthy*
> *of this fertile country . . .*
So Spaulding, Whitman . . . which? the barkeep
everywhere adroit conducts the Hallelujah
chorus, making the world safe for Providence
& Enterprise, Ltd., bigger
than the Hanseatic League Rothschilds Krupp or
Caesar himself Grandaddy to General
Motors the great neo-Platonic synthesis
of God and man
in a Rube Goldberg Whirlygig
raising Commerce from the muck
of its own jackboots
to sit with Him hip by haunch blowing
the very Will of Providence blood
rushing to His obelisk stone hard
with Destiny and Determination most
tremendous tool — opposable thumb and mathematics
notwithstanding — in the pornographic history
of the west. "And say what you will,"
said Buffalo Bill adjusting Joseph's bonnet
in the Hippodrome, "the Big Boy
sure knows how to use it . . ."

> "There,"
says the Voice of America, "*that* ought to hold
the little bastards," and it does it holds us
we love it absolutely
love it . . .

(this diatribe in fact brought to you
by a grant from Exxon simulcast with "Revelooshunairey
Revels"
rock opera starring Marx Lenin
Trotsky Mao Castro and Sun Yat-sen, the
Castrati Chorale, brought to you uninterrupted
because
there is nothing absolutely
nothing to fear)

In Dakotah the Standing Bears the Kicking Birds
the Young-Men-Afraid-of-their-Horses lie down,
alone, where the great plains
slope to rivers — Big Horn, Musselshell, Missouri . . .
And all around them
sky, sky and earth
and the creatures thereof . . . they are one
with the eagle and the mouse
among the hip-high grasses, here
where the great plains slope to rivers
they lie down, alone, at dusk
beneath the Moon-of-the-Geese-Gathering . . .

In the dreams they dream great
flights of geese wheel
in the morning light . . . their breasts gleam,
flashing black and silver
signals from above the rising autumn sun . . .
With each tremendous arcing turn,
like immense arrowheads in the sky,
from north and east and west, they come . . . ghostly
silent apparitions drawn inexorably
to the living wheel, in the Month
of the Gathering of the Geese . . .

When at last they wake
the young men wake to light
more splendid still
than aureoles of August moons, their
very act of waking, mediation,
so stunning is this canopy of arctic lights . . .

They lie still, wide-eyed
beneath basilica more brilliant
than the galaxies . . . Around them
neither owl nor coyote move,
caught by incandescence in
the arching ribs of rare Dakotah nights . . .
Here, where great plains slope
to rivers, are young men more graced
than in their birth . . . and wake
as if to silver geese auroral
in effulgent flight . . . here
where waters of the river stop,
giving back upon itself the sight
young men purify themselves to see,
light and light and light
climbing the holy arch of night . . .

Peter F. Michelson

A GEOGRAPHY OF HOPE

I once said in print that the West — and I mean the interior West of plains, mountains, and deserts — is the geography of hope, the native home of optimism, the youngest and freshest of America's regions, magnificently endowed and with the chance to become something unprecedented and unmatched in the world.

I was probably demonstrating my thesis while I expressed it. I was shaped by the West and have lived most of my life in it, and nothing would gratify me more than to see it, in all its subregions and subcultures, both prosperous and environmentally healthy, with a civilization to match its scenery. Whenever I return to the Rocky Mountain states where I am most at home, my native enthusiasm overcomes me, and I respond as unthinkingly as a salmon that swims past a river mouth and tastes the waters of its birth and feels an irresistible impulse, born I am sure of love, to turn inland in search of the stream where it was hatched.

But when I am thinking instead of throbbing, I remember what history and experience have taught me about the West's past, and what my eyes and nose and ears tell me about the West's present, and I become more cautious about the West's future. Too often, when it has been prosperous, it has been prosperous at the expense of its fragile environment, and its prosperity has been most unequally distributed among its citizens. Its civilization, still nascent, has too often degraded the natural habitat while exploiting it and drawing most of its character from it. So I curb my enthusiasm, I begin to quibble and qualify; I say yes, the West *is* the native home of hope, but there are varieties and degrees of hope, and the wrong kind, in excessive amounts, goes with human disappointment and environmental damage as bust goes with boom.

Historically, visionary expectation was a great energizer of the westward movement — as great, probably, as the sense of being part of a vast mythic adventure. But exaggerated, uninformed, unrealistic, greedy expectation has been a prescription for disaster that the West has carried to the corner drugstore too many times. Ghost towns and dust bowls, like motels, are Western inventions. All institutionalize transience, and transience has, outside Utah, inhibited the development of stable, rooted, Western communities and a shared history that takes in everything from the kindergarten to the graveyard, and involves all kinds and grades of people in the promise of continuance. I believe in the profound influence of places on people, and nobody could miss the effect of people on places. But there remains a doubt: Maybe a continuing cross-fertilization between people and places is not feasible in the West, or is feasible only between a damaged environment and a limited population. Maybe any stable society in the West is destined to be not merely mobile, but sparse.

The Western states do contain some deeply lived-in places, but they are scarcer in the West than elsewhere. Western places are newer, for one thing; for another, many of the people who established them came to pillage, or to work for pillagers, not to settle for life. When the pillaging was done, they moved on. The people who have replaced them are unrelated to the founders, and may be gone with the next bust. They are without history, in the sense that history and place are linked, and they often leave because the country cannot supply them with jobs or because they are themselves too restless to stay. They have no sense of community with their temporary abode; they haven't the shadow of a land ethic. Both of those take time to develop. And as another reason for mobility we should not forget that, however attractive the country surrounding the towns, Western towns themselves are not beauty spots usually, may not be worth living in on anything less than hardship pay.

What makes the West a difficult place to stay put in is aridity. Past and future, the West is a dry subject, and all sorts of social, economic, political, and psychological consequences flow from the fact of too little water.

Environmentally, other regions have been able to recover better than the West from the impact of our high-energy civilization. Vermont, for instance, is a rugged country with a rugged climate, but it *heals*. It wants to be trees. Clear-cut it, and it goes patiently and inevitably back to raspberry bushes and other browse, then to little Christmas trees and crowding stands of little maple, ash, beech, and birch saplings, and then, before you have quite noticed, to woods. The West, vast and magnificent, greatly various but with the abiding unity of too little water except in its northwest corner, has proved far more fragile and unforgiving. Damaged by human assaults on its resources, it is more likely to go to desertification than to restore itself.

Aridity has been a difficult fact for Americans to accept, and an even more difficult one to adapt to. For nearly the first half of the nineteenth century we avoided the dry country that Pike and Long had called the Great American Desert; but by the 1840s and 1850s we were pushing our agriculture onto the dry plains and trying to mythologize aridity out of existence by such hopeful delusions as that rain follows the plow, that settlement improves the climate. When that myth brought on much human misery and failure as well as much environmental damage, we tried to engineer aridity out of existence by damming and redirecting the rivers. (Most of the results of that plumbing job are still to come, but they are coming.) Or, as a plumbing variation, we robbed Peter to pay Paul: We stole the Owens Valley's water to make the subdivision of the San Fernando Valley richly profitable; we conducted water through the Rockies from the Western Slope to permit the urban sprawl of Denver.

Human ingenuity has been manipulating Western water for nearly a century, but all our ingenuity has not increased the amount of water or solved any of the secondary problems that lack of water creates. In 1878, a hundred and twelve years ago, John Wesley Powell in his *Report on the Lands of the Arid Region* warned that there was water enough in the West to supply only about a fifth of the land. Being a man of his time, though considerably ahead of it in many ways, he was thinking in agricultural terms, and the new survey and homestead laws that he proposed would have eased the difficulty of Western settlement. Congress, dominated by boosters and local patriots, ignored his proposals, and settlement went ahead by tradition, habit, mythology and greed instead of by observation and forethought.

Not even yet has it sunk into some heads that the supply of water is finite. We have water only from the time when it falls as rain or snow until it has flowed past us, above ground or below, to its final ocean or underground reservoir. We can hold it back and redirect it, but we cannot add one drop to its total supply. In fact, the evaporation rate in really dry country being as much as ten feet a year, we may lose almost as much of it by ponding it as we save by slowing it down.

Moreover, in the West, "using" generally means "using up." What we put to municipal or industrial use is not coming back into the rivers to be available for irrigation — or if it does, it comes back poisoned. What is used in irrigation largely evaporates, and any percentage that finds its way back into the rivers is increasingly laden with salts, fertilizers, and pesticides from the fields. And no matter what use you find for the water from a river, every acre-foot you take out leaves a lessened instream flow to sustain trout, salmon, herons, ducks, rafters, picnickers, skinny-dippers, or whoever else might find it useful. In

Colorado, as in some other Western states, you can literally dry up a stream if you have prior rights for some so-called "beneficial" purpose.

Aridity means more than inadequate rainfall. It means inadequate streams, lakes, and springs. It means underground water that replenishes itself more slowly than elsewhere. In some places the underground water is fossil water, irreplaceable within any human time frame. And surface and subsurface water are not two problems, but one.

Confronted by the facts of chronic shortage, the decreasing feasibility of more dams, and the oversubscription of rivers such as the Colorado, the boosters sometimes speak of "augmentation" and suggest ever-greater engineering projects, roughly comparable to the canals of Mars, to bring water down to the dry country from the Columbia or the Yukon, or tow it down as icebergs from Glacier Bay to let San Diegans flush their driveways and keep their lawns verdant.

Pipe dreams, arrogant pipe dreams. Why should we expect a desert to blossom? It has, or had until we began to tinker with it, its own intricately interdependent plant and animal species, including the creosote-ring clones that are the oldest living things on earth. The idea of making deserts blossom is something we inherited from Isaiah. It is an idea especially dear to the Mormons, and it has had remarkable short-term successes. But it is open to all sorts of questions when we look very far into the future. For financial and political reasons, more than for technical ones, there are limits to how freely we can move water from one watershed to another. There are ecological and (I would say) moral reasons why we shouldn't. As a Crow Indian friend of mine said about the coal in his country, "God put it there; that's a good place for it." Lots of things have learned to depend on the West's water in the places where it naturally occurs. It would become us to leave them their living space, because if we don't, we are taking chances with our own.

Sooner or later we must accept the limitations imposed by aridity, one of the principals of which is a restricted human population. Western growth has a lower ceiling than the boosters are willing to admit, and people in general, both those native to the West and those lured to it by hope or advertising, have so far not welcomed limitation any more eagerly than the boosters have. From very early on, the West has been a land of Cockaigne, an Indian Valley line where every day is payday, a Big Rock Candy Mountain where the bluebird sings to the lemonade springs and the little streams of alcohol come trickling down the rocks. Ordinary people, making it by guess and by God, or not quite making it, have always understood Western hardship, but they have been at least as susceptible to dreams as the ambitious and the greedy. The dream of the West is the dream of the New World extended into the present.

Everything that bloody and congested Europe ever hoped for seemed realizable in America, where there was free land for the stealing, where ideas as different as the Noble Savage and the Social Contract could blend with the Jeffersonian notion of the freehold yeoman farmer and be galvanized by the Manifest Destiny preached by Senator Thomas Hart Benton of Missouri, among others. Expectation flowered, hope became a vested right. Only in Western America, as Walter Webb pointed out, did the word "claim" acquire the meaning of a land entitlement.

And of course, justifying the hope and at first obscuring the consequences, there was the apparently infinite plenitude of the buffalo herds. There was the California Gold Rush, plus all the subsequent rushes, to consolidate our faith in something for nothing and harden our habit of mass trespass on the public domain. There was the lure of wildness that drew the mountain men and their modern avatars; there was the romantic myth of the self-reliant, chivalric cowboy, homemade by Frederic Remington and Owen Wister; there was the icon of the stalwart covered-wagon pioneer. The West will never live down all that mythology. A thousand years from now boys will probably be running away from the East and Midwest to pursue a dream that the Virginian, or Louis L'Amour, or John Wayne, or Ronald Reagan implanted in them.

Gaudy or humble, fixed on quick fabulous riches or freedom or security, the dream has had both its boosters and its suckers. Promotion of dreams has always been a thriving Western industry and been a foolproof fallback position for Western politicians. For more than a hundred years the West has been oversold as the Garden of the World.

William Gilpin was tooting the manifestly destinarian horn on the bank of Cherry Creek as early as 1858, all but foaming at the mouth over the opportunities available for the plucking in what he called the Central Gold Region. William Smythe, the John the Baptist of irrigation, sang a variant of the same song in the 1890s, and helped bring on the Newlands Act of 1902 that started the remaking (and undoing) of the West. In the 1920s Los Angeles real estate sharks lured the susceptible with the same tune of unlimited opportunity and indefinite capital appreciation. During the energy boom of the 1960s I heard Billings businessmen asserting, with awed conviction, that Billings could become as big as Denver. And in 1988 supporters of the since-repudiated Two Forks dam were predicting a population of four hundred thousand for the town of Aurora, Colorado. Growth is something that has always put a gleam in the eyes of Western boosters; but growth is exactly what the West does not need and cannot stand.

Sometimes it is hard to tell the boosters from the suckers. They may be the same people. There have been plenty of Western buccaneers of the Marcus Daley–George Hearst stamp, but many boosters have been deluded deluders, true believers, wishful thinkers, blindfold prophets, at once the agents, the beneficiaries, and the victims of the vast speculative real estate deal that is Western American history.

We are all to some extent guilty, and we have been narrowly culture-bound in our notions of property and progress. We have been indifferent or hostile to the "lesser breeds" that got in our way. We have been largely ignorant of the special conditions and limitations that any Western enterprise from a homestead to a strip mine must face. We have been careless of what we did to the land, whether we did it with a sodbuster plow or a dragline. Like other forms of communal guilt, our crimes against the land were not intentional, but they were just as real as if they had been. We plowed up buffalo grass that should never have been plowed, tore up mountains and left them pitted with shafts dangerous to walkers, leaking mineral poisons. We clear-cut the most and best of our forests, pumped out the underground water. With enormous federal subsidies designed to protect local jobs with sweetheart leases and permits, we have made semi-deserts out of some wonderful range and forest country, trying to assist a cattle industry that on its own has a most dubious future. We have created an agribusiness that is profitable, undemocratic, and likely to be short-lived, a business built on cheap subsidized water and a pool of dispossessed migrant labor. The mining industry that once raped the land has now, through the new cyanide heap process of extracting gold, become its poisoner. Ironically, what remains to us of the relatively undamaged West has been saved for us by the same feds who helped us half spoil the rest. Which does not prevent one kind of Westerner, generally the kind who has profited most from federal subsidies, from damning the feds whenever anything goes wrong.

I know that historical hope, energy, carelessness, and self-deception. I knew it before I could talk. My father practically invented it, though he qualified more as sucker than as booster, and profited accordingly.

He was a boomer from the age of fourteen, always on the lookout for the big chance, the ground floor, the inside track. As a youth he tried the Wisconsin and Minnesota woods but found only the migratory wage-slavery that has always been one payoff of the American dream. He tried professional baseball but wasn't quite good enough. In the

1890s he floated out to North Dakota on the tail end of the land rush, but found himself in the midst of a ten-year drought and ended up speculating in grain and running a blind pig. If you believe that the world owes you not merely a living but a bonanza, then restrictive laws are more a challenge than an inhibition.

When it began to be clear that Dakota's promises were indistinguishable from Siberian exile, my father dragged us, by then a family of four, out the migration route to the Northwest. His goal was Alaska, but again he was far too late: The Klondike rush was long over, most of the survivors had straggled back. For a while we ran a lunchroom in the Washington woods where now is the Seattle suburb of Redmond. The loggers finished cutting down the trees and left us among the stumps. By 1914 we were up in Saskatchewan, part of another land rush where for a change we *would* be in on the ground floor, and make a killing raising wheat.

In 1915 we plowed up a hundred acres or so of buffalo grass, and for a while we were a wheat farm. Then, because Saskatchewan is part of the arid West and we were in what we called Palliser's Triangle, the driest part of it, we became a tumbleweed patch and a dust bowl. Then we were on the road again, first to Montana, then to Utah, ultimately to California and Nevada. Rainbows flowered for my father in every sky he looked at; he was led by pillars of fire and cloud. In Salt Lake City he met some men who had a doodlebug that would reveal the presence of gold and silver in the earth, and as a consequence of that I still have in my safe-deposit box deeds to various square rods of Nevada gravel and mountainside that my father believed would one day make us rich.

While we waited for one of those bonanzas to materialize, he ran a gambling house in Reno, an occupation as symbolically right for him as for the West. And finally, like Clarence King and many another gambler no worse and no better, he died broke and friendless in a fleabag Western hotel. Out of his life I made a novel, *The Big Rock Candy Mountain,* my first and most heartfelt commentary on Western optimism and the common man's dream of something for nothing.

But, some will object, if the boosters promise too much and the suckers expect too much, should that make us knockers? In any human effort there will be risks and casualties. But obviously not everyone has failed in the West, or there wouldn't be 45 or 50 million people living there, the Pacific Coast would not be conurbia from Seattle to San Diego, and Denver, Salt Lake, Albuquerque, Phoenix, and Tucson would not be spreading like impetigo. If the West weren't a little in our favor, we wouldn't have survived it. What if Searchlight *is* dead, and Butte dying? Billings is going to be as big as Denver; and Aspen, Park City, Jackson, and Telluride are reborn as ski resorts and cultural centers.

True, many people live successfully in the West, and many of them could not be bribed to live elsewhere, and more keep coming. They come looking for opportunity, but also they come following the hopeful dream of escape from industrial civilization and its discontents. They want healthful space, clean air, sun, skiing, a vigorous outdoor life, access to mountain and desert wilderness, emancipation from the dirt, crime, and crowding of the cities.

True, modern communications have annihilated space and broken down the former isolation. Western towns and cities, those that haven't been overwhelmed by an oil or coal or uranium boom, have grown up. There are Boulders and Bozemans and Logans and Missoulas as well as Rock Springs's and Gillettes. In-migrants have sweetened the local cultural kitty. The National Endowment for the Arts and the National Endowment for the Humanities have brought art, theater, music, and dance to communities where in my childhood a box supper was a prime-time cultural event. Western writers have begun to learn their history and their geography, and are writing books that leave the myths to the horse operas, the movies, TV, and the politicians. A little city like Missoula becomes an authentic literary center. New Mexico, out of its multiple cultures, begins to produce Indian and Hispanic writers able to compete on a equal basis throughout the English-speaking world. Up to now, as I have noted elsewhere ad nauseam, Western literature has been pretty much a literature of movement, of the road. Now it shows occasional signs of growing out of deeply lived-in places and traditional cultural climates.

Western writers, it seems to me, are learning to use all their tools and explore their real possibilities. They can deal with both the sanctuary of towns on water and in shelter, and with that awesome space that surrounds them, and the mobility it enforces. That script says that the West is dynamic, hopeful, on the right road, assured of a rich future. But while many believe and adopt it, revisionist historians such as Earl Pomeroy, Howard Lamar, Donald Worster, and Patricia Limerick suggest another, reminding us of the history which, if we ignore it, we will be doomed to repeat.

For the Western past was not the triumphal march that the myths and the romantic chroniclers have made it. Not all of the advertised amenities of the dream are available to all Westerners now, nor were they ever. The mountain man's celebrated and colorful savagery involved a

kind of indentured wage-slavery, bad food, constant hardship, an un-
payable debt to the company, and the opportunity to die young. The
cattleman might live a baronial free life, but the cowboy, that symbol of
personal independence, was and is a hired man on horseback, working
long hours for low pay, his liberty the liberty to quit one job and take
another just as bad, his future in the hands of the chiropractors. The
miner, once the placers played out, had to move on or go to work for a
corporation — Anaconda or the Homestake or the Empire or the Silver
King — and what he found there swiftly brought on the Western
Federation of Miners, a militant and angry union unthinkable in the
mythic West of personal independence. The homesteader, having bet his
life against 160 acres of dry ground, fell back in confusion, or was
gooned off by cattle outfits claiming the range and controlling the water.
The Indians — and a lot of Westerners are Indians, as we sometimes
forget — were first robbed of their land and their living and then stuck
on a poor farm, where they still are, enjoying unemployment rates up to
60 percent and still waiting for the water due them under the Winters
Doctrine. And a very large number of Westerners, mostly Hispanic,
follow the crops as migrants, homeless and dispossessed and without what
the West used to call a Chinaman's chance of becoming free, independent, landholding farmers of the kind that Thomas Jefferson, the Homestead Act, and the Newlands Act all had in mind.

The West, as Walter Webb pointed out, is an oasis civilization. The
overwhelming majority of Westerners are urban. Their cities have the
ills that cities elsewhere do — family breakup, slums, homelessness,
drugs, crime, smog, violence — and some that are peculiarly their own.
For one example, San Diego, one of the fastest-growing cities in America,
has been growing for years on water that legally belongs to Arizona.
When the Central Arizona Project begins diverting all the Colorado
River water it is entitled to, water that until now San Diego has been
enjoying, then San Diego will be scrambling for augmentation, which will
be hard to find. And it will probably blame the feds for the fix it is in.

An oasis civilization. People settled where there was water and left
essentially empty the wide dry spaces in between. It was aridity that
made those empty spaces, and that also brought into being the federal
bureaus charged with managing a public domain largely unfit for human
habitation. Human engineering let us move out a little into the empty
spaces; but altogether, in all its history, the Bureau of Reclamation
reclaimed only an area about the size of Ohio. Now we are at the end of
the dam-building era and close to the end of our exploitation of underground water. The water table around Tucson and Phoenix, where 90
percent of the water comes from wells, has been pumped down several

hundred feet. In the central valley of California, though there is substantial water from reclamation dams, it is likewise pumped down. The
Ogallala Aquifer under Nebraska, Kansas, and Oklahoma will soon be
pumped dry. I don't know about other states, but in California there is
no control whatever of pumping. The answer to a dry year or a light
snowpack is to deepen the existing wells and drill new ones. The logical
end of that practice is not hard to imagine.

There is a point to all this calamity howling. As Patricia Limerick
has pointed out in *Legacy of Conquest,* Western booms have almost
always been raids on a single extractive resource — beaver, grass, gold,
coal, whatever — and they have always been followed by busts, either
because the resource ran out or because fierce Western conditions of
heat, cold, or drought came down on the hopeful like the wrath of God
on Sennacherib's army (remember the Big Die-Up on Western ranges in
the winter of 1886–1887, or the other one exactly twenty years later in
the Montana-Alberta-Saskatchewan country?), or because the world
market broke, as the beaver market broke on a change in hat styles
about 1840. A year or two ago I would have had to put Dallas and Fort
Worth on my list of Western cities that are spreading like ringworm. Not
now, even in spite of Saddam Hussein's adventure in Kuwait. The point
is, things that happen in the Persian Gulf, in Basrah or Bahrain or
Baghdad, can cool off a Western boom or heat it up as surely as can the
petering out of the resource or an attack of local weather.

In Bernard DeVoto's phrase, Western economics have always been
the economics of liquidation. Even presumably renewable resources
such as timber and grass have been mined, not nourished. The blame
has often been laid on Eastern capitalists, but whenever they have had
the chance, Westerners have happily plundered themselves. From the
very beginning, Americans approached the West not as the Children of
Israel approached the Land of Canaan (except the Mormons, who did
just that), but as Egyptian grave robbers might approach the tomb of a
pharaoh.

No boom seems to learn much from the previous ones. In a
country where our most precious resource is water, we treat water
wastefully and short-term. If drainage from our adits threatens to
poison the West Rosebud, satisfy protesters with the lowest possible
denominator of prevention. If in a dry year Montana streams run low,
the governor justifies the ranchers who drain them completely to
benefit a second-rate alfalfa crop, while the trout and salmon — and
the tourist industry, which is worth six times the alfalfa crop — flop in
the gravel. If our clear-cut slopes fill the spawning streams with silt and
our dams cut off the Columbia River salmon run by two-thirds, too

bad; with our winnings we can go fishing in Iceland or New Zealand. If we know that the flood irrigation in desert valleys will eventually turn the fields into alkali flats, all the more reason to mine crops out of there while we can. If our runoff ponds are on the way to Kestersonization, we had better get on with our looting and polluting before some interfering Fed tries to stop us.

If large areas of the West are well on the way to becoming desert, and if overgrazing is one of the principal causes, push in more cattle and get the BLM to chain more square miles of piñon-juniper forest to create more range for us to make into desert. Time is short. If our smokestacks, as at Four Corners and Page, dirty what was once the best air in America, why that's the price of progress. And if our strip mines cut into coal beds that are also aquifers, with consequences no one can predict, we can't stop our draglines for such hypothetical reasons. We must take opportunity by the forelock and scalp it. We must keep pushing our coal leases into the Powder River valley and into the Crow and Northern Cheyenne reservations, though if we succeed we will displace both Indians and ranchers who have been there since George Armstrong Custer was a corpse.

If I thought the American Dream was only the dream of bonanza that my father lived by and that contemporary energy conglomerates live by and that agribusiness and the stockmen and the mining industry live by and that politicians applaud as the spirit that won the West, I could be pretty pessimistic about the West's future. It could easily, under the attacks of those who will not admit its limits, degenerate and deteriorate until not even massive engineering can keep it liveable. It could achieve its proper population sparseness the hard way and end up supporting far fewer people and cattle and sheep than it would if it were treated, in the cant word of contemporary environmentalism, "sustainably." For we cannot forget that the dry country heals, if at all, very slowly. You can still see General Patton's tank tracks, left from the desert training exercises of World War II. Poisoned earth stays poisoned for the lack of rain to leach and flush it. Bare earth erodes in every thunderstorm for lack of roots and plants to bind and hold it. The American West is one place where an ounce of prevention is worth a ton of cure.

In the summer of 1926 we made an excursion through the southern Utah national parks and the north rim of the Grand Canyon. All through the Kaibab National Forest, in every lagoon and meadow, there were deer in tens and hundreds. My brother and I, trying to keep count, lost track in that wilderness of animals. What we were seeing was a classic instance of a population explosion, when the wolves and mountain lions that normally kept the deer numbers down had mainly been killed off. Without natural enemies, and with hunting prohibited in the national park, the herds proliferated like laboratory mice. They were a splendid sight, a spiritual exhilaration such as I have not had since, except in Tanzania during the wildebeest migration. But there was a catch, one we knew too little to understand: The browse that the deer depended on was all gone. We saw bucks standing on their hind legs to reach the untasty hanging sprigs of ponderosa pines. That winter those deer in their thousands were all dead, starved to death. What was almost worse, they would not recover for a long long time, because before starving to death they had destroyed their own habitat.

That, I submit, is what the people of the plains and mountains and deserts had better not do. If I knew the answer to the West's future, I would carry it to every legislative hall from Helena to Santa Fe. But I don't. All I know is that whatever combination of ranching, mining, logging, and taking in each other's wash the West finally comes to, all of the extractive industries are going to have to be far more scrupulous about the environment than they have been in the past, and that the permanent population of the Western states is going to be a lot smaller than the boosters project.

When I ponder the effects the dream has already had on the country I knew sixty-five or seventy years ago, I remember the advice that Satan gave the world at the end of Mark Twain's *The Mysterious Stranger*. "Dream other dreams, and better!" Satan advised. He was speaking of the dream of human life, and speaking as a real pessimist; but as a person of wide experience he should be listened to, and his wisdom applied wherever it works. Dream other dreams, and better.

Wallace Stegner

HOME ON THE RANGE

for Wallace Stegner

———————

[sing:]   Home, home on the range
    Where the deer and the antelope —   [ ]

              Choke on fumes
part carbon dioxide part airborne asbestos
y aire of fewer and fewer parts oxygen.

Home on the range where
on a coldbright March morning
they nibble grassblades *y moras*
sparkling frost and lacey edges
of uranium, shiny
as fluorescent slime on rancid ham.

[sing:]   Where seldom is heard a discouraging word —   [ ]

        Great Miami River contamination
        Rocky Flats   Three Mile Island
        Fernald Ohio   Butte Montana
        Black Mesa toxic waste hazards
        contaminants radioactive leaks
        nuclear accidents —

Time to hear the encouraging STOP!
    Stop burning coal!
    Stop cutting trees!
    Stop spraying aerosols!
    Stop driving your car every day!
    Stop ignoring gov't/corporate crimes
        against air lake tree soil!
        The same crimes that gave us

Indian sorrow/slave sorrow/
mestizo sorrow/all sorrow.

That's the path toward a society to match
the scenery: turn the encouraging word
into a seed of *esperanza*
for an angle, not a whole, but an angle
of repose, for a future

[sing:]   Where the skies are not cloudy all day.   [ ]

Cordelia Candelaria

PART SEVEN

Mr. Jefferson in 1990

THE AMERICAN WEST:
THE DREAM FROM THE VANTAGE POINT
OF COLORADO IN 1990

I am given a rather difficult challenge this afternoon. I am instructed to respond respectfully to each of the papers that has been delivered; to answer certain charges, some of them polite, others rude, leveled against me this afternoon; to entertain a range of audience questions and give the citizens gathered here their first real opportunity to participate in a democratic dialogue today; to sum up on a cheerful note; and to dismiss you. All in about eight minutes. I am tempted, as I did in all of the arenas of my life, to shrink from such a challenge and to run out and buy a laptop computer, the logical impulse for the man who tinkered with portable desks and the many-writer, the paper polygraph still on display at Monticello. I am reminded of Geoffrey Chaucer's prologue to *The Canterbury Tales* in which he epitomizes the character of his clerk with the phrase, "and gladly would he learn, and gladly teach." Those of us from the past have more to learn from your culture than to teach you. I will be brief. And then I will turn to you for your comments and questions, although after witnessing a few fragments of the yeasty stuff of modern democracy here today, I will admit to sensing the advent of one of those migraine headaches that plagued me all of my adulthood.

First of all, let me say that I am in sympathy with the crusty humility of Wallace Stegner, whose extraordinary letter Professor Wilkinson read aloud earlier. Mr. Stegner, whose crabby but honest prose style reminds me agreeably of my old friend John Adams, asks, "Has anybody carved my face on a mountain in South Dakota?" In my view, this is something not to be wished for, not merely because it needlessly defaces nature, and (in my case) in a rather bad likeness, but more importantly because it perpetuates the myth of a "Golden Age of

Founding Fathers," demigods particularly prudent and farsighted. Encouraging that myth disables you from taking back your lives in your
own time. A secular nation must not create saints. Shakespeare somewhere says that we are all men frail, and capable of frailty. As an
Enlightenment optimist, I say equally that we are all men bold, and
capable of refashioning the world of human affairs.

Second, I want to get in my sole theme early and emphatically.
Nothing is sacred but the rights of man; all else is negotiable. Everything
I struggled to achieve is essentially encapsulated in that simple creed. I
have articulated once today my pastoral vision, a Virginian picture of a
quiet people living unobtrusively on the land, minding their own business and living in a nation that minds its own business away from the
arenas of mercantilism and Bonaparte. This portrait of a nation, where
happiness and freedom are more important than power and wealth, may
or may not seem appropriate to you in the late twentieth century. It is
not for me to say. The earth belongs to the living and not the dead.
Perhaps my vision was fundamentally in error. The photographic images
I saw today suggested to me that perhaps my understanding of the
climate and physiognomy of the West was misguided. In my own time I
saw Louisiana as a kind of infinite expansion of the Ohio valley: lush,
fertile, well-watered, contoured like the Garden of Eden. The rugged-
ness and the aridity that have been brought home to me today, by
technologies impossible to conceive when movable type was still thrilling
and a horseless carriage produced no motion, would perhaps lead me to
rethink some of my pastoral vision, at least in the trans-Mississippi
West. (On the other hand, I had better admit, before a neo-Hamiltonian
counts coup on me, that I tended to cling stubbornly to favorite ideas,
even when the weight of evidence made them hard to sustain.) Let us at
least consider my pastoralism debatable.

What then remains of my achievement for you to cling to in your
own troubled times? The answer is simple: Nothing is sacred but the
rights of man; all else is negotiable. Your economy is an artifice, a
construct, and there are undoubtedly many other economies you might
successfully try. I am told that economic opportunity is very unevenly
distributed in your times and that millions of Americans are homeless,
incapable of finding work or reduced to forms of labor not in harmony
with the dignity of man. Your constitution is merely a recipe for
government. I was not at the Constitutional Convention of 1787, but I
know from my friend James Madison and the great General Washington
that few of the Founding Fathers (a convenient term, but one I dislike)
thought the new constitution likely to last more than about a quarter of
a century. It was a start at national government. The document of '87

would eventually be replaced by something better. You have made it instead a semi-sacred document, like the ark of the covenant, too sacred to be touched. In my view, that is a great mistake. Constitutions, political systems, tripartite structures of government, methods of writing, enacting, enforcing, and amending laws — all these are negotiable. They are artifice. Nothing is sacred but the rights of man. Keep your Bill of Rights, or rather *recognize* the rights of man and articulate and rearticulate those rights as often as necessary, but experiment boldly and even irreverently with everything else in life. History on the whole only teaches us what bad government has been. History is a record of failures, of an irrational obsession with tradition, received ideas, sacrosanct notions, and unnatural habits. We may as well wear as adults the suits that fitted us when we were boys as live according to the barbarous regimen of our ancestors — and that includes Mr. Madison's regimen and indeed mine. You ought to experiment boldly, you ought to seek to make your politics equal to your dreams of justice, you ought to repudiate the past as often as necessary. Your charge as you move into the next century is to complete the revolution at last, to fulfill the promise of the Declaration of Independence. That promise is twofold: First, that every human being born on this continent be treated equally in the machinery of the law and, second, that every human being born on this continent be entitled, not by the grace of God or by the generosity of government, but by the law of nature, to something like roughly equal economic opportunity. Unless everyone has a solid chance to thrive as an American citizen, you must not permit unusual accumulations of power and wealth in the hands of the few. This is the world's only true meritocracy. That system works best — only works, in fact — with little or no government interference. But the natural aristocracy, as I called it, can only rise to humble leadership if you level the playing field so that artificial privilege does not lord it over a purposefully oppressed citizenry. Until you reach those two simple but elusive goals, you ought to revolutionize this society as often as necessary, and certainly once each generation. I like a little revolution now and then.

I have heard today a chorus of anxiety, a consciousness of deep failure in American history, a series of descriptions of exploitations, sometimes systematic, of land and people, particularly the aboriginal inhabitants of this continent. And I have seen glimpses among the citizens of the West of an unhappy awareness of a dependency upon power and financial centers elsewhere. Freedom and economic dependency are a contradiction in terms. My answer to your dread and resentment is not that you wring your hands in despair, but that you begin the business of revolution, including possibly bloody rebellion. Let me offer you six or seven quick strategies for revolution. Almost alone among the so-called revolutionaries of 1776, I am not afraid of blood-shed and terror if liberty is at stake. I said, "The tree of liberty must be refreshed from time to time with the blood of patriots and tyrants. It is its natural manure."[1] Alone among the founders, I went to my grave defending the French Revolution, including the Reign of Terror. A people that wishes to enjoy its natural rights must never renounce terrorism. Still, perhaps you need not resort to bloodshed, not yet.

You have at your fingertips constitutional mechanisms with which to revolutionize your political landscape almost overnight. You have the polls: an election every two years for all members of the House of Representatives in your national Congress, the election every fourth year of the president, and the election every sixth year of U.S. senators. The root-bound incumbency of your own time is a shameful repudiation of republican principles. Amateur government and rapid rotation in office are the heart and soul of a republican system. Careerism is the death of self-rule. "Whenever a man casts his eye longingly on public office, a certain rottenness of character is sure to creep in." The simplest approach to revolution in your time is simply to return all national officers to private life at the next opportunity, good men and bad. Then start fresh. You have that mechanism of revolution in your hands. Why wring your hands when you can wield such power with them?

Perhaps you might attempt a few cheerful impeachments now and then. As a lifelong enemy to the judiciary, that corps of sappers and miners dedicated to the destruction of American liberties, I suggest that you begin with the judges. Life tenure is an affront to self-government. So is judicial review, one of my Virginia cousin John Marshall's dubious gifts to the American political system. The will of the people is expressed in their elected legislatures. Legislative bodies must, in a constitutional crisis, be supreme. I find it appalling that you permit an oligarchy of nine unelected, unaccountable, and virtually unimpeachable jurists to determine what is constitutional and what is not. In a democratic republic the will of the majority must in all cases prevail, even, I feel compelled to insist, when that majority is insensitive to the will of the minority.

You might also try to amend your constitution. In my own lifetime I feared that the amendment process had been made too difficult, but it is nevertheless possible and I urge you to attempt it. As a firm believer that the truth is great and will prevail when left to itself in the free marketplace of ideas, I urge you to build a majority for change by way of education, persuasion, the gradual spread of enlightenment and the light of science.

If amendment doesn't suit you, tear up your constitution. I suggested that every constitution be written in plain English, that it be strictly and not broadly interpreted, that it be amended when it ceases to be useful, that when it ceases to be amendable it be torn up, and that, under any circumstance, every constitution — state, local, and national — be torn up every nineteen years (once per generation). Insist upon that simple mechanism of peaceful revolution and you can start the world over again in your time.

If that doesn't work, secede. The compact theory of government guarantees that each state is a sovereign entity and that the confederation is a voluntary compact of sovereign constituent states. Whenever any state feels that it is not being treated well in the national confederation, it has a sacred right to secede. Try it. It will at least get the attention of Washington. As a rival republic you may discover forms of government and pursuits of happiness that will inspire states more timid than your own. As a lone republic you will of necessity learn again the painful but virtuous lessons of self-sufficiency, and you will learn that much of what you consider essential to your material happiness not only does not make you happy, but in fact enslaves and enervates you with the luxuries of corrupt empire.

And finally, and more seriously, when you have exhausted all peaceful means of building a self-reliant agrarian utopia — and a utopia in my view is not a literary illusion, but an urgent demand for all humanity — then you may (and must) begin to employ terror. It may even be necessary to kill innocent people in the streets. I prefer peaceful change, and when bloodshed is necessary I prefer surgical violence to indiscriminate slaughter, but you must never forget that bloodshed and terror are the price of human liberty. If you abdicate terror, you will not long remain free. History teaches us no more clear and emphatic lesson.

To all of the gloom and helplessness that I have heard today, I answer that there are simple mechanisms of revolution in your hands. If you choose not to use them, it is you and not your social structure that is to blame for your dependencies. Painstakingly exhaust peaceful means first and then break forth your muskets and pitchforks. Violence is not to be indulged for light and transient causes. Nor is it always to be eschewed by men of humanity and peace.

There is a suggestion, implicit in our conversations today, that there has been something inevitable about American history. The logic seems to be that although you often brought good intentions to the West, nevertheless inevitably you exploited the resources and the peoples that you encountered. *Inevitably* you displaced the aboriginal sovereigns, *inevitably* you lost sight of the pastoral vision, *inevitably* you eroded the republic and put empire in its place, *inevitably* you replaced small family farms with Mr. Hamilton's industrial estates, *inevitably* many of the most sublime places of the continent had to be "developed" in the name of human progress. Nothing could be further from the truth. We are masters of our destiny. That is the chief glory and perhaps the curse of the American experiment. It is this myth that I wish to combat especially. You chose the America of 1990. There are no iron laws — economic, political, social, environmental — of history. The American people had it in their power to create a pastoral, decentralized, peaceful and isolationist nation, a pluralistic nation, a nation that prized diversity and liberty and dissent. You chose not to maintain the republic. This was not inevitable. You are slaves to no king and no principles of culture. You wrought your America by choice. There was a fierce debate in my time between Mr. Hamilton's vision of America and my own. We fought like two cocks in the cabinet of the great General Washington. There were other visions at large in the marketplace of eighteenth-century ideas, some of them attractive to me, others repellent to my vision. In my time the people preferred my vision, though even then they had begun to vote with their purses and their feet for principles not in harmony with the Enlightenment. Sometime after my death in 1826, a majority of the citizens of the United States gave themselves over to Mr. Hamilton's dream of a world military and industrial empire. You are now a thoroughly Hamiltonian nation with a thin Jeffersonian veneer, and it shows. The people of the United States have voted. The world belongs to the living and not the dead. I have not come today, like Hamlet's father, to whet your almost blunted republican appetite. If you are content with Mr. Hamilton's vision, then I intrude upon your world only as a pathetic antediluvian with a quaint pastoral dream. As a democrat and an optimist — some say a fatuous optimist — I can have no quarrel with the future.

If, however, you oppose the empire and its dislocations of the rights of man here and in your client states, if you prefer decentralization to consolidation, and happiness to getting and spending, if you believe that the purpose of America is to expand the Enlightenment and never again permit human progress to be darkened by the forces of unreason and authority, if you wish to live according to the dictates of nature, and — above all — if you wish to govern yourselves, then you are at odds with Mr. Hamilton and you must begin the revolution today. There is nothing inevitable in human affairs. It strikes me as the oddest of all paradoxes that Americans — the argonauts of human freedom — would descend into the convenient myth of inevitability. For if America stands for anything, it stands for liberty and possibility. For a people who have prized their freedoms, fought for them, erected a Bill of Rights to protect them, in 1990 to shrug their shoulders and say, "We had no choice, this is how societies work, it was inevitable, what could we have done?" is in my view a pathetic abdication of enlightened responsibility and a suggestion that the lofty rhetoric of the New World was as empty as the sophistry of the old order, the babble of kings and the righteousness of priesthoods. Thomas Paine said you have it in your power to begin the world over again. I'd start tonight.

Finally, although I have pages of notes on the papers that I have heard and wish to respond to them all, I have time to respond only to Davíd Carrasco, professor of religious studies, because I think he asked the most important of all the questions we have heard today. He argued, if I understand him, that although American civilization is the story of extraordinary violence, nevertheless the myths that we live by — freedom, justice, and opportunity for all, the constitutional order, the rule of law, the extension of the franchise of happiness — are myths that condemn violence and exploitation and promise higher standards on this side of the Atlantic. According to Professor Carrasco, resolving the American paradox, coming to terms with our violence rather than papering it over with Jeffersonian pastoralism, should be the business of American integrity. Perhaps he is right and perhaps he isn't. His portrait of American history sounds bleak in the ears of an optimist. But he does raise the great question of the humanities: Is it possible for a nation like the United States to break with the past, to lift the standards of human behavior? Or is human nature constant and in some sense even more evil in America because of all the free resources and infinite spaces that were available to exploit with that dark human nature he describes? My own view is quite different from his. I believe that humans are basically good, that when they do evil it is not through their nature but because they are distorted by bad institutions and bad habits. And if we will only reform institutions to be equal to human dignity and reason, and educate the people liberally, then humans will rise to the challenge of living in good sense and forbearance and mutual understanding. In short, I do not believe that human nature is constant. I believe in progress. Like the more moderate philosophies of France, I propose that we are indefinitely, although perhaps not infinitely, perfectible. A friend, late in life, wrote me a letter saying: Mr. Jefferson, you have given your life to the destruction of the four pillars of the old order: monarchy, aristocracy, the priesthood, and standing armies.

What then is left to hold our society together? In response I gave a simple and characteristic answer. I said: Sir, the glue of a great culture is education. If we enlighten the people generally, every form of tyranny, both of mind and body, will disappear like fog and witches when the sun rises in the morning. But if you expect to be a nation ignorant and free, you expect something that never has been and never can be in the history of the world. Restraint in a democracy is the essential virtue. The question you take into the twenty-first century is: Can a self-governing citizenry restrain itself? If not, the West is in grave trouble.

There are three prerequisites for restraint in a self-governing society. First, education is the foundation of everything that matters in a free society. Contact with nature, life in a state of nature, is the second desideratum. And the third necessity is something I like to call our moral sense. You might call it conscience. I believe we our born with a moral sense that is as acute as our sense of taste, smell, or hearing. And if we will only consult it on all occasions, justice and good sense will burst forth all over the planet. In short, in spite of what I have heard today, I remain an optimist. I hope you will not dismiss me as a naive optimist. You have it in your power to begin the world over again. It begins with you. Indeed, where else?

I will say one more word before turning to whatever questions you have. Philip Burgess, with whom I agree in large part, said earlier today that we must insist that our citizens take responsibility. I disagree. That is an *imposition* of enlightenment. We will only be a great nation when our citizens *spontaneously* take responsibility. That does not require any government at all.

The President graciously agreed to entertain a few questions from the audience. Here is a sample.

Question: Mr. President: You have learned that your Louisiana Purchase has not yet been digested by the people. Large parts of it remain in federal hands, as you know, at a fearful loss to the federal treasury. You have heard the mayor of Missoula, Montana, suggest that this should be changed. I wonder if you would advise the mayor of Missoula to lead a secession, to form a new country, perhaps called Jeffersonia, and to take the remnants of the Louisiana Purchase and other federal installations with him.

Answer: Do I suggest secession? The world belongs to the living, not the dead. If you do secede, however, I urge you not to call this country Jeffersonia.

Question: Sir, I would like to know your definition of man. If nothing is sacred but the rights of man, I wonder if you would be willing to expand your definition of man to include women, blacks, all human beings and also life and structure — in other words, trees and mountains and canyons and animals. . . . Is it possible that their rights are sacred?

Answer: By man I mean all human beings, of all colors, of all creeds, of all economic bases, and both genders. This is an absolute statement. Had my countrymen known of how absolutely I meant my felicitous phrase in 1776, they would probably not have approved of the Declaration of Independence. We are identical at birth in the eyes of the Creator; we are entitled throughout our lives to be treated identically in the political arena. In the machine of the law, the rights of all human beings are equal. Rights may not always be adhered to equally by government, but that is only a measure of the corruption of government, not of the limits of this principle.

Having said that, I will now proceed to confirm your implied criticism of my achievement, which I take to be the point of your question. My candid view was that black people and white people would never live together in harmony on this continent because of the poison of the institution of slavery. White slave masters would always fear reprisal after emancipation, and freed slaves would always resent their former masters. It was my hope that once emancipation came, our black brethren would choose to repatriate themselves in their native Africa. If they did not wish to do this, I suggested a black homeland somewhere in the American West. But it was my candid belief that there would be permanent racial tension in this society because of the plague of slavery with which we began our national experiment. This is not at all a pleasant subject for discourse. I always remembered the British moralist Samuel Johnson's statement during our revolution. Isn't it interesting, he said, that those who yelp loudest for liberty are also the drivers of Negro slaves?

Indians I saw somewhat differently. I saw them as every bit our equals, in many respects our superiors. Their governments were superior to our own. They enjoyed true anarchy, no government at all. Their religions were no more irrational than ours, and in many ways less. These people were living according to the dictates of nature and they were proof that John Locke, Rousseau, and other theorists were not simply fictionalizing when they spoke of man in a state of nature. Here were people living in a state of nature. They thrived. It was our duty not to exploit these people, but to learn from them and at length to intermingle and intermarry with them.

The legal rights of women of course must be protected. When I revised the laws of Virginia in 1777, I included provisions to ameliorate the property laws and other legal rights of women. My daughters were among the best-educated women in the United States. But if you are asking whether women should vote or hold public office, then I must indeed be a man of my own century and remind you that the tender breasts of ladies were not formed for political convulsion.

Question: May I briefly follow up that question? Are life and structure part of your definition of man? In other words, do you have regard — legally — for animals and the land itself?

Answer: I prided myself on being on the enlightened side of every question, to stay a step or two ahead of my countrymen, but always to stay roughly within the boundaries of their own sense of things. I was an eighteenth-century man. I subscribed to the idea of an intricate chain of being. I believed without any apology that humans occupy the top of that chain of being and, although the earth does not exist for us alone, we are its primary constituents. If the world around us must be adjusted, it is better that it be adjusted by humans rather than sponges or wolves. You may disagree in your time, but remember that I saw the world from before the Industrial Revolution, and that makes all the difference. I'm unabashedly a humanist. Still, the concept of usufruct suggests that we must use our exalted status on the chain of being with respect and restraint. It would not be natural for us to behave in a way that impaired the earth's capacity to support future generations, including human generations. I was fortunate to live in a simpler time. I was so enamored of the chain-of-being theory that I did not believe that any species ever created could become extinct. That would effectively break the chain. I instructed my explorers to keep their eyes open for the woolly mammoth in northern Louisiana.

Let me tell one more story before you depart, a parable about the New World and the Old. There was a theory put forth by French scientists in my time that American animals and plants were comparatively degenerate. The view was that North America emerged from the last flood later than Europe, and therefore our climate was cooler and moister, and so our animals were less virile, less fertile, less magnificent. We in America knew this was nonsense, but convincing European skeptics was extraordinarily difficult. When I went to France as the American minister in 1784, I took with me a rather large panther skin, which I presented to the Comte de Buffon, the greatest of European scientists, as proof that our fauna were every bit the equal of their European counterparts. He didn't bother to reply to this gift. Later I had a chance to meet him at one of his dinner parties in Paris. My friend the Marquis de Chastellux, who had visited Monticello at the close of the

Revolutionary War, introduced me to the celebrated savant and said this: "Sir, this is Mr. Jefferson from America, who in his book *Notes on Virginia* has refuted your theory of American degeneracy." The great scientist did not even bother to look me in the eye. He merely went to his shelf, pulled down his latest published volume, handed it to Chastellux, and said, "When the American shall have read this, he will see that he is entirely in error." This troubled me. Here was a man of science refusing to engage in open debate. So I scouted him and said, "Sir, it seems to me in your books you have confused the American elk with the European reindeer, much to the prejudice of our elk. Secondly, you have said there is no antler or rack in North America longer than two feet. Our nation, sir, abounds with beasts whose antlers extend beyond two feet to four and five feet." He said, "If you show me the antler of an animal larger than two feet I will burn my library." And finally I said, perhaps going too far, "Sir, it seems to me that your European reindeer could walk under the belly of an American moose with some inches to spare." Well, the conversation ended abruptly and so did the dinner party.

But now my pride was engaged. I wrote to my young friend Mr. Madison, whom I burdened all of my life with my sometimes zany requests, and said, among other things, "Send me a moose." Well, Mr. Madison had no moose, so he wrote to the governor of New Hampshire, John Sullivan, a Revolutionary War hero and good Republican, and said, among other things, "Mr. Jefferson requires a moose." And Sullivan got it. He took out a war party of twenty armed men in a blizzard in New Hampshire and found a small herd of moose, separated out a rather magnificent bull, shot it, and then discovered to his chagrin that they must now drag that two-thousand-pound carcass twenty miles to the nearest village. He said in his long and somewhat whining letter about the affair that the party had to cut a road through the wilderness to bring back my moose. He had it cleaned, the bones separated, the peltry made ready for travel. He boxed the entire carcass and shipped it to Thomas Jefferson, Minister Plenipotentiary, Court of Louis the Sixteenth, Paris, France, and he shipped it COD. Well, this was more than a year and a half after my original request to Mr. Madison, and I had in the press of business forgotten all about the moose. One day a minor official from the port authority came to me and said, "Sir, there is a rather large crate waiting for you and it will cost you forty-five pounds sterling to redeem it." That would be about twenty-five hundred of your dollars in 1990, and in my time the government did not routinely reimburse such expenses. Nevertheless, I redeemed the moose and took it to the Parisian equivalent of a taxidermist and had it prepared after a fashion, and I sent it to the Buffon with my compliments. The great man sent a polite letter of thanks, which led me to assume that he would correct this grievous error in future editions of his work. But he didn't. He died just six months later, and his errors were entailed upon the future.

I tell this story to remind you that the European community looked with derision and even contempt upon the New World and our fragile little experiment in self-government. We had to prove to a skeptical and not-often-candid world that humans could govern themselves, without kings, priests, first ministers, and the corruptions of the old order. You are still proving that great truth to the old world, particularly in Louisiana. Your challenge is to learn to restrain yourselves, to prove to the world that a free people can live in peace and prosperity without exploiting the life around them. There is still time to prove that Mr. Hamilton was wrong — wrong in his reading of human nature, wrong in his sense of national priorities, wrong in his principles of government. This is the nation that should never know despair. I trust that you will regain your Enlightenment confidence and show the world that utopia is not the "nowhere" of literary texts, but an elusive approach to government that the world finally found manifest in America, and Louisiana. I close by quoting from my last letter, written a few weeks before my death in 1826: "All eyes are open or opening to the rights of man. The gradual spread of the light of science has already laid open to every view the palpable truth that the mass of mankind were not born with saddles on their backs, nor a favored few booted and spurred, ready to ride them legitimately by the grace of God. Let this be the ground of hope for others."[2]

Thank you very much.

Clay Straus Jenkinson

CONTRIBUTORS

Bruce Babbitt served as governor of Arizona from 1978 to 1987. He was a candidate for the 1988 Democratic presidential nomination, currently practices law in Phoenix, and lectures and writes on the American West.

Philip M. Burgess is the director of the Center for the New West, an independent, nonprofit research and consulting organization. The Center focuses on public policy and strategies for economic development in the West.

Adrian Herminio Bustamante has a Ph.D. from the University of New Mexico in American studies with emphasis on ethnohistory of the southwestern United States. He is the author of various articles on Hispanic life in New Mexico and teaches at Santa Fe Community College, where he is head of the Division of Arts and Sciences.

Cordelia Candelaria is the author of *Chicano Poetry: A Critical Introduction.* She is an associate professor of English at the University of Colorado at Boulder, and associate professor of Chicano studies for the university's Center for Studies of Ethnicity and Race in America (CSERA).

David L. Carrasco is a professor of religious studies at the University of Colorado at Boulder. He is the author of *Quetzalcoatl and the Irony of Empire* and *Religions of Mesoamerica: Cosmovision Ceremonial Centers.*

James A. Carrier has had two of his series from *The Denver Post* — "Letters from Yellowstone" and "Journey Down the Colorado" — published in book form. He has been a journalist since 1966.

Jo Clark is director of programs for the Western Governors Association. Her areas of concentration include water, state-tribal relations, waste management, and rural development.

James N. Corbridge, Jr., became chancellor of the University of Colorado at Boulder in 1986. A professor of law, he has written numerous articles on water law, mining law, and real estate property.

Edward Dorn, poet and author of *Hi-Plane, Slinger,* and other books of poetry, is a professor of English at the University of Colorado at Boulder.

John E. Echohawk was the first graduate of the University of New Mexico's special program to train Indian lawyers. He has lectured on Indian law at the University of California, Berkeley, and serves as the executive director of the Native American Rights Fund.

Walter Echo-Hawk is a senior staff attorney with the Native American Rights Fund. He has received national recognition for his path-breaking work on cases involving religious freedom of American Indians, prisoner rights, water rights, and Native reburial rights.

Sally K. Fairfax is a professor in the College of Natural Resources, University of California, Berkeley. The co-author, with Samuel Dana, of *Forest and Range Policy*, her article "Beyond the Sagebrush Rebellion: Emerging Patterns in Public Domain Federalism" appeared in the *Ecology Law Quarterly*.

Thomas Hornsby Ferril is poet laureate of Colorado and author of numerous books of poetry.

Estevan T. Flores is an assistant professor of sociology and CSERA's Chicano studies research coordinator at the University of Colorado at Boulder. He has published in, among others, the *International Migration Review* and the *Hispanic Journal of Behavioral Science*.

David H. Getches, professor of law, has written extensively on water law, Indian law, environmental law, and public-land law. He edited *Water and the American West*, is co-author of *Federal Indian Law* and *Water Resources Management*, and was a founding director of the Native American Rights Fund.

Camille Guerin-Gonzalez is an assistant professor of history specializing in labor and immigration history at Oberlin College. She is a co-author of *Politics of Immigrant Workers* and the author of *Proletarians in the Garden: Mexican Wage Labor in California Agriculture*.

William H. Hornby is a senior editor of *The Denver Post*. In addition to extensive news experience, he is a director of the Buffalo Bill Historical Center, Cody, Wyoming, and a past chairman of the board of the Colorado Historical Society.

Evelyn Hu-Dehart is the author of "Immigrants to a Developing Society: The Chinese in Northern Mexico, 1875–1932," *Journal of Arizona History*, among other articles. She is director of CSERA and a professor of history at the University of Colorado at Boulder.

Thomas Jefferson was the third president of the United States of America.

Clay Straus Jenkinson is a Rhodes scholar currently working on his Ph.D. in classical studies. Since 1981 he has directed the Great Plains Chautauqua, a traveling humanities tent show. Among other achievements, he portrays Thomas Jefferson.

Raymond Dean Jones, a graduate of the Harvard Law School, is a judge of the Colorado Court of Appeals.

Daniel Kemmis is the mayor of Missoula, Montana; senior fellow and project director for the Northern Lights Research and Education Institute; and a former Montana state legislator. He has worked, both theoretically and practically, on community building and is the author of *Community and the Politics of Place.*

William Kittredge is a professor of English at the University of Montana. He has written numerous works of Western fiction and nonfiction, some of which are collected in *Owning It All* and *We Are Not in This Together.* He is co-editor of *The Last Best Place: An Anthology of Montana Literature.*

Patricia Nelson Limerick is an associate professor of history, specializing in the history of the American West, at the University of Colorado at Boulder. She is author of *Legacy of Conquest* and *Desert Passages.*

Betsy Marston, a graduate of the Columbia University Graduate School of Journalism, worked in the East as a television news producer prior to moving to the West in 1975. She is editor of the award-winning bimonthly newspaper *High Country News.*

Edwin H. Marston was a professor of physics before turning to journalism in the Rocky Mountains. He founded the *North Fork Times* in 1975, the *Western Colorado Report* in 1982, and since 1983 has been publisher of *High Country News.*

Peter F. Michelson, author of *Pacific Plainsong,* is associate professor of English and creative writing at the University of Colorado at Boulder.

Charles R. Middleton is dean of arts and sciences at the University of Colorado at Boulder. He is a professor of history, specializing in nineteenth-century British social and political history.

Richard Misrach, author of *Desert Cantos* and *Bravo 20: The Bombing of the American West,* has used his skills as a photographer to document, study, and appraise nature and human nature in the American West.

Thomas J. Noel is co-author of *Denver: The City Beautiful and Its Architects* and *Colorado: A Heritage of the Highest State*. He is a professor of history at the University of Colorado at Denver, and in 1987 received Historic Denver, Inc.'s Award of Honor.

Wallace Stegner, author of more than thirty books, is the Jackson Ely Reynolds Professor of Humanities at Stanford University, where he founded the Stanford Writing Program.

Barbara Sudler, a third-generation Denverite, served for ten years as the president of the Colorado Historical Society. She is a boardmember of the American Antiquarian Society.

Mark Trahant, former editor and publisher of the *Navajo Times Today* and reporter for the *Arizona Republic*, is now editing and publishing the weekly *Navajo Nation Today*. He is co-author of the award winning "Fraud in Indian Country," an eight-part series on federal Indian programs.

Charles F. Wilkinson is the Moses Lasky Professor of Law at the University of Colorado at Boulder. His books include *American Indians, Time and the Law; The American West: A Narrative Bibliography and a Study in Regionalism;* and *The Eagle Bird: Searching for an Ethic of Place.*

Terry Tempest Williams is naturalist-in-residence at the Utah Museum of Natural History, University of Utah. She was project director for "Navajo Storytelling: Perceptions of Culture and Landscape," 1983–1985. Her books include *Pieces of White Shell, The Secret Language of Snow,* and *Coyote's Canyon.*

NOTES

PART ONE

Holthaus, et al.

1. Joseph Wood Krutch, *More Lives Than One* (New York: William Sloan Associates, 1962), p. 211.

PART TWO

Jenkinson

1. Marshal to C. C. Pinckney, March 4, 1801, quoted in Dumas Malone *Jefferson the President: The First Term, 1801–1805* (Boston: Little Brown Publishers, 1970), p. 22.

2. Thomas Jefferson, *Autobiography of Thomas Jefferson, 1743–1790* (New York: G. P. Putnam's Sons, 1914).

3. Jefferson to duPont de Nemours, March 2, 1809, in *The Writings of Thomas Jefferson*, Vol. 12, eds. Andrew A. Lipscomb and Albert Ellery Bergh (Washington, D.C.: Thomas Jefferson Memorial Association, 1903), pp. 259–260.

4. Merrill Peterson, ed., *The Portable Thomas Jefferson* (New York: Penguin Books, 1975), p. 217.

5. Thomas Paine, *Common Sense*, ed. Isaac Kramnik (London: Penguin Books, 1976), p. 120.

6. Jefferson to James Madison, January 30, 1787, in *Portable*, p. 417.

7. Jefferson to Madison, September 6, 1789, in *Portable*.

PART THREE

Limerick

1. Donald Worster, et al., "*Legacy of Conquest*, by Patricia Nelson Limerick: A Panel of Appraisal," *Western Historical Quarterly* 20, no. 3 (August 1989), p. 305.

Williams

2. Luther Standing Bear, *Land of the Spotted Eagle* (Boston: Houghton Mifflin, 1933), p. 26.

3. Terry Tempest Williams, *Pieces of White Shell: A Journey to Navajoland* (New York: Scribner's, 1984), pp. 4–5.

4. D. H. Lawrence, "Introduction to Studies in Classic American Literature," *The English Review*, Vol. XXVII, July–December 1918 (November 1918), p. 330.

5. Herman Melville, *Moby Dick* (New York: Harper & Brothers, 1950), p. 69.

6. Lawrence, "Introduction to Studies in Classic American Literature," p. 331.

7. *Portland Oregonian*, June 7, 1988.

8. Ralph Waldo Emerson, "The American Scholar," in *American Literature Survey, Vol. 2: The American Romantics, 1800–1860,* eds. Milton R. Stern and Seymour L. Gross (New York: Viking Press, 1962), p. 285.

W. Echo-Hawk

9. Felix S. Cohen, "The Erosion of Indian Rights, 1950–1953: A Case Study in Bureaucracy," *The Yale Law Journal* 62, no. 3 (February 1953), p. 390.

10. Virginia Irving Armstrong, *I Have Spoken: American History Through the Voices of the Indians* (Chicago: Sage Books, The Swallow Press, 1971), pp. xi–xii.

11. Chief Seattle, "The White Man Will Never Be Alone," in *Literature of the American Indian,* eds. Thomas E. Sanders and Walter W. Peek (Beverly Hills, Calif.: Glencoe Press, 1973), pp. 284–285.

Flores

12. James Coates, *Boulder Daily Camera,* January 15, 1989, p. 4A.

Kemmis

13. Robinson Jeffers, "Shine Perishing Republic," in *Roan Stallion, Tamar and Other Poems* (New York: Horace Liveright, 1925), p. 95.

14. John Winthrop, "A Modell of Christian Charity written on board the *Arabella* on the Atlantic Ocean 1630," *Collections of the Massachusetts Historical Society* Vol. 27 (Boston: Charles C. Little & James Brown, 1838), p. 47.

15. Wendell Berry, "Work Song," in *Clearing* (New York & London: Harcourt Brace Jovanovich, 1977), p. 32.

PART FOUR

Kittredge

1. Gae Whitney Canfield, *Sarah Winnemucca of the Northern Paiutes* (Norman, Okla.: University of Oklahoma Press, 1983), pp. 47–48.

2. Jarold Ramsey, ed., *Coyote Was Going There: Indian Literature of the Oregon Country* (Seattle: University of Washington Press, 1977), p. 229.

3. Canfield, *Sarah Winnemucca,* pp. 60–61.

4. D. H. Lawrence, Introduction to *Bottom Dogs,* by Edward Dahlberg (San Francisco: City Lights Books, 1961), p. viii.

5. Lawrence, Introduction to *Bottom Dogs,* p. x.

Clark

6. Stewart L. Udall, "Pausing at the Pass: Reflections of a Native Son," in *Beyond the Mythic West,* Stewart L. Udall, et al. (Salt Lake City: Peregrine Smith Books in Association with the Western Governor's Association, 1990), p. 20.

Carrasco

7. William Kittredge, "Owning It All," in *Owning It All* (St. Paul: Graywolf Press, 1987), pp. 55–56.

8. William Kittredge, Introduction to *Montana Spaces: Essays and Photographs in*

Celebration of Montana, ed. William Kittredge (New York: Nick Lyons Books, 1988), p. xv.

9. Kittredge, "Owning It All," p. 58.

10. Rene Girard, *Violence and the Sacred*, trans. Patrick Gregory (Baltimore: Johns Hopkins University Press, 1977), p. 31.

11. Kittredge, "Owning It All," p. 61.

12. Kittredge, "Owning It All," p. 57.

13. Paul Wheatley, "City As Symbol," inaugural lecture (London: University of London, 1967), p. 9.

14. Thomas Wolfe, *Of Time and the River: A Legend of Man's Hunger in His Youth* (New York: Charles Scribner's Sons, 1935), pp. 415–417.

Misrach

15. Richard Misrach, text for "Snow Canyon State Park, Utah, 1987," in *Richard Misrach: Photographs 1985–1987* (Tokyo: Gallery MIN, 1988).

16. Richard Misrach, text for "The Pit," a traveling photography exhibition (1987).

PART FIVE

Babbitt

1. 16 U. S. C. 21 (1982).

2. Act of March 3, 1891, ch. 561, 24 Stat. 1103, repealed by 16 U. S. C. 471 (1982).

3. Frank Burt Freidel, *Franklin D. Roosevelt, Vol. 4: Launching the New Deal* (Boston: Little, Brown, 1952), p. 352.

4. 16 U. S. C. 528 (1982).

Corbridge

5. Wallace Stegner, *The Sound of Mountain Water* (New York: E. P. Dutton, 1980), p. 13.

6. David H. Getches, "Putting a Western Brand on Legal Education," paper presented at the annual meeting of the Mid-Continent Association of Law Schools (Keystone, Colo., July 28, 1986).

7. Paul T. Bryant, "Western Literature: A Window on America," paper presented at the annual meeting of the College English Association (San Antonio, March 31–April 2, 1977).

8. Philip D. Ortego, "Which Southwestern Literature and Culture in the English Classroom?" *Arizona English Bulletin* 13, no. 3 (1971), pp. 15–17.

9. Fred Erisman, "Western Regionalism and Awareness of Place," paper presented at the annual meeting of the National Council of Teachers of English (San Francisco, November 22–24, 1979).

10. Charles F. Wilkinson, "Law and the American West: The Search for an Ethic of Place," *University of Colorado Law Review* 59, no. 3 (1988), pp. 401–425.

Guerin-Gonzalez

11. John Winthrop, "A Modell of Christian Charity," in *Winthrop Papers, Vol 2*,

1623–1630, ed. Stewart Mitchell (Boston: The Massachusetts Historical Society), p. 295.

PART SIX

Stegner

1. Mark Twain, *The Mysterious Stranger: A Romance* (New York & London: Harper & Brothers Publishers, 1916), p. 150.

PART SEVEN

Jenkinson

1. Jefferson to Col. William S. Smith, November 13, 1787, in *The Writings of Thomas Jefferson*, Vol. 6, eds. Andrew A. Lipscomb and Albert Ellery Bergh (Washington, D.C.: Thomas Jefferson Memorial Association, 1903), pp. 372–373.
2. Jefferson to Roger C. Weightman, June 24, 1826, in *Writings*, Vol. 16, pp. 181–182.

BIBLIOGRAPHY

Abbey, Edward. *The Monkey Wrench Gang.* Philadelphia: Lippincott, 1975.

Berry, Wendell. *Clearing.* New York & London: Harcourt Brace Jovanovich, 1977.

Berry, Wendell. *The Unsettling of America.* San Francisco: Sierra Club Books, 1977.

Clark, Walter Van Tilburg. *The Ox-Bow Incident.* New York: The Press of the Readers Club, 1942.

Dahlberg, Edward. *Bottom Dogs.* San Francisco: City Lights Books, 1961.

Girard, Rene. *Violence and the Sacred.* Baltimore: Johns Hopkins University Press, 1977.

Hegel, Georg Wilhelm Friedrich. *The Philosophy of History.* Translated by J. Sibree. New York: Willey Book Co., 1944.

Heilbroner, Robert L. *The Future As History: The Historic Currents of Our Time and the Direction in Which They Are Taking America.* New York: Harper, 1960.

Hopkins, Sarah Winnemucca. *Life Among the Paiutes: Their Wrongs and Claims.* New York: G. P. Putnam's Sons, 1883.

Illich, Ivan. *Deschooling Society.* New York: Harper & Row, 1971.

Jackson, Kenneth T. *Crabgrass Frontier: The Suburbanization of the United States.* New York: Oxford University Press, 1985.

Jeffers, Robinson. *Roan Stallion, Tamar and Other Poems.* New York: Horace Liveright, 1925.

Jefferson, Thomas. *Autobiography of Thomas Jefferson, 1743-1790.* New York: G. P. Putnams Sons, 1914.

Jefferson, Thomas. *Notes on the State of Virginia.* New York: Harper & Row, 1964.

Kittredge, William. *Owning It All.* St. Paul: Graywolf Press, 1987.

Kittredge, William, and Smith, Annick, eds. *The Last Best Place, A Montana Anthology.* Helena: Montana Historical Society, 1988.

Krutch, Joseph Wood. *The Modern Temper: A Study and a Confession.* New York: Harcourt, Brace and World, 1956.

Krutch, Joseph Wood. *More Lives Than One.* New York: William Sloan Associates, 1962.

Limerick, Patricia Nelson. *Legacy of Conquest: The Unbroken Past of the American West.* New York: Norton, 1987.

Lipscomb, Andrew A., and Albert Ellery Bergh, eds. *The Writings of Thomas Jefferson.* 20 volumes. Washington, D.C.: Thomas Jefferson Memorial Association, 1903.

Misrach, Richard. *Bravo 20: The Bombing of the American West.* Baltimore: Johns Hopkins University Press, 1990.

Mitchell, Lee Clark. *Witness to a Vanishing America: The Nineteenth-Century Response.* Princeton, N.J.: Princeton University Press, 1981.

Morris, Charles R. "The Coming Global Boom." *The Atlantic,* October 1989, pp. 51–64.

Nichols, John. *The Milagro Beanfield War.* New York: Holt, Rinehart, and Winston, 1974.

Paine, Thomas. *Common Sense*. Woodbury, N.Y.: Barron's Educational Series, 1975.

Peterson, Merrill, ed. *The Portable Thomas Jefferson*. New York: Penguin Books, 1975.

Powell, John W. *Report on the Lands of the Arid Region of the United States*, Executive Document No. 73, 45th Congress, 2d Session. Cambridge: Belknap Press of Harvard University Press, 1962.

Standing Bear, Luther. *Land of the Spotted Eagle*. Boston: Houghton Mifflin, 1933.

Stegner, Wallace. *Beyond the Hundredth Meridian: John Wesley Powell and the Second Opening of the West*. Boston: Houghton Mifflin, 1954.

Stegner, Wallace. *The Big Rock Candy Mountain*. New York: Sagamore Press, 1943.

Stegner, Wallace. *The Sound of Mountain Water*. New York: E. P. Dutton, 1980.

Turner, Frederick W. *Beyond Geography: The Western Spirit Against the Wilderness*. New York: Viking Press, 1985.

Udall, Stewart L., et al. *Beyond the Mythic West*. Salt Lake City: Peregrine Smith Books in association with the Western Governors Association, 1990.

Weatherford, J. McIver. *Indian Givers: How the Indians of the Americas Transformed the World*. New York: Crown Publishers, 1988.

Winters v. United States, 207 U.S. 564 (1908).

Wolfe, Thomas. *Of Time and the River: A Legend of Man's Hunger in His Youth*. New York: Charles Scribner's Sons, 1935.

Worster, Donald E. *Dust Bowl: The Southern Plains in the 1930s*. New York: Oxford University Press, 1979.

Worster, Donald E. *Rivers of Empire: Water, Aridity, and the Growth of the American West*. New York: Pantheon Books, 1986.

INDEX